SAI BABA

The Holy Man . . .

. . . and the Psychiatrist

SAI BABA
The Holy Man . . .

. . . and the Psychiatrist

Samuel H. Sandweiss, M.D.
Birth Day Publishing Company
San Diego, California, USA

This book may be obtained at your local bookstore or you may order it directly from Birth Day Publishing Company, at a cost of $4.25 for the paperback edition or $8.25 for the hardbound copy, plus $1.00 for postage and handling. Send check or money order to Birth Day Publishing Company, P.O. Box 7722, San Diego, California 92107.

Library of Congress Catalog Number: 75-28784

ISBN 0-9600958-1-0

Printing rights for the use of quotations and passages from Sai Baba's discourses granted by the Sri Sathya Sai Education Foundation, Brindavan, Bangalore, India. I wish to thank Sai Baba and the Foundation for this privilege.

Published by Birth Day Publishing Company
P.O. Box 7722, San Diego, California 92107, USA

Acknowledgments

I would like to acknowledge with a very special sense of gratitude Dick Croy, Los Angeles writer and film-maker, whose talents and painstaking efforts as writer and editor played such a major role in the production of this book. It was through his efforts that a deluge of loosely organized material from a novice writer was organized and molded into a finished product. Also, a special thanks to my secretary Mary Alice Berning, who typed and retyped the manuscript an untold number of times and whose positive attitude, selfless service and helpful advice proved invaluable throughout the writing.

My heartfelt thanks goes to Larry Smith, San Diego artist and designer, who added a whole artistic dimension to the book by providing his original art in the form of the sensitively done line drawings which appear throughout the book, and who single-handedly designed and laid out the book from cover to glossary; also to Lee Gerlach, Nancy Sandweiss and my mother Freda Sandweiss, who assisted with the final stages of editing; Homer Youngs, who provided the glossary; The Sai Baba Center in Los Angeles and the Lite Storm Singing Group, for providing many of the photographs in the book; The Sri Sathya Sai Baba Book Center of America in Tustin, California, for providing the four-color separations for the color photographs in the book; Howard Murphet, for allowing the use of passages from his book *Sai Baba: Man of Miracles;* and Indra Devi, Elsie Cowan, Dr. V. K. Gokak, Dr. S. Bhagavantam and Dr. John Hislop for the use of material related to their personal experiences with Sai Baba.

And an extra-special thanks to my dear wife Sharon, who has been a constant support throughout, giving such loving attention to me and to the children when I was busy with the book. Her helpful comments and constant encouragement have been a deep and continuing source of strength.

A word from the editor

My work in this book is dedicated to my parents, whose ever-expanding love has given me a basis for beginning to comprehend the ineffable relationship between Sai Baba and his devotees.

Dick Croy

CONTENTS

A Word To The Reader

All of Sai Baba's own statements, and passages from his discourses are italicized without the use of quotation marks. The Western reader will probably find some of the selections a bit esoteric at first. A careful reading, however, will reveal that they express basically the same age-old and universal message found in the literature of all the world's major religions. Many passages are strikingly similar to the teachings of Jesus Christ.

A clear and concise English translation for all Sanskrit and Telugu words—indicated by *italics*—accompanies them in parentheses in the text, and further clarification is provided in the glossary. Throughout this book reference will be made to other works by and about Sai Baba. For more information about them and where they can be purchased, please refer to the Appendix.

For the sake of clarity and convenience, the familiar usage of "him" and "his" will be applied throughout the book in reference to the spiritual aspirant. This should in no way be taken as an indication that the female is somehow less likely or less able to succeed on the spiritual path. Sai Baba's view on this issue should be stated at the start: *Woman is equipped equally with man to tread the spiritual path. But still there are many who worry when they see women taking up spiritual pursuits or hear them reciting the* pranava *("Om"—the primordial sound). They forget that sound itself is fundamentally* pranava, *that all breath has* pranava *immanent in it. How then can women avoid or keep away from "Om," which is ever present in the ether in which their breath is reciting every moment? ... Women have equal chances and equal rights to attain Godhead.*

FOREWORD

Dr. Samuel Sandweiss, in his thought-provoking book on Bhagavan Sri Satya Sai Baba, has opened up three main avenues of communication: a fascinating narration of his own experiences with Baba; his probe, as a psychiatrist, into the roots of psychiatry and his consequent discovery that what passes as psychiatry is an incomplete science and that quite essential additions have to be made to it from the field of spiritual awareness to make it truly effective; and the reproduction, from Baba's writings and speeches, of passages which are regarded by Dr. Sandweiss as key passages for an exploration of Baba's teachings.

Turning over the pages in which these key passages are printed, one can easily see that Dr. Sandweiss' choice is a happy one. Baba on Avatarhood; Baba on the nine forms of devotion; Baba on the relation of the individual to society; Baba on Sadhana: these and other pivotal quotations take us to the heart of Satya Sai philosophy.

Dr. Sandweiss' own experiences with Baba are not only interesting but fairly typical. He is first rendered unsettled and "unmade" and then remade in the light of spirit. The "monkey mind" crumbles gradually and gives up its struggle and is replaced by a genuine sensitiveness and receptivity. Allowing his skepticism to fly as high and as long as it can, he still realizes that, if there is any honesty in doubt, it has to admit and accept the existence of a soul and a transcendental reality—a new spiritual dimension to the universe. He also grasps the truth about the role of the Avatar in human affairs. In short, Dr. Sandweiss undergoes a profound transformation. He becomes a different person, gaining as he does a new spiritual dimension.

This change is reflected in the consequent attitude toward his own profession—that of a psychiatrist. A scientist of consciousness is required. Psychiatry itself has to change into an art of healing based on the science of consciousness. Dr. Sandweiss may raise a hornet's nest around him by this strange assertion. But truth has to be accepted as truth even if the heavens move around you and fall.

It is his sensitive discernment, his honesty and forthrightness in the course of his exploration that will endear Dr. Sandweiss to the readers of this book. A transparent sincerity permeates this piece of writing. The writer takes his readers into confidence regarding all the changes in his thoughts and moods. We come to know every bend of the road he has taken and the direction of each step. This is what makes it a genuine document of human sensitivity and of the psychology of profound inner changes.

Dr. Sandweiss is a valued friend and we cherish many deep interests in common. I am very happy that I was given the opportunity to write these few lines by way of an appreciation of his book.

Vinayak Krishna Gokak

Brindavan
Whitefield
Bangalore, India

INTRODUCTION

I first met Satya Sai Baba three years ago. I went to India as a Western psychiatrist to study the psychology of religion at first hand and left with a deep sense of mystery about a being I could not comprehend.

Sai Baba says, *My life is my message.* He teaches about spirituality in a universal language, attracting the attention of people from all over the world, all walks of life and all religious beliefs. He is breathing new life into age-old truths for millions. *There is only one caste,* he says—*the caste of humanity; there is only one language—the language of the heart; there is only one religion—the religion of love; there is only one God—and He is omnipresent.*

What is it about this world teacher that is so captivating? His followers believe him to be much more than a revered spiritual leader. Scientists, educators, leaders of government and public figures, as well as the poor, the weak and the sick—the whole spectrum of humanity—attest to the claim that Sai Baba is capable of the most extraordinary feats. It is reported that he can materialize objects from thin air and is capable of remarkable clairvoyant, telepathic and healing powers; that he is able to transform himself into other forms and identities and transport himself great distances instantaneously; that he has been seen in two or more places at once.

The scope of his reputed powers boggles the mind; it is in fact thought by his followers to extend beyond the limitations of time and space. To them, this charismatic and mysterious man is an *avatar*: a superhuman embodiment of the divine in human form.

It is hard, to put it mildly, for most Westerners to take such claims seriously. Yet the caliber of people convinced of Sai Baba's paranormal powers, and the increasing documentation available on him, are impressive. Dr. S. Bhagavantam, for example—physicist, former scientific adviser to India's Defense Ministry and past-president of the Indian Science Congress Association—describes himself as "a rational man, practically an agnostic, who would not accept anything without a scientific explanation." This is how he has resolved what was once a conflict between his scientific training and the evidence of his senses:

"In our laboratories," he says, "we scientists may swear by reason, but we know that every time we have added a little to what we know, we have learned of the existence of many other things, the true nature of which we do not know. Thus while adding to knowledge, we add more to our ignorance too. What we know is becoming a smaller and smaller fraction of what we do not know.

"How do I reconcile my background of science with what Satya Sai Baba does? I have seen miracles performed by Baba perhaps in the thousands during the fifteen years that I have known him: materializations of an infinite variety of physical objects, healings of every description. I must confess that with the logic I know and the training I have, I cannot accept that Sai Baba is like you and me. He can transcend the laws of physics and chemistry. I have therefore to describe and to declare that he is a phenomenon, that he is a transcendental being, that he is divine."

The world today appears on the brink of insanity. Half its population may be starving or undernourished. We are witness to shootings on the streets, suicides and terrorist attacks on a daily basis. The most grotesque inhumanities to man and a virtual rape of the land are practiced by us as a way of life. We are caught up in an absurd infatuation with weaponry and war and a selfish preoccupation with ourselves.

Everyone is a *guru*. The bookstores, filled with books supposedly showing the way, attest to this fact. But nothing seems to work. We are lost in a myriad of ideas, a confounding whirlwind of impressions and experiences without direction or discipline. It is crucial that we learn to discern truth and find direction. Yet to many of us, a search for fundamental answers to personal and social problems seems futile and meaningless.

My own search for meaning and understanding led to a medical education and then into the field of psychiatry. But nine years of psychiatric training and practice, and a comprehensive investigation-by-participation of what one might call the "human-potential movement" provided few answers.

Promises of the attainment of deeper insight and an "expansion of consciousness" proved shallow and without substance. Is there really such a thing as humanity's infinite potential—an ability to so transform one's consciousness as to discover and merge with a divine, infinite or eternal dimension of being? I was beginning to be convinced that such a search was an exercise in futility.

In such a mood I turned to the East . . . and came upon Sai Baba. Here was a teacher—a scientist of consciousness—who taught that our true nature is not bound by time or space, and is in fact infinite, immutable, eternal. Who proclaimed that behind all forms and objects there is spirit, and that all creation is based upon the will of the spiritual dimension . . . that our truest identity is an incorporeal state of pure bliss and love. His followers believe that Sai Baba's life itself is concrete proof of his possession of knowledge profound enough, and energy sufficiently powerful, to help them achieve the deepest kind of self-realization.

But how can one determine whether this Indian mystic and holy man, still obscure to the West, is even a fraction of what his followers believe him to be? The crux of the matter for many Westerners is whether or not he can in fact demonstrate powers that concretely prove the reality of those dimensions of which he teaches.

This book is an attempt to describe my direct observation and personal experience of some of these powers. It is the outcome of a soul's struggle to comprehend phenomena in which the West does not generally believe. I have tried to prepare the Western reader for the alien territory which he will encounter here and to relate what I observed to psychiatric concepts with which most of us are at least somewhat familiar.

This is in spite of the fact that I came to find modern psychiatry quite limited in its capacity to understand this type of phenomena. The reality of this holy man—his apparently advanced level of consciousness and his manner of relating to people and environment—could not be satisfactorily contained or explained by the concepts and principles I have learned in my years of psychiatric experience. Until recently, the phenomena which are so much a part of his way of life have been almost exclusively the domain of saints and mystics. These are scientists, if you will, whose field of investigation is the dynamics of expanded consciousness—described by mystics as cosmic awareness, by the world's religions as divine or God-consciousness, and by Western psychology in the twentieth century as super-consciousness.

"Non-ordinary" levels of awareness first became subject matter for Western psychology in 1908 with William James' great classic and seminal study, *Varieties of Religious Experience*. A decade later, Carl Jung introduced the concept of the collective unconscious and the idea that we may well extend beyond space and time and ultimately be part of a higher dimension of reality than that represented by the physical world. He believed that our consciousness could tap into this higher reality, drawing from it intuitive and creative insight, wisdom and direction.

Developments within the past twenty years in psychology, at first loosely combined under the general heading "the new psychology" and more recently "humanistic" psychology, have explored the possibility of expanding awareness to enhance creativity and reveal a deeper meaning and purpose in life.

Fathered by Abraham Maslow, humanistic psychology ushered in the human potential movement and in 1973 was accepted by the American Psychological Association as its newest branch. Maslow was the first major American psychologist to postulate that man is an evolutionary creature whose higher nature seeks actualization just as surely as does his lower nature, and that sickness arises when this upward evolution, this need for self-actualization, is blocked. "The higher nature," Maslow said, "includes the need for meaningful work, for responsibility, for creativeness, for being fair and just, for doing what is worthwhile and for preferring to do it well." This is in contrast to man's lower nature, which seeks gratification of the animal drives and instincts.

Terms of this new psychology—such as "peak" and ecstatic experiences, self-transcendence and self-actualization, energy flow and energy fields, love, and consciousness ... the spiritual dimension—create a language similar to that of mystics, saints and spiritual leaders. Its attitude toward self-exploration and personal involvement is opposed to the requirement of the classic scientific method for an objective observer. Investigators in this newest branch of psychology believe that one can go into states such as meditation, hypnosis, sensory deprivation and other altered states of consciousness and still make valid observations and collect worthwhile data.

No less than a revolution in human consciousness is occurring in our culture, with research being conducted into the nature of mind and consciousness from almost every scientific and humanistic viewpoint. Reflecting the scope and diversity of this new field of interest, courses are turning up on campuses across the country. Experimental Johnston College, at the University of Redlands in California, bases an entire four-year course on a new transpersonal psychology—which combines the humanistic and the spiritual. The curriculum committee of Harvard University recently approved an undergraduate course in altered states of consciousness. Once a year a diverse group of medical doctors, psychologists, anthropologists, physicists, philosophers and holy men from around the world meet at Council Grove, Kansas, to study the subject of expanded consciousness. The meeting is co-sponsored by the Association for Humanistic Psychology and the Menninger Foundation.

My own experience with this burgeoning movement, however, has not been of much help in my struggle to comprehend Sai Baba. How is it that although appearing to recognize man's spiritual nature, many therapists still get caught up in what to my intuition and common sense seem such absurd and conflicting issues. For example, the topic "Should a professional therapist go to bed with his patient if they are mutually attracted?" was actually aired at a forum of the Association for Humanistic Psychology.

Such misplaced concerns are absolutely contrary to the atmosphere which surrounds Sai Baba. The direction for so many seems toward increasing emotional expression, at the expense of a disciplined code of morality—in which I include the surrender of oneself to God, relegating the physical plane of existence subservient to a higher relationship with the divine. Is such a code outdated or, worse, a pathological denial of one's basic identity? Or is there indeed hidden truth in a spiritual morality considered repressive by most Western behavioral scientists?

Surprisingly enough, the phenomena of expanded consciousness seen from the point of view of the poet are the dynamics of love. Love and consciousness, I found, are intimately related—perhaps one and the same. Yet even here, in investigating a central aspect of the human condition, which one would think of major interest and importance to psychiatry, I found modern psychiatric knowledge grossly limited.

The love that I witnessed in India extended beyond the concepts of emotions and feelings as defined in psychiatry. In Sai Baba's presence I learned that the deepest and most profound experience of love grows out of a devotional attitude toward the divine—a principle which, it goes without saying, is almost completely absent from modern psychiatric theory and practice. In India I was taught that our basic identity is in fact pure and selfless love. In its pure form, love may be best defined in spiritual terms: as the divine spark at our very center—the essence of our identity, the manifestation of our truest nature—which, like consciousness, reaches out and expands until it embraces all that we perceive or know. For psychiatrists who believe that human nature is fundamentally animalistic, motivated by the pleasure-pain principle and the need for some form of self-gratification, Sai Baba's demonstration of selfless love is an impressive revelation.

In my attempt, then, to integrate what I observed with what I know of psychiatry, I have tried to define areas of limitation in modern psychiatric theory and practice . . . to point out how a growing body of knowledge concerning the dynamics of consciousness and love is revealing an added human dimension which psychiatry needs to consider and investigate seriously.

I must warn you that although I have tried to describe my encounter as objectively as possible, I found during the first of my five trips to India that the method of being an objective and nonparticipating observer was an absolute obstruction toward understanding. I could not afford to take shelter in the role of visiting expert. To understand these phenomena, I had to become a part of them.

Indeed, I took the direction from Sai Baba himself: *You must dive deep into the sea to get the pearls. What good is it to dabble among the waves near the shore, and swear that the sea has no pearls in it and that all tales about them are false? So also, if you must realize the full fruit of this* Avatar, *dive deep and get immersed in Sai Baba.*

To the most rigid in the scientific tradition, this will seem a terrible transgression. But in the main body of the behavioral sciences there is a healthy regard for this approach and acceptance of its validity. For even in the heat of intense internal and external reactions it is possible to maintain a position of witness and observer. In my encounter with Sai Baba I believe I maintained that position. And in so doing, I feel that I bring to this account an added dimension: a first-hand observation of experiencing my own soul in transformation.

Who is Sai Baba? If his powers are genuine, how can he lead one deeper into the innermost mysteries of our existence? These were the basic questions with which I started my search. If you are still with me, I invite you to join my journey toward this holy man . . . to explore an exciting and inspirational realm of human possibility through this enigmatic figure.

PART I The Journey

1
SWEETS, SWEETS

What am I doing here? I stood listlessly beside my friend, Alf Tidemand, in the vestibule of the large summer house where Sai Baba resides when he is in Bangalore. It was evening. Bugs aimlessly circled the lights, and a lizard was scurrying in fitful zigs and zags up the wall. I wondered how he was able to hold on. My eyes strained, looking for the suction cups on his feet.

I was exhausted. My bones and rear end ached from sitting for long tedious hours cross-legged on the ground. My stomach grumbled in reaction to unfamiliar hot Indian dishes. I had lost ten pounds in ten days. A primitive ceiling fan revolved in annoying monotony overhead—barely circulating the air and not stirring my sluggish, dejected spirits at all.

Two large wooden elephants on pedestals, trunks raised, guarded the door from the vestibule to the inner house. To one side in front of me was a footstool and a chair covered with bits of red velvet, which resembled a small throne. Frequently occupied by Sai Baba, it was almost the only piece of furniture in the barren room.

"You wouldn't catch me dead in India," my brother Don had graciously and sympathetically volunteered on my departure. "Sam, what are you looking for? You're a successful psychiatrist with a nice university position. You have a healthy and happy family. You're living by the ocean in the best climate in the world. What in the world more could you want? You're acting foolhardy and crazy going to India after some dream, jeopardizing your health and making your family sad."

I had often questioned this inner discontent myself, this old yearning inside to find a deeper meaning in life. Now all the recent literature bubbling up in the West regarding clairvoyance, telepathy and people with apparent healing powers—the question of other levels of consciousness, other dimensions of reality: did such phenomena actually exist? And even if they did, could they shed any light on the meaning and purpose of life? Wasn't it just neurotic to travel halfway around the world in pursuit of a man reputed to know the answers to these ancient questions—and supposedly able to perform miracles besides?

I had been involved in psychiatry for nine years. In addition to my private practice, I was an assistant clinical professor in psychiatry at the University of California in San Diego; had treated thousands of patients and in the process of my training gone through my own treatment, searching for many years for a way to deeper meaning and deeper peace—and still I was yearning and searching.

I hope you're happy now, Sam, I thought miserably. This Sai Baba, supposedly in possession of Christ-like powers, hasn't given you a second glance. He doesn't know you exist.

"But he can materialize objects," I had been told. "He is omnipresent, omniscient, omnipotent—all love."

After ten days in his presence I remained doubtful. Every once in a while he appeared to be "materializing" something, but I was too far away to see what he was doing. In any case, who in his right mind could actually believe another human being capable of producing something from thin air? Of course, magic tricks and deception are another matter.

Sai Baba had just delivered a ninety-minute discourse to some 500 people that was totally unsettling to me. What he had said was not just contrary to contemporary psychiatric thought; it seemed years behind the times and psychologically unsophisticated. His uninformed challenge to my system of beliefs was the last straw. How could I even for a moment consider this foolishness?

Trained in the most advanced country in the world, in the best schools; exposed to the leading theories, the latest practices and techniques in psychiatry, how could I expect to find anything worthwhile here? I knew more about the mind and emotions, the way to inner peace, than anyone in this primitive, under-developed country. Sai Baba teach *me* anything about the way to inner peace? This whole trip was just an exercise in self-torment!

In a few moments Alf and I would retreat down the walkway from the *ashram* (spiritual community) to our cab and head back to Bangalore. Several walls separated us from the back of the house, where loud and lasting applause signaled the end of the talk. We stood silently.

"I'm feeling terrible, Alf—like being torn apart. I might even have to go home early." Alf nodded, a tired smile on his face.

I looked down at the floor, at my bare feet, wiggling my toes for entertainment. My trip had been a failure. I had come seeking the meaning of life and had found confusion. I had seen no miracles, no superhuman powers. I was one of thousands, unrecognized by Sai Baba. I was a fool and it was time to go home.

Then suddenly he appeared. Quickly and gracefully he walked up to us, smiling and full of joy. He held out two pieces of candy, saying *Sweets, sweets*. His blissful, loving gaze held my own transfixed. What a message in those eyes! They seemed to tell of an understanding beyond my comprehension. I felt a chill and the clear impression that this man actually knew and was responding to my sense of despair.

In ten days he hadn't given me a sign of recognition. How could he now know who I was and what I was thinking when a moment ago he had been surrounded by hundreds and I had been nowhere in sight?

What was communicated in that brief moment? The world! Something broke inside of me. Some of Sai Baba's joy and love penetrated my soul and I felt myself laughing like a child. There was such love and gentleness and caring in this man's presence.

Who *was* he?

Puffed up self-worth and egotistical attachment to my own particular values and beliefs seemed to shatter into dust, suddenly giving way to a sense of awe and mystery. I felt somehow transformed in one dazzling, incredible moment . . . then realized that *everyone* can be transformed in this way, *everyone* has such glorious potential.

Baba turned swiftly and disappeared the way he had come, leaving me with my mouth hanging open, feeling dazed and humble.

"What was that?" I finally managed to ask Alf, staring blankly into his beaming face.

"Well, if you believe that's ordinary candy, Sam, you're sorely mistaken," he said. "Eat." I ate the candy, feeling its sweetness in my mouth matched by a most marvelous sensation welling up inside my body. As I looked at Alf, I could feel the radiance on my own face. "I'll stay," I said.

However high a bird may soar, it has sooner or later to perch on a tree top, to enjoy quiet. So too a day will come when even the most haughty, the most willful, the most unbelieving, even those who assert that there is no joy or peace in the contemplation of the Highest Self, will have to pray: "God, grant me peace, grant me consolation, strength and joy."

[1]Dr. Y. J. Rao, head of the Geology Department of Osmania University in Hyderabad, was an appropriate witness of the apparent transmutation of solid rock to something quite different—with a valuable spiritual lesson added for good measure.

One day at *Puttaparthi*[2] Baba picked up a rough piece of broken granite and, handing it to Dr. Rao, asked him what it contained. The geologist mentioned a few of the minerals in the rock.

Baba: *I don't mean those—something deeper.*

Dr. Rao: "Well, molecules, atoms, electrons, protons . . ."

Baba: *No, no—deeper still!*

Dr. Rao: "I don't know, *Swami*."

Baba took the lump of granite from the geologist and, holding it up with his fingers, blew on it. Dr. Rao says that although it was never out of his sight, when Baba gave it back, its irregular shape had changed to a statue of Lord *Krishna* playing his flute. The surprised geologist noted also a difference in color and a slight change in composition of the rock.

Baba: *You see? Beyond your molecules and atoms, God is in the rock. And God is sweetness and joy. Break off the foot and taste it.*

Dr. Rao found no difficulty in breaking off the "granite" foot of the little statue. Putting it in his mouth, he discovered, he says, that it was candy.

From this incident Dr. Rao says that he learned something beyond words and far beyond modern science; in fact, beyond the limits of the rational mind of man today: "Science gives but the first word; the last word is known only to the great spiritual scientists like Sai Baba."

[1]Howard Murphet, *Sai Baba—Man of Miracles;* Frederick Muller, Ltd., London, 1971 (p. 156).

[2]Puttaparthi: village in Southern India where Sai Baba was born and grew up, and the location of his ashram.

2
GOOD
NEWS

In late 1971 I began looking for someone to teach me yoga and meditation. I had been experimenting with a number of "newer" psychotherapeutic techniques and felt that in some of these the West was actually approaching yogic or "spiritual" practices known for thousands of years in the East. How had these ancient cultures understood human nature? And how did "spiritual practice" lead to improved mental health?

I learned that Indra Devi, a woman with an international reputation in yoga, had a ranch and yoga retreat in Tecate, Mexico, only fifty miles from San Diego, and it was my good fortune to be invited graciously to her home for a talk. It was destined to be an interesting and important meeting.

After crossing the border, my wife Sharon and I made our way through the small town of Tecate and onto a narrow dirt road which wound through foothills to a large area, open and quiet, at the base of a mountain. This was Rancho La Cuchuma. I had the strange feeling of entering another world, removed by more than distance from the hustle of San Diego. The warm sun was gentle and soothing, the silence penetrating.

Indra Devi's large old Spanish home was an experience in its own right. As Sharon and I entered the house, we were met by a large poster: an Indian man with Negroid features, a natural Afro hairstyle and brilliant orange robe stood amongst seated admirers, who gazed up at him with reverence and devotion. I found the poster and its placement a bit unusual, having never before come across this sort of display on entering someone's home.

Indra Devi came down to greet us, and she was like a breath of fresh

You might have heard people talk about the miracles of my "taking" this and "giving" that, of my fulfilling all your wants, etc., of my curing your illness. But they are not so important as the sathwaguna *(spiritual quality of steadiness, purity and unselfishness) I promote and appreciate and instill. Of course, I confer on you these boons of health and prosperity so that you might, with greater enthusiasm and with less interruption, proceed with the spriritual* sadhana *(spiritual work).*

air. She was wearing an unusual, very interesting scent, almost like incense, and I had the impression that she was marvelously open, as if I could actually feel a breeze passing through her body. Motioning us to follow, she led us through the house singing a strange chanting song which I later learned to be a *bhajan,* or devotional song.

Our conversation soon turned to the mysterious man of the poster: Satya Sai Baba. It seemed that no matter what I asked, her mind was channeled to Sai Baba. Sai Baba this, and Sai Baba that, until I began to consider how unusual it was for a woman in her seventies to have such a reaction. It is not, of course, all that uncommon for someone who is young and looking for guidance to become devoted to a teacher. But Indra Devi was a mature sophisticated woman. In the course of her extensive travels she had visited most of the major *ashrams* and met some of the most evolved yogis and *sadhus* (spiritual men) in India. For her, suddenly, in the later years of her life, to become so devoted to another person, a mere mortal—this I found quite unusual and interesting.

"Six years ago," she said, "Sai Baba transformed my life. He is a master and teacher whose powers are beyond comprehension." To my growing dismay and disbelief, she began to recount a seemingly endless list of his "powers." He could, for example, materialize things out of thin air.

She described witnessing numerous such materializations, showing me how, by waving his hand in circles, he produced *vibhutti,* or "sacred ash," a substance supposed to possess spiritual and healing properties —similar for the Hindu to the holy water of Catholicism. She demonstrated how he had taken a large metallic urn filled with *vibhutti* right out of the sky, merely by making a few of these horizontal, clockwise circles with his right hand. Baba had told her that the urn would replenish itself and never be emptied. And indeed over the next few years, she said, although she had given out much of this *vibhutti,* and the urn had been almost empty on a number of occasions, it had somehow always replenished itself.

This respected teacher and writer then went on to describe still other superhuman abilities which she attributed to Sai Baba. It was said that he had stopped rainstorms, made a rainbow appear in front of a doubting observer, protected people by influencing the events of men and the forces of nature, instantaneously rescued devotees from danger at a great distance from himself . . . and even that he had raised at least one person from the dead.

After that, it did not surprise me to hear her say that Sai Baba knew the past, present and future of everyone who came before him, that he could transform himself into other (including non-human) forms, or that he could be in two places at once.

In spite of this proliferation of amazing capabilities, Sai Baba's greatest miracle, according to Indra Devi, was the genuineness of his spiritual insight and his ability to turn people Godward. She said that one wishing to feel what it must have been like to experience Christ or Buddha or *Krishna* should go to Baba, because he embodies them all. "One is enveloped in such a highly charged aura of love in his presence, such a profoundly spiritual and holy atmosphere, that many are transformed on the spot. And almost everyone coming into his presence can feel this deeply moving climate."

She spoke of her own personal experiences, such as that concerning a photograph she had taken of Baba and had developed in the United States. Someone leafing through her album came across the picture and asked, *"Mataji* ("Mother:" a name of respect given Indra Devi), why is it covered with dust?" She looked at it and became almost speechless; the "dust" to her was obviously *vibhutti*, materializing on the photograph 12,000 miles from Sai Baba. "I framed it and the *vibhutti* continues to be produced," she said reverently.

She showed me the now-framed photograph. Clumps of caked dust-like material filled the space between photograph and glass: quite unusual perhaps, but hardly convincing evidence of a miracle. She thinks I'm going to believe all these stories because of this "proof"? How easy for someone to have tricked her; or she may have done it herself for all I know—certainly no evidence that the Messiah has come, I thought.

"Very interesting," I heard myself say.

On and on went Sai Baba's ardent devotee, speaking at such length about his greatness and his limitless power and telling such unbelievable tales that I finally couldn't absorb any more and my mind became dulled. She continued to speak in this electrified manner, taking us around her home and pointing out numerous objects which Sai Baba had supposedly materialized. What a strange experience! Here I was, bombarded, knocked almost silly by all these stories and knowing all along that they could not possibly be true.

While it was true that others there confirmed her accounts —and she gave me names of reputable people who, she said, had seen Sai Baba and been transformed—this was simply not my reality. Indra Devi was probably experiencing a "fugue state" in which, from her great need to believe, she would run around in a sleep-like trance placing objects here and there and sprinkling *vibhutti* around, and then on waking, unconscious of her previous behavior, would attribute the occurrences to Sai Baba.

She smiled at me knowingly. "When I first heard of Sai Baba I couldn't believe that such a person really existed either," she said. "People filled me to the brim with stories until I couldn't believe another word. It was as if I had eaten too much sugar and couldn't stomach any more. I had to get away from it to let all the information settle."

I went home and, as Indra Devi had said of her own reaction, simply couldn't digest the whole thing right away. I made a couple of inquiries of people to whom she had directed me, to see if this man actually did exist. I was informed that he not only existed but that millions of people followed him, and a great deal had been written about him.

I was fascinated—a spiritual leader of millions alive now in India yet virtually unknown in the Western world. How could this be, in an age of electronic global communication, especially if even one-thousandth of what was reported about him was true?

It happened very quickly for me. I decided to go to India to see Sai Baba for myself. Of course I was familiar with other accounts of the kind of phenomena credited to him: clairvoyance, telepathy and other so-called "psychic" powers, such as the stories of Christ's miracles. I had always assumed them to be tricks of perception recorded by gullible or careless historians and reporters.

To my way of thinking, a belief in miracles grew out of psychological phenomena, such as mass hysteria or group delusion or the ability of someone to wield an uncanny influence over others to the point of altering their perception of reality.

The opportunity of observing such events at first hand and of investigating their psychological mechanisms myself was very appealing. I felt that observing Baba in person would give me an idea of what might have happened at the time of Christ to propagate those incredible stories.

Isn't it strange, I felt, how much an individual's system of reality can be compromised by the need to believe? We're such small, insignificant and vulnerable beings, too frightened to accept reality as it is, having to manufacture a God and other realms of existence in order to feel safer, more secure.

I had always believed much like the pragmatic existentialists that life is rather absurd, incomprehensible and meaningless; that we are some sort of freak mistake of nature coming from nowhere, going nowhere—born in a dark, confusing setting in which people are constantly warring and fighting, being cruel and unfeeling to one another. I had always felt that, at best, we could get a few kicks out of life, some fleeting momentary pleasures—and that was that.

But still and all . . . what was this strange, eerie, almost electrifying feeling inside at the thought of the possibility of a higher reality, a higher order of consciousness and love?

No, no—that was just neurosis. I had put those ideas away a long time ago, maybe even before I was a teen-ager, because it was weak to give in to the need to believe in something beyond the perception of the senses. Nor was there any proof that anything beyond the senses existed.

It so happened that Indra Devi would be going to India a month after our first meeting. I decided to go with her. I would go as a scientist, to study and understand the psychological realities of a situation shrouded in mysticism . . . to prove that miracles do not exist.

Everyone has to be asked to approach me and experience me. In order to get an idea of a mountain, it is not enough if you show a stone and say, "The mountain is a million times the size of this." You will have to see an actual mountain, at least from a distance.

3
LETTERS
HOME

London: 7 a.m., Tuesday, May 9, 1972

Dear Sharon,

Everyone's trying to convince me that it's 7 a.m. The sun is out, everyone is shouting and eating breakfast, but they can't fool me—it's 1 a.m. San Diego time. I'm terribly tired. I can't eat breakfast because I just ate supper two hours ago.

I'm actually enjoying my situation though. Mataji is really nice and very protective. She has made this trip often and is looking after me like a hawk. She actually ran up and down three flights of stairs searching for me in JFK Airport.

I have eaten all the food you packed but for one tangelo. Sorry to have awakened you so early in the morning when I called on arriving in London. My thoughts are with you all the time and I love you very much. My feeling of love is intensified, or I'm becoming more conscious of it, as the distance between us increases. I don't know what kind of strange situation I'm getting myself into—I'll have to wait and see.

Love, Sam

Bombay: 6 a.m., Thursday, May 11

My dearest love,

It is now six in the morning and my sleeping cycle has changed; I had a fairly good rest after a hectic day's shopping in Bombay yesterday. I miss you and want you not to worry about me. My thoughts are with you always.

The trip was fairly smooth, although 29 hours in the air gets a bit old and tiring. We traveled from New York to Bombay in a large 747, and I could sleep comfortably anytime by lying across four seats. After much internal questioning about why the trip; should I be here and is Baba real; what will happen? etc., etc., we arrived in Bombay at 3 a.m.—12½ hours' difference from San Diego time.

It was hot, humid and very uncomfortable upon stepping outside the plane. My first and continuing impression is that I dislike Bombay and have a strong desire to return, but for Baba. The airport was dirty and dingy, uncomfortable and barren. Bare walls, dirty with smears and handprint marks; primitive facilities, overcrowded with skinny, protein-deficient, ill-looking people. I was tired and sweaty and dazed and felt the potential for malaria, hepatitis, "su gong fu fever" and any other illness existing. I didn't want to touch anything.

I got my bags and was pleasantly surprised to see that nothing was stolen and I still had my money. After passing through customs and a crowd of people, with a number of them begging for money and some wanting to make illegal exchange of it, we entered an old 1942-looking taxi and headed for the city. Some of my impressions: Two small mosquitoes in the car, and I pray for health. Rickety roads. Cab driver turning off his lights to save battery power, then coughing—I move away from cab driver and again pray for health.

Skinny, emaciated people sleeping on the road, limbs twisted this way and that. Hot. Hot. Humid. . . . Oppressive. Wandering dogs and cattle. A man broken and bent, washing himself at the side of the road in waste water.

My spirits were low and I was tired. I settled at the West End Hotel in Bombay and will stay here two or three days, as we learned Baba is coming to Bombay to greet people in a ceremony at a large stadium here.

Thank God my room is air-conditioned and I am comfortable in it. The first day here I went shopping and my spirits were further lowered; the city is crowded and dirty and the people look malnourished. The rich and comfortable say, "These people are paying for their sins." I don't know . . . I don't think this way, but who knows—maybe Baba can show me.

Leaving the hotel the first day to go sightseeing, I was concretely struck with the cultural shock; I could feel myself dazed and unsteady after the long trip and the vast change in setting. The sun was bright, hot, glaring. A myriad of smells, sounds, movements and activities made me reel and sway. All kinds of smells: incense, dung, food cooking, people and animals.

Cows and dogs and monkeys were about, with people moving this way and that in all directions—confusing, overpopulated. Sights and sounds of every dimension gave a kaleidoscopic impression, and I felt that all my senses were being bombarded. Jingle, jangle, tinkle, tankle . . . smelling here, smelling there . . . glaring sun, reflections off windows, a monkey jumping . . . a dog here, a cow there—people staring at me from all over. Tipsy and a bit giddy, I enjoyed letting myself float with the experience, engrossed with the sensory challenge.

I almost bumped into a cow as I wandered around dazed, looking at everyone, and I soon realized that I wasn't the only one sightseeing. There I was dressed in full western regalia, looking as totally out of place as a creature from another planet.

Early in the day Mataji picked me up by cab, and we ate at the house of people involved in planning the program which Baba will attend at the stadium. They were influential people—one a wealthy industrialist by the name of Kamani; another, a tall friendly Norwegian man named Alf Tidemand. I understand he is the focus of a chapter in "Man of Miracles," the book by Howard Murphet. When I questioned him about his first meeting with Baba, he said that it would take too long to tell and referred me to Chapter 16. Maybe later, if we have more time together, I can get his personal account. He actually was extremely nice, helpful and caring and said things about Baba, and life in general, which raised my spirits.

It's strange that when my spirits become low and I begin to feel I'm chasing some meaningless dream, if I talk to a devotee of Baba, my spirits are lifted. I don't know whether it's the exuberance they all share, or what—but something genuine and electrifying comes across and immediately uplifts me. There is a strange similarity of feeling and expression communicated by people who have contacted Baba, as if they are all experiencing some common vibration which they are able to reflect. To me, this is a very optimistic sign.

My feelings vacillate from pessimism to elation, and I can almost sense that something is about to happen to me. Something very important, something central to my life and to your life—to our lives, my dearest, dearest love. You also are always with me.

Love, Sam

Bombay: Friday, May 12

Dear Sharon,

Today will be busy. A friend of Mataji has made an appointment for me for a reading from the Book of Bregu. This is my first experience with such a situation and I am excited. I hadn't known, but the Book of Bregu is a very respected spiritual manuscript with quite a reputation. It was supposedly written 7,000 years ago, by someone at a higher level of consciousness with access to other dimensions of reality.

Everyone's life is supposed to be written in this book—a real mind-blower to a scientific man, and of course, if it were true, quite a blow to our Western conceptualizations of time and reality. What's just as unusual is the way the reader picks the page or chapter to be read. He measures your shadow, any time of the day you come—nothing more specific than that. He makes calculations in some mysterious way from his shadow-reading and then comes up with the correct page.

Think of the forces necessary to accomplish this phenomenal feat from what would seem to be such a simple, haphazard procedure. I certainly would have to be shown a great deal from the readings to believe them—not just vague generalities but specific "unknowable" facts. Still, I am assured by Mataji that this is exactly what happened to her: the accurate telling of many unusual facts about her past and present, as well as specifics about her future.

I understand that Sai Baba has said that past, present and future are the same, and that it is only because of our human condition that we see only a small section called the "present." Perhaps if I have some exciting experience with the Book of Bregu, my feelings about time may change —who knows?

Sai Baba is coming to the ceremony today and I'll have the good fortune of going with one of the people responsible for setting up the function. I don't expect to see him at close range though, since thousands of people will be there.

Mataji has already gone to Bangalore, a mountain town 450 miles southeast of here, and I'll meet her there in a few days. Baba's summer residence, *Brindavan,* where he is conducting a summer course for college students, is located just outside of Bangalore.

I have been thinking about you and the family frequently, if not always. I feel your presence with me and kiss each of you warmly. Please don't worry about me. I am okay, although a bit lonely.

Love, Sam

4
FIRST
MEETING

My first meeting with Sai Baba, as unusual as it turned out to be, was to prove fairly typical of all those that would follow. After landing in Bombay, we learned that Baba was to appear at a stadium there, and then would return to his summer residence near Bangalore. I decided to see this religious leader at the stadium. How would he present himself, and what would transpire between him and such a large crowd?

The morning of his appearance I was invited by one of Baba's devotees for lunch at her apartment someplace on the outskirts of Bombay. She gave me directions to the stadium and left early to get a good seat; I could rest awhile and leave later in the day, as I was still tired from the long trip. Now Bombay is a city of some six million people; I was in a small apartment lost somewhere in this sprawling metropolis, quite a distance from the stadium. Baba was going to present himself at six o'clock. At about five-thirty I walked out to catch a taxi to the stadium.

As I was leaving the building, I noticed some people rolling out a tattered little red rug and placing flowers over the entrance. I stopped and asked what this meant. The answer, given casually to this Westerner who couldn't be expected to comprehend its significance, produced an eerie sensation similar to that of *deja vu.* And the longer I thought about it, the more my confusion grew. Who but Sai Baba himself was expected at this very building—to visit a devotee, someone on the ninth floor whom I did not know. What an extraordinary coincidence! . . . But then again, highly unlikely. Wishful thinking surely.

There were a handful of people here, rolling a tattered red rug out on the ground, and tens of thousands waiting somewhere in a stadium. How foolish even to consider the possibility of Baba's making an appearance here! By this time, however, I was open enough to consider any-

To a worldly man, a God-intoxicated person will appear mad and he will laugh at him for it. But, to the God-intoxicated man, the worldly appear insane, foolish, misled, blind. Of all the insanities that harass man, God-madness is the least harmful, the most beneficial.

thing possible in a culture so unlike my own, and decided to wait around just to see what would happen. I was directed to the apartment on the ninth floor and a small group of mostly older people and their younger children, no young adults and no one from my culture.

I was reassured by a man standing at the door that Baba was indeed coming; the lady of the house had told him so and we should just wait patiently. A glance at my watch informed me that in fifteen minutes Baba was to present himself at the stadium. How crazy I was getting—to believe he was actually coming here. Purely wishful thinking on the part of these people; this was probably how all the stories of Sai Baba got started. To think he would show up just when I was walking out, in the very place in all of Bombay where I happened to be—minutes before he was supposed to appear at the stadium. What foolishness!

I descended the nine flights of stairs and walked toward a taxi, then stood there, wavering between going and staying. My better judgment was to go to the stadium; Baba was to be there in about ten minutes now. But . . . wouldn't it be nice to see him here, up close, without the clamor and confusion of a huge crowd? Sam, strange things are happening to you, I thought—to be tempted by such an unlikely occurrence.

Yet, as I was about to step into the taxi, a white car passed within three feet, and I saw the characteristic orange robe and bushy hairstyle and knew that Sai Baba was indeed going to visit that apartment. Before I knew it, I was running after the car like a madman.

I stopped myself almost in midflight; here I was, beginning to act like a religious fanatic. I had to remind myself that I didn't believe much in Sai Baba. Although this was an unusual coincidence, I should proceed at a more leisurely pace and not let the situation go to my head, overwhelm my senses. I rode an elevator back to the ninth floor and found that Baba was in the back room, with everyone silently awaiting his reappearance.

Some devotees had told me that upon first meeting him they knew Baba to be divine, and I had heard of people falling into a swoon or experiencing other dramatic emotional reactions when coming face to face with him for the first time. I waited expectantly . . . and then out he came: graceful, smiling, radiant —nodding to all present, appearing extremely confident: a man with great presence and control, very fluid and graceful in movement.

He was slender and just over five feet tall. I wasn't struck with any overwhelming emotional reaction and really didn't think him particularly unusual. I had seen artists and entertainers and indeed my own teachers and professors show as much confidence and command as much respect.

Nevertheless, people pressed to get closer, to touch his feet. Embarrassed at the thought of participating in this kind of display, I shrank to the edge of the crowd and watched. He approached one man, looked into his eyes and spoke something, and then off he ran to the elevator.

The visit had lasted no more than a couple of minutes.

On the way to the stadium I reflected on the probability of such a chance meeting. I was sure that had this happened to a devotee, it would have soon become an example of Baba's control over the direction of people's lives. For an individual who still believed in coincidences, however, that's all it was, unusual though it might have been.

I arrived at the stadium too late to get in and had to content myself with observing through a gate. Far in the distance, making a slow circular gesture with his hand, palm up—raising it slowly in a gesture directing attention heavenward—was Baba. I watched him for a moment and then he began to walk slowly in my direction.

His face reflected gentle compassion and love and an unusual inner gaze, an expression seeming to mirror his being both in this world and in another. I felt that he radiated some sort of inner rhythm, as if the chanting of *bhajans* by the crowd actually originated within himself. People reached out to touch his feet. He stepped back gently, motioning for them to stop.

I saw the intensity of man's deepest desires and innermost needs reflected in the pleading, searching eyes of the crowd, arms and hands out-stretched desperately for contact. Then, without noticing me at all, he turned and walked back, some hundred yards away.

The Lord has to come in human form and move about among men, so that He can be listened to, contacted, loved, revered and obeyed. He has to speak the language of men and behave like human beings, as a member of the species. Otherwise, He will be either negated and neglected or feared and avoided.

5
FROM
THIN AIR

Although only 110 miles from *Puttaparthi*, the village where Sai Baba grew up, Bangalore is 3,000 feet higher in altitude and blessed with cool mountain breezes and tolerable temperatures. In contrast, *Puttaparthi* lies in a basin of surrounding mountains, which reflect the hot Indian sun like the walls of an oven. Temperatures soar to 110 or 120 in the shade, stifling and seeming literally to bake everything in sight.

Baba was conducting a school for spirituality at *Brindavan* when I arrived. This was the first session; the school was to be held annually. Approximately 300 hand-picked college students representing all areas of India had been invited and would stay on the grounds. As teachers, Baba had invited educated and productive men and women from all over India to lecture. This was the setting in which I was going to be viewing Baba for the next two weeks.

I would be living in a hotel some twelve miles from *Brindavan* and would come in daily by taxi to sit amongst the students, hearing lectures on the spiritual history and heritage of India. I'd be able to watch Baba frequently, as he would be present at many of the lectures and would be giving students a good deal of attention. I would be having lunch with him daily and attending an hour and a half discourse by him each night.

Within this setting—viewing Baba in many different roles, moods and situations—I hoped to get both a rounded picture and a close view of this enigmatic individual. I would observe and record closely and carefully. If there was anything unusual, deep, mysterious, transcendental or godly about him, I should be able to catch a glimpse of it. Although still filled with doubts, I felt the possibility of something significant about to unfold.

Bangalore: 7 a.m., Sunday, May 14

Dear Love,

I'm in a cramped, stuffy room filled with little moving creatures. Big black ants on walls and floors, musty and dingy smells, and rain outside. Have traveled here from Bombay even though Baba is still there, simply to get away from the huge crowds and the feeling of futility in trying to see him. I hope to move from this place soon, but the town is busy and no place has vacancies.

Baba will return here today and I am awaiting this event with a mixture of frustration and eagerness. I went to his ashram yesterday, fifteen miles from here. I like riding in cabs, find the scene psychedelic and a bit bizarre. Scenes shift from the maddening activity of the city to the peace of the countryside: old cows and horses shambling about; emaciated, crippled beggar children; cab darting in and out of pressing crowds, around buses spewing black fumes, driver incessantly honking—missing people and animals only by the grace of God. At times shacks and squalor and then the smell of grass, and a small field appears. I sit back, letting it all happen, and am moved.

Brindavan was unexpectedly beautiful—the trees, their movement and color, almost defying description. Their gently swaying motion in the breeze was peacefully religious. They lift beautiful red flowers toward the sky. In contrast: people without shoes sitting amongst flies and ants, and mangy dogs roaming the grounds. I met some Americans, a man and wife and their children, and their stories of Baba's greatness and their strong devotion to him lifted my spirits.

Shopping yesterday, I bought two beautiful handmade rugs woven by Tibetan refugees. They were striking and must reflect my present mood. The pattern is stark and the colors are bold and intense: mysterious dragons and creatures in swirling, unraveling design, as if a core of energy is about to spring, erupt, evolve.

I am wondering more and more why I'm here. I keep hearing that there is some design in all this but even that thought fails to hold much charm now, and I wait in a rather dazed and hurt mood for Baba. So far I have gained entrance to the outer grounds of the ashram but haven't been permitted through the inner gates to the area where Baba spends most of his time. I must have hope that I'll be allowed closer. Perhaps Mataji will help.

I conjure up images of you and the kids all the time and am amazed at how these pictures bring me back all those thousands of miles to you. Then I look up at these blank dull walls and the primitive room and find myself moving back and forth between these two worlds with amazing speed. I'm left with confusion, trying to relate this world to our own. I miss you all and will be back with you soon.

Love, Sam.

Two views of grounds at Brindavan.
Top: picture of outer grounds.
Right: driveway leading to inner grounds and house where Sai Baba receives visitors.

p.s., When I see Baba I will ask him to wave his hand and give Ruthie, Rachel, Bethie and Judy something nice. I love my sweet girls so much.
Love, Daddy.

7:30 a.m., Tuesday, May 16

Dear Sharon,

It was nice to hear your voice over the phone. I initially felt so far away; it took a few seconds to bring myself back to you. I miss you and the children a lot and am thinking of you often. I will be back very soon. Let me recall some of the incidents of the two days since I wrote last.

I was lucky to meet Alf Tidemand again. He and Mataji talked to Baba and I was finally allowed past the stop gate. I am permitted to eat with the students and even to enter Baba's house. This is supposed to be a great honor; I've met people who have been here six months without receiving a glance from Baba. It was certainly an honor for me, as I'd been sitting cold and alone in the rain outside the gate, and had begun to imagine that I'd come all this way and wouldn't be allowed near him.

But it seems that each time frustration occurs something then lifts my spirits. I've been allowed close to Baba and I keep my eyes glued to him. He's exciting to watch. I'm fascinated by his style, his energy—his fluid, spontaneous reactions. He uses no notes when giving a speech and tells interesting down-to-earth stories to make his points clear.

His talks are very entertaining and informative, although his strict morality puts me off a bit. The lectures at the school emphasize a morality that is jarring to my more modern orientation. Strict control over sex and aggression, no hostility, always do good. . . . It seems to me that the students are squirming in their seats. The lectures are 55 minutes, one after the other, all morning and afternoon. Baba sometimes appears and then things get interesting.

At one point, during a discourse on states of consciousness, I grew impatient with a lecturer who was saying so many things contrary to my strong beliefs. Finally the man said something about thought being the same as action. He suggested that thinking a "bad" thought is the same as doing it. This is absolutely contrary to psychiatric thought. I began to wriggle and strain and then suddenly the lights and microphone went off. Then out of the commotion Baba appeared, inviting the speaker, Alf Tidemand, a few other people and myself into his private eating quarters. What a stroke of good luck—another example of good fortune arriving right after a feeling of distress.

Baba's actions appear somewhat out of the ordinary. He is very alert and almost always full of humor. He has a high smooth voice, bright eyes and the quickness of a cat. He often acts with childlike innocence but can change in a wink to a commanding, powerful figure. Filling plates with food and serving us, he seemed at one point to playfully scold an old, mostly toothless man with painted lines on his face, quite primitive looking. He said something and patted his stomach, then left.

I asked this man with the aid of an interpreter what Baba had said. Baba had invited him to lecture tomorrow and asked whether he had anything in his guts to speak about. The man smiled and said he never knows what he will say, just raises himself to the podium and feels that Baba speaks through him.

Later in the day I again crossed Baba's path and made the sign of respect, clasping my hands together in front of me, like praying. He touched my hands and told me to come back tomorrow. So far, I find him warm and extremely interesting to watch and hear, but certainly not to the point of feeling that he is a god. I will write again soon.

Love, Sam.

8:15 a.m., Wednesday, May 17

Dearest Sharon and family,

Had a long day yesterday. I've yet to see any miracles, although I'm privileged to be in Baba's house and around the important people gathering close to him. Yesterday I saw one of the greatest dance instructors in India give a talk and demonstration. I spoke with an elderly man who had spent many years working closely with Mahatma Ghandi, including a good deal of time spent in prison with him. A great honor for me and I felt moved.

Whoops! Alf Tidemand just joined me for breakfast and I have to stop writing now.We eat breakfast together daily and then leave for the ashram. Will continue tomorrow.

Thursday, May 18

Dear Sharon and family,

I'm feeling discouraged, even though I've been spending long days in the ashram and seeing a lot of Baba. People tell me I am very lucky. I still see no miracles although I'm impressed by the caliber of people here. Baba is not so easily impressed. An important military general from New Delhi came yesterday to see him and was just turned away.

I met one of India's leading scientists in nuclear physics, Dr. S. Bhagavantam, a former scientific adviser to the Ministry of Defense. Yesterday the governor of one of the states came. Still, when I sit cross-legged in pain on a hard floor, trying to eat rice and bread with my hand and fingers, drinking water which is potentially polluted and feeling nauseous from the smell of the spices . . . and sit next to a primitive toothless, painted man in pajamas who grabs large handfuls of food, licking his hand with a huge tongue—I begin to wonder what in the world I'm doing here.

Yesterday I spent a good deal of time during one of the slower lectures watching the flies and ants crawling around on a scab on Alf Tidemand's foot. All this and still no miracles, and my spirits drop. My fantasy changes from feeling that I will be a great bringer of the word of God back to the States and be hailed a champion of justice—marched down the streets of the USA on shoulders of admirers—to returning adrift on a life raft, penniless, empty-handed and depressed.

I'm feeling less convinced that I will see Baba alone, to say nothing of getting what I want in the way of spiritual insight. If he does see me, the pattern has been with others that this takes place only when you are about to leave.

Although I've tried to keep my eyes glued to Baba, every time he supposedly materializes something I've always just missed it. Either I develop an itch and turn away or I'm struck by something off to the side. All of a sudden Alf Tidemand whispers in my ear, "Did you see that, did you see that?" and again I'm frustrated after missing another materialization.

People tell me Baba is even able to arrange things this way, perhaps to

whet the appetite, or test one's stamina. But I'm reluctant to accept the grandiose idea of some scheme and design in frustrating me. Oh well, at least it's bright out and I'm fresh and ready for another tedious day. I hope something happens.

Love, Sam

10:15 p.m., Thursday, May 18

Dearest Sharon,

Today has been trying but extraordinary. In a ceremony this morning Baba walked amongst a crowd of the gathered poor, giving food and clothing. It was beautiful. He was so impressive. Even though I haven't seen a bona fide miracle so far, tears came to my eyes as I felt strongly for the first time the possibility that a Father, all-knowing and-comforting, could exist in human form.

I remembered that a few months ago, while sitting in meditation and seeing a small light in the distance, I had wondered whether I could be looking through a very distant window, and had imagined God on the other side. I felt that if only I could get close enough, I would see Him. And all of sudden I was struck with this experience as I watched Baba give lovingly and caringly to the poor. I felt that I was looking directly through the window at a loving Father, and tears welled up inside me.

Baba has amazing energy. He handles almost all functions on his own, in this instance giving out clothing tirelessly himself. His followers believe he knows each and everyone he passes. And they say that when he gives discourses he can immediately sense questions in his audience and weave answers into the fabric of his talk. They say he does this frequently, answering hundreds of questions this way. I saw him pass and greet literally thousands today with great energy, and indeed there is an uncanny sense of familiarity and recognition between the crowd and Baba.

The evening program was very trying for me. I have been getting tired and lonesome for home. People tell me that the natural state of affairs is for God not to give gifts too readily. There is usually a period of testing until an individual is ready. I certainly can identify with most of the people of the world who are asked to believe in God without seeing direct proof. I wonder why I should even hope to get a glimpse of a miracle or a clear vision of a higher reality—yet I try even through the frustration.

This evening Baba spoke again about right behavior and morality. I feel that he is so contrary to modern psychiatric thought, encouraging repression and over-control, a Victorian morality. I was so frustrated I began planning an early return home. He spoke about not wearing tight pants, no long hair, no fads, controlling thoughts and emotions, and all kinds of should's and should not's. At the end of the speech and chants the crowd mobbed him, falling to the ground, kissing his feet. I felt left out.

I followed Alf to the house and waited inside with a few others while Baba was busy greeting many visitors in the back. We were separated by a number of walls and quite some distance. This was probably the greatest moment of my distress, as I felt that Baba's teachings were directly threatening my way of life, even the way I practice my profession. I was seriously considering leaving.

Then all of a sudden he appeared before us, holding two pieces of candy and saying, *Sweets, sweets*—and then just as quickly he left. Within two seconds I was all smiles. My mood completely turned. I stood there chuckling like a child, confused and awed by my feelings. I was overcome by the fact that he could recognize my pain and respond to it, even while in the midst of hundreds and from another part of his house.

I've been reconsidering Baba's moralistic approach since this remarkable incident. I now wonder why I have such faith in my value system, for this system is the reflection of a culture which isn't doing very well. Half the marriages in Southern California now end in divorce; people are raping the land, polluting the air and water and killing each other, and there seems little regard for love or for God.

Why then should I cling so strongly to "modern" ideas about morality: freedom of expression in sexuality and aggression . . . involvement with the senses and the sensual to the point of pornography or the bizarre . . . following all thoughts and fantasies in an exciting chase into the absurd, doing always what one wants to do rather than what one has to do . . . putting great reliance, almost to the extent of worship, on the rational mind, with deemphasis on religion and God?

On the other hand, Baba speaks of work, duty, responsibility, dedication, devotion, love of God. He is a consummate disciplinarian, who speaks tirelessly about control over, and detachment from, the senses, and the importance of fixing one's sights on higher goals. I have long silently wished that these attitudes toward life reflected underlying truth and thus should be followed, but my cultural experience has been that being too much a goodie-goodie doesn't get you anywhere. These attitudes don't "pay-off;" in fact, they only make you more vulnerable. Now, I am beginning to feel that there is greater reason to believe in these perhaps old-fashioned but very important, solid and real-life attitudes.

I am being taught here that right actions and right attitudes bring one closer to God and closer to the meaning of life. Baba gives people the strength to believe in these forgotten attitudes, and the strength to lead lives illumined by devotion to such high ideals. I am beginning to see myself melt before him, beginning to see some of his magnificence. I love you all and will be writing again soon.

Love, Sam.

6 p.m., Saturday, May 20

Dear Sharon and family,

Well, I clearly saw a miracle—a materialization. I have little doubt now that Baba has this power. Matter appeared out of thin air—right before my eyes.

I don't know why it should happen now; perhaps his approaching me the other day in my deepest despair was the turning point. I am beginning to feel terribly blessed. Perhaps there is something to the story that God waits and tests, allowing certain experiences only when one is ready.

I was sitting there awaiting the program when the speaker announced that Baba would say farewell to a visiting professor. Baba rose about eight feet from me, turned in my direction, made a few circles in the air with his hand, and out came a very large religious necklace. Then he placed it around the professor's neck. What a sense of genuineness and love accompanied this unbelievable act! So matter-of-fact, with so little fanfare—an everyday occurrence with Baba. Yet how shocking! Can you believe that he can actually materialize objects?!

This morning I had a chance to talk to Dr. Bhagavantam. I've referred to him before; he is a distinguished physicist with an international reputation—an impressive figure, educated at Cambridge and quite grounded in science. He met Baba as a skeptic, feeling holy men were doing nothing to raise the standards of life in India. Although having no interest in meeting Sai Baba, he found himself talking to him one day while walking beside a river bank.

Baba said, *You scientists have a distorted outlook on life and always look at things which are of a transient nature. Scientists think they are discovering important laws and learning something about reality, but, in fact, the important things about the meaning of life—this they know nothing about.*

Baba continued, *Do you believe in God? Do you believe in the Indian tradition?*

Dr. Bhagavantam felt provoked and replied, "Why does one need to become a scientist to become ungodly? There are many non-scientists who are ungodly. I am proud of our traditions. My father and forefathers were all Sanskrit scholars and they respected Indian tradition."

He began quoting the distinguished American scientist Robert Oppenheimer, who is often called the father of the atomic bomb. When the first atomic bomb exploded in New Mexico, newsmen asked him to express his reaction. Oppenheimer quoted a passage from the Indian scripture, the *Bhagavad-Gita*. When *Arjuna* (devotee and friend of Lord *Krishna*) had a vision of God he described it like this: "It is like one thousand suns, all of them shining at the same time in the sky." Oppenheimer compared the light generated by the atomic explosion to *Arjuna's* splendid vision of the Lord.

Bhagavantam said: "If an American scientist with no Indian background quoted from an Indian text at the moment of his highest scientific achievement, why do you accuse scientists of being ungodly?"

Bhagavantam's discussion with Baba about the *Bhagavad-Gita* did not end there. Soon afterwards during a conversation in which Bhagavantam brought up the topic Baba asked, *Do you believe in the Bhagavad-Gita? Would you read Gita if I gave you one?*,

Bhagavantam replied, "I would not make a fetish of reading it today but I would certainly treasure it."

Well stretch out your hand, Baba said, and then picked up a handful of sand and poured it into Bhagavantam's hand. The sand, Bhagavantam claims, changed into a small text of the *Bhagavad-Gita*.

He told me: "I am a rational man, a near agnostic. I was utterly amazed, but I will not accept anything without a proper scientific explanation. I agreed within myself that the printed text must have come from a press somewhere and in my bewilderment asked Baba where the book had been printed. Baba replied: *It was printed at Sai Press. I have chosen* Telugu *script because it will be easier for you to read.*

Dr. Bhagavantam laughed as he told me that it was still four years before he was convinced of Baba's divinity. During this period he saw many more amazing miracles and spent a great deal of time and energy trying to figure Baba out. At times Baba would walk up to him and say that he was thinking along wrong lines, or that what he was thinking at that instant was correct, seeming actually in touch with Bhagavantam's thoughts.

The final straw was an incident that happened four years later, when Baba was at Bhagavantam's house. He walked over to a large sheet of stamps lying on the table and slowly moved his hand across the surface. Bhagavantam said that as he looked on, each image on the sheet turned into that of Sai Baba. He knew that Baba hadn't produced this from his sleeve and was finally convinced that Sai Baba was beyond his comprehension.

My belief in these stories is growing. I hear them from everyone, miracle after miracle, and now I have seen up close with my own two eyes a very dramatic example myself. People tell me of Baba's ability to know everything in their past and present, what they are thinking and what will happen in detail in the future. I say to myself that I can't fully accept this by word of mouth just because I saw the execution of one power (with the chance that I could have been fooled). But I am beginning to believe that Baba is this powerful, and that I am most fortunate to be in the presence of such a being.

Amazing! Unbelievable! Unthinkable! The most mind-blowing, extraordinary experience—as if the most far-fetched science fiction were actually seen to be true.

All of this delivers a crushing blow to my previous beliefs and value system and it is painful to give them up. But when I see what appears to be concrete evidence of our existence beyond time and space in a human being who not only demonstrates this reality, but teaches us how to attain realization of this higher self—then I must listen. I am witnessing here no abstract college argument or cerebral debates about whether or not God exists. I am seeing concrete evidence of such a reality.

When one finds a teacher of this caliber, all one can do is follow him, and this means full surrender as exemplified in the Bible. Those Bible stories evidently are not symbolic but true. There *is* a right and wrong way of behaving. The divine *does* become manifest in order to teach. God *does* appear on earth. There are forces in the universe, powers of being, that we cannot even imagine.

Alf says that Baba's mission is to cut out the cancer that is devouring society, that this is not easy and he is preparing people for the operation. Alf thinks there will be a worldwide catastrophe and that people will be given the chance to lead a righteous existence or else.

I am becoming humbled now in the feeling that I am really not in charge of my own destiny, that I am not the doer; God is the doer. I must nevertheless muster whatever strength I have to do my duty as best I can, to live a righteous life and do what a great master such as Baba says. There is no other choice.

Give up attachment to world possessions, he says. *Work hard, do your duty, overcome the five senses. Be loving, begin to perceive your inner voice and follow it. Meditate and find God, who resides above, below, around and within.*

I am saddened and frightened by the feeling that I may have to give up so many of the things that I thought brought me pleasure. I feel a great sense of helplessness and vulnerability in the face of Baba's awesome power. My basic beliefs are shaken. I have begun to realize that evil power must also exist, and I feel a little helpless in not being able to understand the dynamics and mechanisms and laws of such a power beyond my senses.

Since I am not sure of Baba's plan and pattern, I also at times fear that he himself might be an element of black magic and I become frightened.

Last night I crept into my dark hotel room, slowly opened the bathroom and closet doors and peeked around—and was happy and thankful that no goblins or ghosts were there to jump out at me.

I am really like a newborn baby, awed at what I see and beginning to recognize this new reality without knowing exactly how to become a part of it. Even though I am comforted by stories of Baba's protective powers, at present I do not have the great faith in his grace that many devotees have, and therefore do not feel protected by it.

. . . Well, I'm written out. I know I shouldn't let first impressions so completely dominate. I'll let them settle and will be looking for more evidence and writing again soon.

Love, Sam.

6

SHATTERED
ROCK

Almost immediately after writing the foregoing letter—as if a hammer had struck and shattered solid rock—I underwent a sudden cataclysmic change inside myself. Call it an alteration of consciousness, a shift in my mental perspective of reality, a religious conversion or a transcendental experience—it's far easier to label than to describe. My letters to follow illustrate this change. In the meantime, I'd like to stop for a moment to reflect upon and investigate the factors contributing to such a profound psychological and spiritual reaction—both from my personal point of view, as a thinking, feeling human being, and from my professional stance as a psychiatrist.

One of the important motivations behind the writing of this book is my desire to communicate some of the uplifting nature of my experience, and to share it with those who are yearning for light. Even though at present we know little about the various factors and mechanisms involved in a spiritual transformation, it is almost enough to be aware that such a phenomenon exists at all. Knowing that many people have undergone or been witness to this extraordinary experience can bring joy, and the strength to continue, into the lives of others who are searching.

What factors can lead a person to adopt a radically different view of reality? Why is it that one person can change almost completely upon simply seeing Sai Baba, while for another it takes a certain amount of time to measure and study him . . . and still another—no matter how much contact he has with Baba, experiencing the most incredible demonstrations of his greatness—changes not one iota? I have tried to analyze this but have given up; the answer is simply beyond me.

I remember reading something Baba said about this when he was questioned about why some people stay at the *ashram*, disciplining themselves, becoming involved in meditation and good services and appearing to be very devoted—yet still not experiencing much of a change inside—while others will stay only a short while and suddenly be overwhelmed with bliss and joy and become completely transformed. He has used the analogy of a rock that has a specific breaking point: let's say twenty-two blows with a hammer. It might already have received twenty blows in a previous lifetime so that in this one it needs only two more to shatter, while a similar rock may have had only two blows and so require twenty in this lifetime.

Such concepts involving another dimension of reality are beyond my level of consciousness, and so I am simply unfamiliar with many of the factors operating here. I now realize my limited capacity to communicate my experience in a way which allows others to share in the transformation. But I can shed some light on these reactions by tracing the steps along my journey . . . and I can assure the reader that there is possible a profound inner reaction in which an amazing new vision of the world opens up . . . and one feels that he is coming home again. This magnificent transition took place within me.

When I returned from India after the first trip, I was higher than a kite from my experience and thought that everyone would be interested in and excited by what I had witnessed. It was incomprehensible to me that, instead, most people seemed to shrug their shoulders and go on their way. Was I leaving out of my narrative some essential element, or were they simply not seeing something?

Soon after my return, my wife and I held open house for some 250 friends and colleagues. I had asked a number of reputable people —perhaps to protect myself—to join me in relating their experiences with Baba and in describing their impressions of his stature. We also showed beautiful films demonstrating Baba's powers and his magnificent way with people.

I was amazed to find how few people were really interested. On the other hand, I found that I had lost much of my credibility amongst my medical colleagues—to the extent that some of my psychiatric students were contacted to determine just how crazy I had become and whether or not I was still capable of teaching.

Having lived it so intensely, I had forgotten how incredible and upsetting my story was bound to be for those who had little or nothing with which to compare it in their own experience. I had forgotten my own reaction upon hearing Indra Devi for the first time speak of her experience with Sai Baba. I had forgotten all that I had gone through in India before I could accept what my eyes and heart were telling me. And if I found it difficult to believe my own eyes, then why should you find it easy to believe that what I say I saw did in fact happen as I will report it? What are my qualifications in evaluating psychic and psychological phenomena?

Let me fill in a little of my medical and scientific background . . . and trace some of the steps leading to my spiritual transformation.

I was born into a medical family, my father being a rather prominent gastroenterologist in Detroit. He told me years later that soon after my birth he lifted me to his face, his mouth to my ear, and whispered, "My son, you will be a doctor." I remember frequent visits with him to the hospital, where I was introduced to his bedside manner and the relationship between doctor and patient. At an early age I was his sidekick in sometimes embarrassing, often exciting moments as we wandered through the hospital peering into people's lives.

I entered medical school at the University of Michigan in 1958. My initial goal was to be able to help people in crises, and I felt that I would either like to work in an emergency room where activity, excitement and drama were at an intense pace, or else be a surgeon, dramatically saving people's lives. But in two years of medical training I discovered that surgery and medicine were practiced in a way which I felt reflected some of the shortcomings of our culture. That is, there was a high degree of specialization at the expense of concern for the total man. Somehow priorities seemed to get mixed up in all the fascination with subspecialties and gadgetry. I felt that there was something too mechanical and too super-scientific about the approach.

I remember one experience that epitomized this situation for me. It took place during a neurology lecture in which one of the professors brought a patient into the lecture hall before some 150 students to demonstrate certain limitations in his facial movement. This man was confused and unable to speak, obviously quite disabled by his physical impairment. Looking at the class, without making any personal human contact with the patient, the professor asked us to observe an impairment in facial movement while he inflicted pain on the patient.

Then he dug his knuckles deep into the man's chest, pinching the skin and applying great pressure on the bone. The result was a tremendous grimace but on only one side of the man's face, the other side being paralyzed. The situation was hyperscientific and without a trace of human warmth. To me, more had been demonstrated here than a condition of paralysis.

My interest in more abstract questions about the nature of existence, and in making deeper contact with my patients, led me toward psychiatry. The residency program in which I participated had a very strong psychoanalytic orientation because many of the supervisors were from the Detroit Psychoanalytic Institute. I became interested in this approach and was anticipating my own analysis when my plans were interrupted by two years of military service.

My medical experience in the military was primarily in hospital psychiatry at Fort Sam Houston in San Antonio. There I was in charge of two, sometimes three, psychiatric wards. All told, I have treated thousands of people in psychotherapy and have gone through individual and group therapy myself. I am Board Certified, having passed this highest test for competency in the field of psychiatry in 1969. I have training and experience in many psychiatric techniques, including psychoanalytically-oriented therapy, Gestalt therapy, Bioenergetic therapy, behavioral modification and conditioning therapies, relaxation techniques, group and family therapy, and marriage counseling, as well as experience in community psychiatry, drug therapies and liaison psychiatry in a general hospital.

In 1968 my family and I moved to San Diego, where I now maintain a private practice. With the title of Assistant Clinical Professor, I teach hospital-applied psychiatry and supervise psychiatric residents at the University of California. I am also the psychiatric consultant to the university's Hemodialysis and Kidney Transplantation Program.

My interest in the phenomenon of other levels of consciousness dates back to medical school years. Even then I was struck by the fact that although some people were intensely curious along these lines, most were not, and I couldn't understand why. I remember in particular reading William James' *Varieties of Religious Experience* while in medical school and being deeply moved. I was surprised that the responses of many of my friends frequently did not parallel mine and was curious about this difference in reaction.

My fascination with the possibility of spiritual transformation, of seeing more deeply into the nature of reality, continued even after I entered psychiatric training. For the most part, I was bored reading the usual psychiatric texts and found myself instead attracted to spiritual and mystical writings. I wondered why there wasn't more psychiatric interest and investigation in these areas, since they seemed such appropriate subjects for a psychiatrist, interested as he is in psychological change in general and how it comes about in therapy.

The reaction connected with a religious conversion appeared to be different in quality from the change occurring in psychotherapy. How were they related, and what did spirituality have to do with psychiatry?

7
PSYCHIATRY
& SPIRITUALITY

Early in my experience with psychiatry I had been attracted to the psychoanalytic approach. It was my observation, however, that although many people who were emotionally handicapped improved in this approach, many others who entered it relatively healthy but curious about their existence and interested in investigating themselves at a deeper psychological level, did not appear profoundly changed by the treatment. Nor did they themselves believe they had undergone a significant qualitative alteration in attitude or behavior, although many did claim to have gained some personal insight.

Another observation was that many analysts, instead of growing more spontaneous, human and approachable with the development of their professional careers, became rather austere in manner, cerebral and intellectual in meetings, and distant in social gatherings. Did this reflect certain basic limitations in the analytic approach?

I came to understand these observations in this way. In our development one can define two major processes: that of becoming more differentiated and highly defined, and that of becoming *less* differentiated, losing definition and organization.

The first process is expressed in the incredible development of an individual human being from the fusion of two single cells—egg and sperm meeting in the womb to form undifferentiated cells, from which then develop organ systems, arms, legs, eyes, etc. At this early stage the cells repeatedly divide to form a group of cells called the morula, each individual cell of which is multi-potentialed, with the capability of changing into any of three basic tissue types: ectoderm, endoderm and mesoderm.

Then a fascinating organization begins to occur, at the command of some still unknown director, in which the major tissue systems begin to unfold and differentiate. This continues, with greater and greater differentiation, until the miracle of the completion of the physical organism, with all its diversity of functions, has been accomplished.

This same process continues in the development of our emotional and mental bodies throughout childhood, as the early, poorly defined expression of emotions and perceptions slowly becomes more highly differentiated. We develop a fine sense of individuality and separateness from all that appears to be not-us: "the other." After we have left the mother's breast, we develop increasing self-sufficiency, becoming more and more able to carry on by ourselves.

The second process—which perhaps can actually be called dying—is characterized by becoming more *un*differentiated: *losing* one's sense of separateness and self. This is expressed on the physical level in the deterioration of physical organs and the eventual death of the total organism itself, followed by the body's slow disintegration into dust.

Although on the surface this process appears negative, I felt that it reflected or paralleled the process I had read about in spiritual literature; that is, the breaking down of the small individual self so that one can merge into a greater universal self. It seemed related to the spiritual path one takes in order to transcend the consciousness of duality: to merge into a fundamental oneness or unity in the universe. "One has to die in order to be reborn."

"Duality" is that consciousness where everything is seen as separate and distinct unto itself, and it appears that the spiritual process attempts to break down that separateness, to supersede distinctions, until one actually merges with "the other" and the subject-object boundary is transcended.

Now in psychoanalysis this whole process appeared to be neglected or even contradicted. I felt that psychoanalysis was concerned with establishing the separateness of the individual as a whole entity, vital and strong—helping, in other words, to clarify the self-identity of the individual. Health was seen as rising from this more highly defined sense of individuality. Analysts contended that problems occurred in the early differentiation process if a person had failed by the age of six or so to develop a strong separate identity—whether because of conflict with parents, environmental trauma or for whatever reason. It was the job of analysis to help one develop this finite sense of self by clearing up conflict revolving around the "oedipal stage" of development, which occurs at about this age.

And here was one of the first weaknesses I saw in the psychoanalytic approach. For although it was clear to me that individualization is an essential stage in healthy development, there still remains a *world* of evolution beyond this stage which isn't clearly defined in psychoanalytic thinking. The steps taken to increase a sense of self, separate and individual, with emphasis on mind and emotion (the very core of this "small" self) may be quite helpful only up to a point, but detrimental thereafter if a person is to evolve further. Many psychiatrists, and a large segment of society in general, mistakenly think that the attitudes and processes of the psychoanalytic approach which help a person regain the health and maturity he should have attained at the age of six or seven should be useful in continuing development throughout one's life. Here is where the danger lies. One can easily fall into the trap of over-valuing the mind and expression of emotion, at the expense of morality.

With the analyst curtailing his moral and value judgment, the analytic situation creates an environment of almost total permissiveness for the individual, in order for him to become aware of and to express feelings, desires and needs which have been blocked in his emotional life. A special relationship with one's mind, thoughts and fantasies is encouraged and promoted. This involves free-association: allowing everything one thinks to come to the surface and be expressed, uncensored. One becomes aware of the strong relationship of thoughts to emotions, desires, drives and needs. Allowing this free-association to occur helps bring these elements to clear consciousness, where they can be recognized and dealt with. This is one way to become better acquainted with our emotional and mental bodies.

Such a process is essential in the analytic situation, but as a way of life it can be disastrous. Yet there is ample evidence that these therapeutic principles are being carried over to society as a distorted morality, which contributes to our culturally prevalent preoccupation with self-gratification. Psychiatry may be partly responsible for this cultural borrowing and distortion of psychiatric principles, by its hesitancy to relate itself to morality in its attempt to be non-judgmental, and by its failure to clearly define healthy limitations for the permissive attitude. It is clear that such boundaries must be defined. Our culture in general has gone overboard in testing how far we can go with sexuality, promiscuity and pornography; assertiveness, aggression and violence.

There seems to me no end in sight to our testing—"letting it all hang out." We're getting deeper and deeper into worshiping the senses, emotions and our every fantasy. Instead of becoming masters of ourselves so as to create order and facilitate humanity's evolution of consciousness, we are becoming slaves to our emotional and mental energies and being driven every which way in our craving for sensual gratification. We have deformed the land and polluted our air, food and water. We trade insensitivity and violence with one another instead of sharing our love and giving our help where it is needed. The moral and spiritual precepts of directing our lives with discipline and a sense of responsibility, and the importance of surrendering our selfish wants and desires in order to attain higher goals for ourselves and for the welfare of others, seem to have lost importance for us.

An over-valuing of emotional expression not only leads to social chaos but absolutely curtails spiritual growth. Freedom of emotional expression must be balanced by the spiritual attitudes of giving up attachment to emotions at a certain point (as discussed later in this chapter) and of considering the possibility that our true identity may lie beyond the influence of the emotions. I believe that the psychoanalytic approach will become more balanced and holistic when integrated with spiritual principles. There is a definite need in contemporary society for such spiritual practices as quieting, emptying or controlling the mind in meditation, detaching from emotions, and disciplining and controlling our energies—as expressed on the social level by developing a sense of morality, responsibility and respect for others.

Another orientation and attitude propagated by psychiatry which I came to believe helpful up to a point and harmful beyond, was the over-valuing of the rational mind's ability to know—the faith we have that the rational mind can solve all problems, all difficulties. Although beginning to recognize the mind's limitations, for the most part the psychoanalytic approach still gives it a preeminence among our perceptive faculties which greatly limits any deeper awareness of reality.

It seems that this over-emphasis on rationality grew with the development of science and the industrial and technological revolutions. To the extent that the present state of our technology represents true and unqualified progress in civilization, we may be justified in holding the rational mind supreme. An increasingly more vocal percentage of the population, however, feels that we have had to pay too high a price in human welfare for progress that has been primarily materialistic in nature. Living on the brink of nuclear war and the possibility of annihilation, rather than indicating the infallibility of the rational mind, attests to its limitations.

The psychoanalytic approach appeared to me to embody contradictions and unresolved views concerning the mind. I saw it this way. On the one hand, analysts had quickly become aware that many people do not change as a result of intellectual interpretations or didactic discussions of their problems. We can, however, gain insight into our problems through the nonrational technique of free-association. It appeared that analysts recognized the importance of going beyond the rational mind in order to delve more deeply into the nature of one's existence and *then* to use the rational mind to help evaluate and integrate what one discovered. The analytic approach deems it crucial that the patient understand the genetic determinants of his behavior (that is, how early environmental traumas relate to present symptoms) in order to effect a lasting cure.

Actually, there is growing doubt among psychotherapists that the rational mind even needs to evaluate and integrate what one uncovers in order for healing to take place. In other words, one does not necessarily

It is enough if love is cultivated—the love that knows no distinction between oneself and another—because all are but limbs of the one corpus of God Almighty. Through love alone can the embodiment of love be gained. Here no scholarship is needed; in fact scholarship will be an impediment, for it caters to egoism and it breeds doubts and the desire for disputation and the laurel of victory over others preening themselves as learned!

have to know how his problem is related to early parental or environmental experience to find relief from his symptom. There are psychotherapies being developed now in which the full therapeutic work is done nonverbally, and no attempt is made to explain the why's or wherefore's. Success rates in these psychotherapies seem at least as good as those reported for psychoanalytic therapy. Could it be that the healing force in all the therapies has more to do with love and human caring, that the cerebrating, intellectual gyrations mean very little?

At any rate, analysts seemed on the one hand to have recognized sufficient limitations of the rational mind in the treatment process to have developed the technique of free-association. On the other hand, I was struck by how cerebral and overly intellectual many analysts were in their writing and in meetings, as if they actually thought they could understand and define human nature with concepts and mechanisms as one would an automobile.

Even early in my education I had greatly doubted that one could understand human nature in this manner. But many analysts gave it a good try, and I still remember how boring it was for me to wade through reams of arid professional reading material. I found myself instead reading about mystics, Zen Buddhism and other spiritual doctrines, in which is found again and again the firm assertion that higher levels of reality simply can't be comprehended by the mind . . . in which the mind is considered an obstacle to be overcome and transcended in order for one to see more deeply into his true nature. Identifying with mind, emotions or body leads one more deeply into the world of illusion, into the condition of suffering.

I felt that the Western behavioral scientist's identification of self with mind was the result of a one-sided vision of reality. My attraction to such spiritual concepts as *Atma* (the real self; one's divinity: imperishable, immutable, infinite, eternal) and *moksha* (the merging of the wave with the ocean from which it appears to differ; liberation from delusion, release from the round of birth and death; the attainment of eternal joy) was simply too great to allow me to be bound by the limited conceptions of self adhered to in modern psychiatry. These Eastern views and the spiritual practices growing out of them demanded thorough investigation.

A comparison of the psychoanalytic process of free-association with the practice of Eastern-originated meditation points out in a concrete way the differences between East and West in attitudes and approaches toward mind and self. The aim of both these processes is toward realizing our deepest inner nature, and a central element in each is our becoming aware of being an observer and witness—but for different reasons. In free-association, one becomes the observer as a means to an end, in order to watch thoughts and emotions as they bubble up into awareness. The assumption is that these thoughts and feelings are valuable because they eventually lead to underlying conflicts which when found can be resolved; therefore, one is directed to attend to and follow them.

In meditation, on the other hand, simply being aware of oneself as witness may be an end in itself. The experience of being centered or focused in full awareness in the here and now may lead us into deeper experience of our true nature. Meditation is supposed to take us beyond the mind to the point where we can watch passing thoughts and feelings without being seduced into attending to and following them.

If the mind is to be used at all, it is to be directed by the will of the observer to create an inner spiritual experience, such as that which invokes a sense of awe of creation, or an all-encompassing sense of love and peace. This can be done by mentally repeating one of the many names of God, trying to visualize light, picturing a form of worship, or any number of techniques. These exercises tend to tame the mind, encouraging in one the experience of divinity believed to lie at the center of our identity. By staying in touch with one's self as witness and with an aspect of the divine, one may eventually reach the place where witnesser and the witnessed, the "I" and the "that," merge and become one. At this point the profound sense of the great Eastern phrase *Tat Twam Asi* (that thou art) may be finally realized and one enters the peace and calm that defies understanding.

By contrast, if one is free-associating on an analyst's couch and drops into a place of great peace and quiet, this may be interpreted as resistance to the flow of material, and the individual may be encouraged back into following his thoughts and feelings.

In Eastern thought concerning the nature of man, there is a clear distinction made between mind and real self, a distinction not appreciated in contemporary psychiatry.[1] Baba has said, *The scientist looks outside—and is always saying, "What is this?"* (this which can be perceived by the senses; existing in the world of emotion or mind). *But the saint is always looking inside, and his question is, "What is that?"* (that which is beyond the senses, beyond emotions, beyond the grasp of the mind).

The mind, he says, *is like a cloth, the threads of which are desire. If we give up desire, the cloth falls away, revealing our true nature.*

My most serious misgiving about psychoanalysis arose when I witnessed what happened within myself during early attempts at treating

1. In Eastern literature on consciousness it is written that thoughts begin, develop and end at an extremely rapid pace, on the order of trillions per second. We are able, it is said, through the practice of certain spiritual exercises such as meditation, to reach a level of awareness where we can actually observe the creation of thoughts. Evidently a space exists between the end of one thought and the beginning of another which, when we have attained a sufficiently advanced or expanded level of consciousness, we are capable of moving into—thus going beyond the mind. This condition, called *samadhi,* is characterized as a state of absolute bliss.

patients with this approach. I began feeling less spontaneous, more controlled and isolated from my patients—the exact opposite of the results I had hoped for. I began to search for a way of observing and reacting to the world which was less limiting. This led me to Gestalt therapy, a method I found both interesting and promising. I launched an enthusiastic investigation by undertaking the therapy myself.

On the positive side, this approach dealt more directly with the nature of duality and the possibility of going beyond it, and therefore seemed to recognize, at least, the possibility of man's spiritual nature. There was also less emphasis on the rational mind as a means of gaining deeper knowledge of the world, and more on one's taking responsibility himself for his actions, without blaming mother, father or early trauma. Still, as in most uncovering insight-oriented psychotherapies, great value was placed on freedom of expression, without defining or even raising the issue of where in one's development detachment from emotions becomes desirable or necessary.

The Gestalt therapist is less concerned than the psychoanalyst with the *why's* behind a patient's behavior. This, he feels, only leads to overly intellectual talk *about* problems instead of direct experience of them. His job is to help the patient directly experience, thereby becoming aware of, *what* he is doing and *how* he is *being* in the here and now. Being centered in this kind of awareness, without being unduly limited or constricted by memories of the past, worries about the future, transient emotions or repetitious and distracting thought patterns, is considered growth-promoting.

This seemed to me a rather great change in orientation from analytic therapy. Interpretation and explanation by the therapist was considered a waste of time, serving only to boost the ego of the therapist. His job then became less cerebral as he stopped trying to figure the patient out, and more spontaneous and intuitive as he tried to experience the patient's reality. Gestalt therapists indeed looked different from analysts, seeming to reflect their different orientations to the world. The generally austere, well-tailored, at times up-in-the-air analyst was a contrast to the frequently more spontaneous, sometimes overly casual but more down-to-earth Gestalt therapist.

Gestalt practitioners frequently wanted to be called by their first name. The founder of the movement, Fritz Perls, projected an image of earthy, cantankerous playfulness—sometimes even to the extent of jarring coarseness. At times he wore a jumpsuit and always casual clothing. He wrote a book with the scholarly title *In and Out of the Garbage Pail*. This sort of flavor about the therapist and therapy was quite attractive to me.

The patient in Gestalt therapy is asked to move beyond duality and break the subject-object boundary—to re-identify with avoided or projected aspects of self—by actually *becoming* any object or feeling-state avoided or considered separate and apart from the self—often by acting out the role of the object or feeling, or attempting to develop a dialogue with it. Everything perceived by the senses or conceived by the mind as being separate from the self is considered a projection *of* the self, an aspect of the self which for some reason the self considers foreign and tries to cut off and reject. Frequently the work of the treatment is to direct the patient to re-identify with this shunned aspect, making better contact with it or even merging with it and regaining the energy bound up in the projection process.

Of particular significance are those projections labeled "bad" or those which are in any way avoided or considered particularly alien to the self, and an effort is made to establish channels to these areas so as to end struggling with them. For example, if one is phobic or frightened of barking dogs, he may be asked to play the part of a barking dog. If he is frightened of anger, violence or spontaneous assertive behavior, he may initially find it difficult to be the barking dog. As his reluctance breaks down and he feels more familiar with this task, he may likewise feel more at home with his own impulses and his own assertiveness. What was once a frightening experience may now turn into a source of strength. In this way one may develop the capacity to assert himself when that reaction is called for in everyday life.

It often happens that by playing this kind of game the patient becomes aware that such projections have become symbols and that something important lies hidden within the symbol, something avoided and feared. When one re-identifies and rediscovers those parts of himself which are avoided because of fears or guilts, he becomes stronger and healthier.

Using the previous example: If one is frightened of anger, acting out the motions and feelings of the barking dog, although at first frightening, may become a source of pleasure and strength as one gains experience with such activity and sees that nothing terrible comes of it. In this process as one reestablishes contact with repressed feelings, including them among the choice of responses he has in facing the world, he no longer has to avoid or be frightened of all situations in which a possible appropriate choice of activity is anger or aggression.

Through such treatment I became more deeply aware of the nature of duality, more familiar with some of the techniques that could be used to break down the subject-object boundary. I found usefulness in the techniques but after a while I found some limitations as well.

For instance, in my own experience these techniques did not resolve my fears of death or of physical or mental deterioration with age. I could not get to that state where I was unaffected by such fears; I could not lessen my aversion for weakness. I wanted to feel strong and in control and did not want to feel weak and helpless.

No matter how many times I played these roles, I still ended up wanting one over the other, continuing to fear weakness and struggling to be strong. Although aware of my areas of avoidance, in trying to resolve them I frequently found myself playing parts over and over again without making any headway. There finally came a time when I felt I could go no further in Gestalt therapy. I was unable to break certain problem cycles, and saw myself endlessly repeating certain patterns of behavior and responses without knowing how to get out.

Even though I began to appreciate that what I considered the outside world was really me, and that struggling with it was only a reflection of my struggle with myself—that if I wanted to stop my inner struggle I would have to stop wrestling with the "outside"—I was still unable to stop. It was as if I were stuck in the groove of a record, repeating myself over and over again. The only way of getting out would be to pick myself up out of the groove and place myself somewhere else.

The difficulty and confusion in the therapy seemed to be that in order to break the cycle one had to become unaffected by real pain and the feelings and emotions which accompany it. Psychotherapy may be effective in overcoming an irrational or imagined fear, in which one fears a situation that "in reality" is not painful. But it is quite another thing not to fear a situation which "really" *is* painful. To become unaffected by, and detached from, "real" emotions is generally considered a negative and undesirable process by most schools of psychotherapy. They generally call such a maneuver a defense against, or denial of, reality. On the other hand, this kind of detached attitude toward what we call the "real" or physical world is an indispensable part of the spiritual approach. This is a point over which psychiatry has been so critical of religion.

Most psychotherapies believe that one of the basic principles behind motivation is that of pleasure-pain. Because of our experience of either pleasure or pain, we develop the desire to choose one object over another. Our seeing things as separate from one another and of being more or less valuable is directly related to our anticipation of pleasure or pain. Gratification of wants is pleasurable; frustration of wants is painful.

If there were a way to transcend this whole system, so that one could be unaffected by either pleasure or pain, then everything would be considered equal. The pressure to move in one direction rather than another would end, as all directions would be the same. Duality, the experience of seeing things separate and apart, would then have been transcended.

Psychiatry's position is that to try to become unaffected by such a central system in our lives is in fact a defensive measure, a way of trying to repress or deny our true identity. Psychiatrists for the most part do not believe that there is a higher self or a level of consciousness beyond duality. Their position is that God is manufactured by man; belief in a higher self is a defense against emotions. On the other hand is the spiritual attitude: attachment to the emotions is a defense against realizing one's higher self.

It became apparent to me that at one level of our development—the process of becoming more differentiated and developing a sense of self—it is very important to become aware of emotions and to learn to express them. It is important to be able to feel both the role of the weak and of the strong: to feel all the reactions involved in living both roles and to know how to express the full repertoire of feelings related to each.

But at another level of development—the process of dying, or dissolving the small self in order to merge into a higher self—it is essential to learn to detach from emotions and the senses; to learn not to desire strength over weakness, pleasure over pain or even life over death; to treat all positions as equal. Such seemingly opposing feelings are an illusion. They reflect a dualistic perception of being in the universe.

One of the reasons for psychiatry's failure to integrate or reconcile these two fundamental approaches to human growth seems to be a general misunderstanding of the nature of *detachment,* a confusion of detachment with repression. There is a great difference between the two.

My belief is that at the point in our development when we are trying to become more individual and defined, it may be harmful to detach from the emotions. To do so then would be to repress primary energies at a time when we are just learning about them. It would be like giving up walking before one has learned how to walk; we would become emotionally crippled. One cannot transcend the senses or emotions—cannot surrender them to God—if one is not actually in control of them, if one has not first reached a stage of individuality. They are not ours to surrender.

In effect, we grow toward a merging with the universal or "cosmic" self "up through" the human self, a vehicle for growth like the stem of a plant. And, since the human or small self is as much mental and emotional as it is physical, a strong sense of identity and integration of the emotions are as important in our development as is the stem's cellular growth.

After we have attained a state of individuality and identity, it is time to surrender the ego or personality of the small self in order to merge into the higher self . . . to give up involvement with the senses in favor of a deeper involvement with God . . . to transfer our energy from stem-making and maintenance to blossoming.

In talking about the process of growth and the final stage of release, Sai Baba has said, . . . *It is like the flower of one's individuality growing into a fruit and filling itself with sweet juice out of its own inner essence, and then the final release from the tree.*[1]

---

[1]*Sathya Sai Speaks,* Vol VII, p. 253.

This seems to be the difference, then, between repression and detachment. The first is separating oneself, out of fear, from contact with one's senses and emotions before learning to control and harness these energies—thereby remaining unaware of them. The second is surrendering them willingly as part of our yearning to continue to grow, after we have gained awareness, and a measure of self-mastery, of them.

Religion presents many techniques, orientations and attitudes toward life which help in gaining detachment from feelings, but for most psychiatrists this is regarded as detrimental to emotional stability and sound mental health. The common Western attitude regarding this kind of detachment is that it is a defense against our basic drives and emotions, and as a consequence likely to foster indifference toward human welfare and a selfish withdrawal from society. The spiritually wise say this is not the case. They point to examples of the highest expression of the correct spiritual attitudes as demonstrated in the life style, character, and activities of such greats as Christ, Krishna and Buddha . . . and they assert that in fact one becomes more loving, creative and productive to the degree that he is able to *be* in the world while remaining fundamentally unaffected by it.

So the question arose: how to break out of the hold of duality . . . and was it possible to do so without giving up one's attachment to his senses and feelings?

You must not be a bit of blotting paper, absorbing all the passions and emotions, all the joys and griefs that the actress nature demonstrates on the stage of life. You must be a lotus unfolding its petals when the sun rises in the sky, unaffected by the slush where it is born or even the water which sustains it!

8
MONKEY
MIND

It was the end of a long, hard day, a day which would prove to be a turning point in my life. I had just seen a woman who was quite distressed, and in the course of the hour with her, despite my efforts to center attention on what she was saying, I had felt myself becoming overwhelmed by a powerful and extremely unwelcome sensation. I didn't know exactly how it had begun this time, but all of a sudden I'd felt myself struggling inside in a way that was quite familiar to me by now . . . back into that vicious cycle—here I go again.

The pattern was familiar; I had observed it in many of my patients and seen it develop within myself, witnessing it closely during my own treatment in the course of my training. But recognizing it was one thing, and pulling myself out of this kind of conflict was quite another. How had my energy been sapped? Had my patient in some way transferred her confusion and distress to me? Had her cry for help and my feeling of being unable to meet her needs created this sense of helplessness? I simply did not know.

I felt very scattered and confused after the hour. I disliked the feeling of not being in control, of being lost, which was spreading through my mind and limbs like some sort of paralysis. I struggled to feel strength and power again. This is the nature of duality.

When I want to get rid of one feeling and to replace it with another; when I choose one object over another, then of course there is struggle. If I can accept pain equal to pleasure, sadness equal to happiness, weakness equal to strength, there is no struggling. But when I start desiring and wanting, the struggle begins. How to stop?

At the end of the hour with the woman I was caught and knew I couldn't get out by myself. What a helpless feeling, as if I were com-

On Bondage

In our country, there is a peculiar method of trapping monkeys. This process consists of bringing a big pot with a small mouth and keeping some material which is attractive to the monkey inside the pot. The monkey will put its hand inside the pot and catch hold of a handful of the material. It will then not be able to pull out its hand from within the pot. It will imagine that someone inside the pot is holding its hand. Then it makes an attempt to run away along with the pot, but the monkey is thus trapped. No one is holding the monkey. The monkey has trapped itself, because it has taken in its hand such a lot of material. The moment it lets the material in its hand go, it will be free.

In the same manner, in this big pot of the world with the narrow mouth of the family, man is tempted by the pleasures of the world, and when he gets lost with involvement in these pleasures he thinks that someone or something is binding him down. No other person is responsible for this bondage. The moment he gives up the pleasures and detaches himself, he will be free. That is the way to free himself from the imagined bondage.

pletely destroyed inside—chastising myself for not being in control, wanting desperately to get out . . . outside myself, out of the dilemma of self-examination and self-struggle: a whirlpool of stale, maddeningly repetitive sensations, thoughts and emotions. As I played this frightful game with myself, I only sank deeper into feelings of despair, confusion, frustration and futility. I couldn't begin to think of sleep that night.

"Is there any other way of being in this world?" I shouted silently to the room. "Is there any place inside where there is peace and quiet?"

The harder I thought about this with the mind, the more confused I became; the more confused, the more I struggled to replace confusion with a feeling of strength. The more I tried for strength, the greater my sense of weakness; the more struggling, the greater my exhaustion.

Finally, in my despair I did something that was quite unusual for me. I had to get out of my mind. Scanning my memory for things I might have read or heard about other ways of being in the world, I remembered a book entitled *Through an Eastern Window,* by a psychologist named Jack Huber. He had experienced meditation in the East, and his book described meditational techniques that had lifted him into another state of consciousness. The technique that had struck me as being most interesting was one which concentrated on breathing.

In desperation and the recognition that I was going to have to do something beyond or in addition to thinking, if I was ever to escape the whirlpool my frantic mental activity had created, I began to focus on my breathing, keeping awareness on breathing and nothing else. This went on for a day and a half. Though I was still in touch with what had become an almost self-pitying sense of suffering, my concentration was focused mainly on the breathing process.

Now one might think that concentrating on one's breathing should be relatively easy. But to have enough control over the mind to focus and hold attention on one point for any length of time proved quite difficult—especially with the mind trapped in a desperate and helpless feeling of conflict. To loosen the mind's infatuation with this suffering, so that it could become free and fluid enough to fix on breathing, was a struggle that went on for hours before I began to feel somewhat in tune with the process.

At first I could hold attention for only a few seconds before the mind was pulled to my struggle; then for longer and longer periods but always with the mind in some strange powerful manner drawn in the end back to the struggling. Torn between the two focuses of struggling and breathing, I felt the exercise to be futile, yet I had no choice but to continue, hoping that something was happening beyond my level of awareness, something that was leading me out of the trap.

Then something else occurred. I did something that I hadn't done since childhood, and now it felt very unusual and out of place. I began to pray. At this point I was willing to try almost anything to get away from the grasp of my mind.

"Oh, God, if there is any way of being other than this," I pleaded, "please help me." And something amazing happened. Within seconds, I felt something release inside of me, as if a weight of some kind had suddenly been removed. Waves of energy, expanding and contracting, began to pulse through my body. I felt very fluid.

What a strange experience! What did it have to do with my day and a half of meditation and the short period of prayer? The conflict which had been so intense a second before was completely dissipated; I simply had no interest in it anymore as I felt a wonderful, peaceful calm envelop me.

What in the world was this state in which I found myself? I hadn't resolved anything conceptually or intellectually, but the sense of peace, well-being and energy in my body was marvelous.

There is a good story of Gajendra the elephant, which conveys well the meaning of bondage. In the thick forest of life, a wild elephant, the mind of man, will be roaming about. This mind which is roaming about becomes thirsty for sensuous pleasures. To quench that thirst, it begins to drink in the lake of worldly activities. The moment the elephant puts its foot in the lake, the crocodile of attachment catches hold of its leg. The elephant cannot free itself. With this attachment, the elephant struggles until it becomes weak. When it becomes weak, it prays to God and asks to be saved. When such a prayer, in desperation, is made to God, the grace of God will descend on the person. When the elephant's vision turns toward God, God's vision also turns toward the elephant. This is what is called sudarshana *or holy vision. When you turn toward God, God will turn toward you.*

It wasn't until later that I began to understand what all this meant. The mind is a powerful tool which has to be brought under control. If it controls *us,* we are lost. When the mind engages itself with sensations, emotions and desires, we are caught. My mind had been involved in struggle out of the desire to be strong and to escape a sense of confusion. When I was able to pull the focus of my mental energy away from this struggling and detach from the whole problem, I felt great relief, an upsurge of peace and energy.

Sai Baba has said that the mind need not merge itself with the physical senses or emotions, that it has senses of its own with which it should be concerned. They are awareness, peace, truth, love and bliss. As long as the mind is engaged with these, all is well. And when there is a strong desire for God, negative thoughts, even if they arise, just pass through the mind and are not retained. Baba has said, *That habit of thinking is a long-standing one; even when it is broken, it will continue for some time. The fan continues to revolve, doesn't it, for some time, even after the current is switched off? The best method is to train the thought onto a spiritual goal: perfection, God, Rama*

He tells the story of a poor man who was overcome with many menial tasks by which he felt bound and trapped. One day he met a sage who asked him what he most desired, and he pleaded for a servant to help him. The sage said that his wish would be fulfilled, but with this catch: The servant would labor and be productive as long as the man could provide him with work; but should he be without work and become idle, he would turn upon the man and kill him. The man felt quite safe, however, as he knew there was enough work to occupy a servant for quite some time.

Shortly thereafter a man did indeed come to his house and agree to work for him. At first the man could provide his new servant with continuous work, but soon—and quite a bit earlier than he had anticipated—all the work was done and the servant was about to become idle. The man grew panicky and hurried back to the sage. "What shall I do?" he moaned.

The sage replied: "There is a solution to your problem. When the servant has finished all of his work, have him build a high pillar in front of your house; when he has finished, have him occupy himself by climbing up and down the pillar continuously. In this way you can keep him occupied forever."

Of course the servant in this story represents the mind. Directed along the right path, it can be a powerful tool. But if left idle and without firm direction and control, it can become very dangerous. The pillar in the story is symbolic of God. Engaging our mind constantly with God will tame it and bring it under our control. When I was able to detach the mind from my struggle, and it became stilled and centered in the task of just being aware of my breathing, I felt great calm and relief.

This was the beginning of my fascination with non-cerebrating, non-verbal, *experiential* techniques in psychotherapy. This pivotal experience in my life hinted at other ways of being in the world that I hadn't been aware of which could bring one an extreme sense of contact and peace. I could not conceptualize them; I allowed belief in their existence to develop on the strength of a faculty I had always considered inferior to rationality: my intuition.

I sought out a teacher in a therapeutic technique called Bioenergetic therapy. "Bioenergy" is a current name for a form of energy hypothesized for thousands of years to exist within the body and throughout the universe in a state too subtle for usual human perception.

This cosmic energy or life-force, in one form or another, has been a religious or philosophical element of virtually every human culture in history. It has been known to the Hindus as *prana,* for example, for thousands of years. To Polynesian peoples it is *mana,* and in the pantheistic worlds of most preliterate cultures it is the all-pervasive power which gives life even to what we in the West consider inanimate objects.

Due primarily to the long-standing inability of Western science to detect or measure such a force or energy, Western civilization is unfamiliar with, and skeptical of, its existence. New ultrasensitive solid-state instrumentation, however, now points to evidence that it may indeed exist after all. Russian physicists and psychologists, who seem to be the leaders in the various fields of scientific exploration often combined under the general heading "parapsychology," have given the elusive force a properly scientific name. They call it "bioplasmic energy."

In any case, the modern theory behind bioenergy is that its unhampered circulation through the body, and transference between body and atmosphere, is essential for the ultimate in physical, mental and spiritual health. Most of us have developed blocks to the free flow and exchange of this energy, however. These blocks are represented by certain tensions, contractions and constrictions in body musculature; feelings of discomfort in visceral organs or other organ systems; or conditions of disease anywhere in the body. By interfering with the flow and fluidity of the energy, we develop aches and pains on a physical level; anxieties and depressions on an emotional level; impulsive thoughts, preoccupations and fantasies on a mental level.

This type of energy flow is not unlike that described by acupuncturists; they see the use of their needles as a means of releasing the blocks and allowing proper flow to resume throughout the body. Other techniques, such as placing the body in postures that produce strain and promote involuntary trembling, or by using the infliction of pain, deep massage, touching or movement, can also effect a release from these blocks. Release helps bring about a state of expansion and fluidity which makes the experiencing of oneself and others a deeper, more exciting and penetrating experience.

After freeing energy in this manner, becoming fluid and flexible, one becomes aware of a process called "centering" or "grounding," in which he experiences a feeling of stability concerning his position in life. One develops a fuller experience of himself and others, becomes more confident, feels more secure. This is a concrete feeling, experienced within the body both physically and emotionally.

Wilhelm Reich, a contemporary of Freud, was the founder of this mode of treatment. He thought—and many thought him crazy for this idea—that there was a heretofore unknown energy in the atmosphere called orgone energy. People could become sensitive to it, he believed, incorporating it, perhaps merging with it, thereby gaining a great deal of strength and vigor.

Reich tried to concentrate this orgone energy by building strange-looking boxes and placing people inside them. He even thought that he could cure cancer with this technique. This seemed absurd to many casual observers and to many of his contemporaries. Reich's life ended on a rather low note when he became involved in legal difficulties over his ideas of curing cancer with orgone energy and over some of his other methods of therapy. He died in prison.

Although I had at first found Reich's concepts strange, I was quite interested in them, and became even more fascinated after learning about the similarities between some of the bioenergetic techniques and yoga. This is the case both in the exercises and postures practiced and in concepts regarding energy in the atmosphere and the body. Yogis spoke of *prana* energy in the air; and Reich, of orgone energy.

I became involved in Bioenergetic therapy two months after the "turning point" experience with the patient mentioned previously and soon experienced, concretely, a tremendous opening up of my body and release of energy—a feeling quite similar to that following the earlier period of meditation and prayer. Bioenergetic experience began to teach me a new way of being in the world.

I began to recognize that I had a real alternative to being too much in the mind, emotions or senses. By focusing on this internal energy I could pull myself out of the mind. By meditating on its flow, its expanding and contracting waves, I found that I could become more intuitive in my practice with patients and much happier in my life.

I didn't understand quite how this worked, how I could gain so much from such a non-cerebrating way of being in the world; I only knew that it *did* work for me. Could it be that by tuning in to these energies I was drawing on some form of life-force which was the fundamental source of my strength, creativity and intuition? This I didn't yet understand, nor could I comprehend how this process related to psychoanalysis or other psychiatric theories.

From here I became involved in a variety of other techniques for releasing energy. There are many to choose from; we're becoming infatuated with techniques these days. There are Rolfing, body contact therapy, massage, all kinds of "touchy-feely" groups, encounter and sensitivity sessions, Primal Scream therapy, Tai Chi and on and on. Leaving my family behind, I would go to the "growth centers" and dance around in a rather wild animalistic manner, stomping on the ground, yelling, shrieking, moaning, groaning, howling—getting in touch with primitive feelings that I usually didn't allow myself to express. Then there was rolling on the floor, hugging everyone and sharing intimate thoughts and feelings . . . and lying on the ground on my back with my arms outstretched, reaching for an imaginary mama, lips puckered and sucking from an imaginary breast.

There was no doubt that these techniques-upon-techniques were doing some good. I was witnessing myself becoming less frightened of experimenting with every imaginable drive and yearning, actually feeling myself becoming more alive and sensitive. I found I could pull myself out of old repetitive conflicts; I had a choice and could be different. But I also saw some dangers—a great danger to my home life, my close relationship with my wife and children. There are many temptations for one stomping around up there in the mountains.

I saw many people activating themselves and sharing intimacies, and I could see that given enough time in this setting, one could readily become sexually involved with others. I found myself asking, "Well, here I am with all this energy, but how can I actually structure and focus it so that I can grow without destroying myself and those I love in the process?"

It seemed I had again reached a dead-end. Leaders of the human potential groups had promised expanded vistas and new freedoms, and I had listened with hope to their claims of the possibility of infinite growth. But again, I failed to find the leaders themselves demonstrating in action what they promised in words. And I remained as distrustful as ever of techniques which seemed so lacking in a sense of morality or discipline. Was there indeed something missing in these techniques, or was I chasing some kind of fantasy?

9
CADUCEUS
& KUNDALINI

A week after meeting Baba, I became aware of a message hidden within a familiar symbol: the caduceus,[1] symbol of medicine. A latent but extremely powerful energy called *kundalini,* or "serpent fire," is thought to lie "sleeping" within the body—a hidden potential of which most people are completely unaware their entire lives. The principle of *kundalini* is significant in Hinduism, yoga and virtually all mystical and occult doctrines. The caduceus symbolizes the manner in which this energy is awakened. When I discovered this, I realized that it might provide answers to many of my questions.

Consider for a moment the symbol of caduceus. It is a staff around which two snakes are entwined, intersecting each other at several points. At the top of the staff is a pair of wings. Charles W. Leadbeater, a noted scholar of occult and mystical literature, has theorized that the caduceus represents an ancient secret of the means of achieving transcendence of the body and ego. The staff, he believes, is a representation of the spinal cord, and the two snakes symbolize paths that the *kundalini* takes as it awakens and unfolds from its source at the base of the spine. The path beginning to the left is called *Ida* in Sanskrit and the one to the right *Pingala;* the pathway through the center of the spine to the head is *Sushumna.*

It is thought that by the disciplined practice of meditation, chanting or specific yoga exercises—usually over a period of several years—an individual can liberate his sleeping *kundalini.* As *kundalini* energy awakens

---

[1] The caduceus of Mercury, symbol of medicine; prior to Greek mythology may have originally been the symbol for *Kundalini* or serpent fire.

and evolves, certain areas along the spine, called *chakras,* also awaken or open up, to become centers of organized energy systems. As this energy is developed, the individual's consciousness changes. How he perceives the world, and thus how he reacts to it, changes.

My experience with Bioenergetic therapy made me more open-minded to such a concept than I would otherwise have been and gave me an awareness of how such a transformation might take place. I was beginning to experience strange new vibrations and perceptions myself. Also, I began to come across increasing discussion of this type of energy. Dr. William Tiller, for example, a noted Stanford University physicist, includes the *chakras* in his scientific model of how the human body evolves in response to the radiation of energy and information from the environment.[1] And in *Breakthrough to Creativity* Shafica Karagulla, a Los Angeles neuropsychiatrist, describes in fascinating detail the *chakras* as seen by "sensitives" with whom she is working—people with highly developed sensory, or extrasensory, powers.

There are supposedly seven *chakras,* located not in the physical body but in the *etheric* body, thought to exist coincident with its physical counterpart. (Dr. Tiller refers to the *etheric* body as the "negative space-time frame body" and sees each of the bodies acting as a "tuned circuit via which one may tap energy from the cosmos or communicate with another aspect of self.")[2]

The *chakras* are thought to be intimately related to the body's endocrine system. With the successive awakening of each, there are said to be corresponding changes in one's body, emotions, mind and degree of consciousness. The progressive expansion of consciousness yields an increase of knowledge about oneself and a deepening awareness regarding one's relationship to the cosmos. Finally, when the seventh or crown *chakra* at the top of the head is awakened and opened, the individual is supposedly able to leave his physical body—thus realizing the soul's transcendence of the body.

Coming to realize fully that the nature of one's fundamental identity is conscious energy, or awareness—rather than body, ego or personality—is thought to be the highest human level of knowledge. And actually rising from the normal level of consciousness to this higher level is represented of course by the wings of the caduceus.

What is the relationship of all this to psychiatry? The first and second *chakras,* supposedly related to the adrenal glands and gonads of the endocrine gland system, are said to be located in connection with the anal and genital areas of the pelvis. This seems anatomically to parallel

[1] William Tiller, *Radionics, Radiesthesia and Physics;* A.P.M. Symposium Transcript "The Varieties of Healing Experience," Oct. 1971 (pp. 55-78).
[2] Ibid.

Freud's observation of the importance of these body areas in developing personality. These two *chakras* appear to be related to coarser, more basic energies, such as aggression and hostility—or what Freud called anal attitudes—and to genital or sexual attitudes. According to the theory of *kundalini,* when *chakras* are awakened, the personality takes on certain psychological qualities which reflect the *chakras* corresponding energies. And in fact many of psychiatry's personality types and its description of orientations to life *are* related to anal and genital characteristics in different combinations and intensities.

Most of us are aware of these basic energies, and part of our life's work is to be in touch with them so as to channel them appropriately for our survival. (As a matter of fact, the first *chakra* is often called the "*root chakra*.") There are, however, some people who are not in touch with these fundamental biological or survival energies, as if these *chakras* have not been awakened in them. These people have not experienced aggressiveness or sexuality in their lives; they are in fact almost void of any way of making contact with the world.

Psychiatrists, it seems to me, should be concerned with helping people first to get in touch with these lower energies and then with finding ways of channeling them for better adaptation, adjustment and happiness in life. For the most part, however, psychiatrists make the mistake of awakening these energies *without* dealing with their proper channeling and disciplining. Then we get into some of the difficulties of our age like "letting it all hang out," and worshiping the emotions and drive systems at the expense of learning discipline and control.

I have already discussed the kind of trap into which this can lead us, and we can observe in our culture some of the destructive aftermath of this attitude. In the yogic system, on the other hand, much weight is given to the proper disciplining and channeling of these lower energies. After becoming aware of aggression and sexuality, one is taught detachment from them so that he can then focus on the awakening of higher *chakral* areas. Yogis in fact, when they have attained a certain level of development, generally practice sexual abstinence, together with control of thoughts and emotions—not allowing anger or "bad thoughts." This, as I have said, is generally considered repressive by most psychiatrists.

So much for the first and second *chakras*. The third *chakra* is supposedly located in the abdominal area (and related to the pancreas); the fourth in the chest near the heart (related to the thymus gland); the fifth in the neck by the thyroid gland; the sixth on the brow between the eyes—in the area of the so-called "third eye"—(pituitary gland); and the seventh on the crown of the head (pineal gland). When each of these areas is awakened, one achieves a new level of consciousness and experiences the world differently. The heart *chakra*, for instance, is associated with the capacity for selfless love. When the brow *chakra* or third eye is activated, one might experience clairvoyance and telepathic phenomena; and when the crown *chakra* is awakened, the ability to leave the body and experience oneself as pure awareness or consciousness.

The yogic powers awakened during this upward journey can represent drawbacks and obstacles to be *overcome,* if they tend to draw the spiritual aspirant into attachment to the powers themselves and cause him to lose sight of the primary goal: union with the higher self. This is the same danger which lies in our attachment to such coarser energies as aggression, assertiveness and sensuality. We can get caught up and worship the power in these energies and never grow any further.

If the caduceus and the theories related to it might indeed reflect reality, it is no wonder that I found the theories and practices of psychiatry very shortsighted in their vision of man's place in the cosmos. For after awakening to the lower energies of aggression and sexuality, the subject matter of most psychotherapies, the journey has just begun. There is a whole world of evolution ahead.

In this regard, Sai Baba's teachings of how to pattern our social lives took on greater meaning. Such attitudes as responsibility, discipline, work, duty, devotion, dedication, right action and surrender are important not only for proper conduct amongst people but, most especially, for developing the necessary internal discipline in oneself to handle higher energies when they are awakened. According to all religious systems, these attitudes are absolutely essential for the growth of the self and the stability of world society. And, in contrast, how chaotic individuals and societies become without them.

Even though the religious frame of reference seems old-fashioned and square in relation to our contemporary Western system of values, it began to appear to me to be exactly what is needed in the world—as if no one had ever said that before! It became clear that chaos is what develops when we lose sight of the higher reality most people call God and place in its stead mind, emotion and the material world.

The system represented by the caduceus and the systems expressed in most religions, then, appear to structure our energies—defining priorities and projecting attitudes from a grander perspective than that afforded by the routines and demands of our everyday material lives. But what is lacking in modern culture is a conviction that these religious systems actually represent reality, or *truth.* Religion, it seems, has fallen into such ill repute.

What great experience can bring us back to realization of the eternal truths embodied in the religions of the world, and the resolve to lead righteous lives? What kind of monumental occurrence is required?

10
A SOUL IN TRANSFORMATION

If the caduceus symbol, representing the dynamics of *kundalini* energy, does in fact reflect a deeper vision of reality, it offers us an overview with which to understand Western psychiatry's relationship to spirituality, and gives us a great deal of knowledge about the nature of the path Godward. There are specific pronouncements on how to lead one's life, specific descriptions of guideposts we will pass along the way and comments about the pitfalls and dangers to be encountered. The biggest question at this point appears to be: Does this system actually exist; is it a true expression of "the Path?"

It seems to me that the crucial factor in answering this question for most of us—wrapped up as we are in our scientific, technologically-minded culture—is direct, concrete proof and not abstract ideas. The strongest argument for most is experience that can be perceived and measured by the senses. In this regard, the Russians seem to be way ahead of us. The book *Psychic Discoveries Behind the Iron Curtain*, by Sheila Ostrander and Lynn Schroeder, reports that Russian scientists have experimented with, and are now capable of scientifically evaluating, such so-called "psychic" or "paranormal" phenomena as telepathy, clairvoyance, psychokinesis, psychic healing and the nature of auras.

We in this country have awakened more recently to the possible validity of these phenomena. We are becoming fascinated by them and, at the same time, are trying to find a system of explanation which will allow us to understand them better. Uri Geller, who has been studied by scientists at the Stanford Research Institute, appears on the basis of considerable test data accumulated to possess certain psychic powers or *siddhis*. He has been remarkably accurate, for example, in reproducing drawings seemingly communicated to him telepathically by test subjects. And it would appear that he may be able to bend metal objects at a distance by willpower alone, although this is disputed in some quarters.

Edgar Cayce developed a great reputation for seemingly being able to gather information at a distance, telepathically or clairvoyantly, and then offering medically sophisticated programs of healing for people he never even met. His apparent success with these healing powers received impressive documentation.

"Psychics" such as Geller and Cayce seem able to perceive things beyond the range of the senses. They often relate similar experiences concerning their powers, and many have come to similar conclusions about them. Most feel there is a higher order of reality than that of which we are usually aware, and that for some reason beyond their consciousness they are being used as channels between it and the world with which we are familiar.

Kathryn Kuhlman, the late well-known minister of a church in which many miraculous healings have apparently taken place, also saw herself in this relationship to a higher reality, stating that she could absolutely feel the presence of the "Holy Spirit." She could stand in front of thousands in her congregation and point to areas in the auditorium, making such specific statements as: "There is a gentleman with longstanding cancer in his hip who has just been cured. . . . There is a person with a broken ankle in that part of the auditorium who is now being cured and relieved of pain. . . . There is someone over there who has been in a wheelchair for a number of years and is now cured and can get up. Will these people get up and come to the front of the auditorium?" And in an amazing and emotion-filled demonstration of *some* kind of extraordinary force at work, these people would rise and move forward.

It is beyond the scope of this book to do more than point out such well-known examples of evidence pointing to the existence of paranormal powers, in the possession of individuals claiming to have made contact with a higher reality. But the reader must be aware of the wealth of material available on this subject. Much of it of course is absurd, sensationalistic and exploitational. A great deal of the literature, however, is compelling and eloquent documentation of dimensions of being beyond the physical world.

In the history of man there have been certain rare, supposedly divine figures capable of demonstrating extraordinary powers in a most concrete manner, who have said not only that they knew of such a higher reality, but that in fact they *were* this reality —thus indicating that they had gone completely beyond duality and merged into the oneness of the universe.

All of the concepts with which this book is concerned—the question of the reality behind the caduceus; the limits of man's potential; the purpose of life; the reality of God and the nature of the path to Him . . . all the deepest, most profound questions that lie at the center of our existence and to which we yearn for answers, so that we may adjust our lives accordingly toward truth—all these questions are answered by the appearance of such magnificent beings. Their appearances on earth have had monumental impact on humanity. They are humanity's brightest moment.

They demonstrate by the very nature, quality and rhythm of their lives the reality of higher dimensions, the awe-inspiring mystery of that something beyond. And by the miracle of their love and encouragement they give faith, strength and direction to our lives, creating in many the bliss and love which come from contact with the divine. Only a handful of such divine figures are well known to the world today: among them the legendary *Rama* and *Krishna* in the Hindu tradition, Buddha, and Jesus Christ.

In this book I propose to introduce you to another: Satya Sai Baba, who is in my opinion the brightest, clearest *living* proof of a higher reality—embodying concrete evidence which can be observed and measured. He himself has said that we are indeed uniquely fortunate, as no other *avatar*—incarnation of God or the spirit of God—has moved so freely and openly amongst the people, allowing all to see and experience the grandeur which he embodies. He asks people to come, measure him, sound him out, investigate him—and then draw their own conclusions.

Of all the emotional, psychological and social reactions and phenomena I have observed, all the experiences I have had, none has equalled the mystery and magnificence of my experience of Sai Baba. He has taught me that the deepest, most profound innate drive and yearning in us is not aggression or dominance or sexuality; it is merging: returning home to God.

Sai Baba has shown me where and why other psychological theories I have followed are shortsighted and limited when they fail to recognize the reality of God and the spiritual dimension. He has shown me how to continue, in spite of all obstacles, along the spiritual path. I feel that he is a teacher so profound and deep that no words or concepts can categorize him. He is beyond definition and boundary.

Bangalore: 8 a.m., May 22, 1972

Dear Sharon,

There is no doubt in my mind that Sai Baba is divine. I astound myself to say such a thing. What must I have experienced, a rational scientific man, to say such a thing? I believe I can't even communicate the experience. I know all this isn't hypnosis, mass delusion, hallucination, hysteria, an effect of cultural shock or drug intoxication. It's too simple to say I saw a materialization and then all of a sudden changed. I marvel at the experience, unable to relate it fully, joyful that I'm able to share it with so many who are also witnessing it.

I believe Baba to be an incarnation of God. It appears to me now that all those stories in Hindu, Christian and Hebrew literature are not symbolic; there really *is* a spiritual level of reality that can make itself manifest. One of the most amazing insights I have had has been experiencing how dramatically one can change upon seeing this higher reality. It's like a person jumping from one level of consciousness to another—everything seems different.

When I speak to people devoted to Baba, I can feel now a certain subtle vibration between us which tells us that we have become aware of a new reality; and when talking to those who are not devotees, it is plain that they simply don't perceive or understand certain nuances of meaning and expression used by devotees. I can't describe more clearly what happens during this sudden change—only that I can see my life powerfully affected, with this experience and vision of a new reality coloring everything I see.

If I am strong enough to continue to comprehend the significance of all this, I know that I will be profoundly changed. I now plainly see that there are moral and spiritual laws governing our existence—laws for us to follow—perhaps even more real than scientific laws. Followed, they will lead us closer to ultimate truth, bliss and meaning; and if unheeded, to pain, meaninglessness and suffering. How strange it is for me to so thoroughly believe in a higher reality, a higher level of things, when just a few days ago I was such a doubter and skeptic.

Yesterday I experienced more miracles. It's as if Baba is allowing me now to see this wonderful power close-up. I saw a ring created right in front of my eyes for a visiting professor, also much vibhutti. I have met many, many people who have told me of Baba's uncanny knowledge of their innermost secrets. He will approach people in the ashram who are discussing matters and add instant insight and direction to their conversation, without having been physically present earlier to know what they were talking about.

I mean, in short, that I am witnessing in live color and in the flesh an experience a million times more astonishing than the fairy-tale stories I have been telling my four sweet children. In fact, now I believe that these stories about witches and angels, monsters and gods probably refer to a dimension of being more real than the physical world we consider real life. I am aware now that there really are such things as black magic and evil, angels and gods.

I feel blessed to be here to experience such a phenomenon. I am feeling more of Baba's love and protection; my feelings of a few days ago of apprehension and worry on witnessing such power are quieting. Baba appears all-loving: he is everywhere, giving to everyone with unending energy. I don't see how a human being can perform the tasks that he does with so much energy. His smile is electrifying and he can change from a child to a lion in the wink of an eye. After witnessing his powers and seeing materializations first-hand, I am convinced that the hundreds of stories I have heard about him are true.

I see my task in the near future as having to come to terms with certain elements in my life to align myself more fully with Baba. His teachings are clear: he is showing the way. He preaches constant meditation and contact with God, devoting oneself to godly pursuits and a righteous way of life . . . not allowing bad thoughts or actions; controlling and detaching from emotions; canalizing one's passions. Discipline, discipline; transcending the level of bodily pleasures. Don't waste a second of precious time, remember your spiritual goal, work hard, devote yourself to God, seek wisdom. I struggled terribly against what I thought to be a Puritan moralism, yet after witnessing Baba's greatness I can do nothing but accept fully what he says. He is truly so magnificent.

The time is drawing closer for my return home and I am excited by the thought of seeing you soon.

With all my love, Sam.

6:30 a.m., May 24

Dearest love,

I had a very hard and painful day yesterday. Became very ill with a temperature of 103.6 and aching all over, diarrhea and abdominal cramping. I was dazed and very uncomfortable. Although, as you know, I'm usually very frightened in this situation, I was amazingly peaceful even though suffering a great deal. I had a feeling of being protected by Baba. He came up to me personally, felt my pulse and said that I would be all right. I cried after this, feeling that he cared enough to approach me. This morning I feel much better.

I used to be embarrassed by allowing myself to feel dependent but I am convinced now that this sort of dependency is realistic, as man is in fact very fragile and vulnerable and yearns to make contact with his Father and move into a higher reality. In fact, I think this is probably man's most basic instinct and represents his true life's work.

The lectures here lately have been a bit better. One was about Sri Aurobindo. He is considered a saint who at one time in his life was jailed and locked in solitary confinement because of his activities in resisting English rule. After a short while he broke into another level of consciousness and held a conversation for 14 days with a late great yogi, Swami Vivekananda, who taught him deeper principles in the practice of yoga. After his release he wrote about what he had learned from his contact with this higher dimension, and brought renewed light and life to spirituality. Following his release from prison he started an ashram and lived forty years in a single room without ever leaving it.

Imagine that—only a madman or the divine could do something like that. He is considered a scientist of consciousness, who evidently found everything in inner space and needed to spend no time in the world we consider outer space, except to conquer it. This type of approach to learning is deeply fascinating to me. In contrast to the West's emphasis on cerebration and the acquiring of intellectual knowledge, a yogi might hang from a tree by one arm for ten years and learn all there is to know by that technique. Strange but true.

This cosmic organization of things, this interlayering of realities, continues to electrify and excite me. It is absolutely amazing to me that we as humans can break out of our familiar reality—people here call this illusion—and ascend to a greater consciousness, in which we are actually in touch with great spirits of the past or future. I have read about higher levels of consciousness, and I'm witnessing daily concrete proof of the existence of them, and the qualities one can develop as he evolves higher and higher.

Evidently man has to cast aside his attachment to the material and sensual life and strive toward the spiritual. Baba has stated that his purpose is to bring the righteous life back to people and back to the world. He says that he will not fail. It is clear that my job is to change myself and become a spiritual man.

Love, Sam.

8 a.m., May 25

Dearest Sharon and family,

I am learning new things each day. Yesterday Dr. S. Bhagavantam, a very well-known nuclear physicist with an international reputation, came here. His reverence, softness, humility, gentleness and respect filled me with awe. I saw this man lie face-down at Baba's feet, then later humbly approach him to sheepishly ask a question. Baba smiled, then went over to a basket containing packets of *vibhutti* and gave him a handful. The renowned scientist then turned and walked away with a smile reflecting complete fulfillment.

10 p.m., May 27

Dearest Sharon and family,

It's late, I'm tired, have been up a long time: today began at 3 o'clock in the morning. I participated in *Nagara-Sankirtan,* a custom revived by Baba which is becoming widespread in India. I walked with the male students barefoot at 5 a.m. through the streets of a nearby town singing *bhajans*—devotional songs repeating the names of the many different aspects or forms of God as He has appeared to man throughout history. Baba says it is good to awaken to such holy vibrations as the singing of God's name, and it is quite impressive to see this band of men walking through town in such a spiritual and devotional attitude. But I am very tired now and can hardly describe the activity further.

Also, today for the first time I saw energy pulsating from Baba's head; and I could clearly see his aura. This must be the halo described around an angel's head. What an experience!

Love, Sam.

9 a.m., May 29

Dearest Sharon,

Yesterday was again hectic. Woke again at 3 a.m. so we could get to Baba's in time to sing in the streets. I have been feeling chronically weak and tired because of this schedule.

An exciting thing happened though. I'm becoming anxious because I've arranged to leave on the 31st and haven't had a personal interview with Baba yet. I began thinking that I wouldn't get this opportunity and have been asking people what I should do. Alf felt that because he was watching over me it was his duty to ask Baba; when he did, Baba said that I would not leave on the 31st, but on the 1st. So I must run around now and change all my plane reservations. I guess this means that I should stay to see the ceremonies for the end of summer school, which will take place on the last day of the month. I'm also hopeful that he'll be seeing me. My spirits are lifted.

Love, Sam.

12:45 a.m., June 2—sitting in an airplane awaiting takeoff from Bombay to New York.

Dearest love,

I'm awaiting takeoff for home, looking forward eagerly to seeing and being with everyone. The past two days have been hectic and unusual. Delaying my departure to June 1st allowed me to see the ceremony for the end of the summer school course. It was impressive and drove home the fact that Baba is vitally interested in education and that many top people in India are among his followers. Numerous high officials were present, with some speaking at the ceremony.

I have also become aware that many people would like to see Baba, but few get in to visit with him intimately. I have advised a number of young Americans to visit him, and they came—only to sit at the gate for long hot hours, finally to leave discouraged. I have been extremely fortunate to be so close to Baba and especially to have such a great guide and now close friend in Alf. Anyway, hoping to have a personal interview, I had been waiting expectantly . . . but Baba hardly gave me a glance.

I went to the ashram early this morning before takeoff and he didn't come downstairs to see me. To make a long story short, I haven't had a personal interview and am leaving rather downhearted and hurt but for a few strong exceptions. One, I know that Baba knows more than I do, and what I want might not be what I need. What he does shouldn't be questioned. Secondly, I have gotten all that I came for, and more. He has awakened me to the existence of a higher reality and has convinced me of his greatness. His significance and meaning for me are very deep. He has given me a precious gift, and his not seeing me individually must be right.

So here I am in a rather stuffy plane awaiting takeoff and thinking always of you. Oops! the plane moves and I must fasten my seatbelt. I'll see you soon.

Love, Sam.

F*or the protection of the virtuous, for the destruction of evil-doers and for establishing righteousness on a firm footing, I incarnate from age to age. Whenever* asanthi, *or disharmony, overwhelms the world, the Lord will incarnate in human form to establish the modes of earning* prasanthi, *or peace, and to reeducate the human community in the paths of peace. At the present time, strife and discord have robbed peace and unity from the family, the school, the society, the religions, the cities and the state.*

The arrival of the Lord is also anxiously awaited by saints and sages. Sadhus *(spiritual aspirants) prayed and I have come. My main tasks are fostering of the* Vedas *(Hindu scriptures) and fostering of the devotees. Your virtue, your self-control, your detachment, your faith, your steadfastness: these are the signs by which people read of my glory. You can lay claim to be a devotee only when you have placed yourself in my hands fully and completely with no trace of ego. You can enjoy the bliss through the experience the* Avatar *confers. The* Avatar *behaves in a human way so that*

mankind can feel kinship, but rises into his superhuman heights so that mankind can aspire to reach the heights, and through that aspiration actually reach him. Realizing the Lord within you as the motivator is the task for which he comes in human form.

Avatars like Rama and Krishna had to kill one or more individuals who could be identified as enemies of the dharmic (righteous) way of life, and thus restore the practice of virtue. But now there is no one fully good, and so who deserves the protection of God? All are tainted by wickedness, and so who will survive if the Avatar decides to uproot? Therefore, I have come to correct the buddhi, the intelligence, by various means. I have to counsel, help, command, condemn and stand by as a friend and well-wisher to all, so that they may give up evil propensities and, recognizing the straight mark, tread it and reach the goal. I have to reveal to the people the worth of the Vedas, the Sastras and the spiritual texts which lay down the norms. If you will accept me and say "Yes," I too will respond and say, "Yes, yes, yes."

If you deny and say "No," I also echo "No." Come, examine, experience, have faith. That is the method of utilizing me.

I do not mention *Sai Baba* in any of my discourses, but I bear the name as Avatar *of Sai Baba. I do not appreciate in the least the distinction between the various appearances of God: Sai,* Rama, Krishna, *etc. I do not proclaim that this is more important or that the other is less important. Continue your worship of your chosen God along lines already familiar to you, then you will find that you are coming nearer to me. For all names are mine, and all forms are mine. There is no need to change your chosen God and adopt a new one when you have seen me and heard me.*

Every step in the career of the Avatar *is predetermined.* Rama *came to feed the roots of* satya, *or truth, and* dharma, *or righteousness.* Krishna *came to foster* shanti, *or peace, and* prema, *or love. Now all these four are in danger of being dried up. That is why the present* Avatar *has come. The* dharma *that has fled to the forests has to be led back into the villages and towns. The* anti-dharma *that is ruining the villages and towns must be driven back into the jungle.*

I have come to give you the key of the treasure of ananda, *or bliss, to teach you how to tap that spring, for you have forgotten the way to blessedness. If you waste this time of saving yourselves, it is just your fate. You have come to get from me tinsel and trash, the petty little cures and promotions, worldly joys and comforts. Very few of you desire to get from me the thing that I have come to give you: namely, liberation itself. Even among these few, those who stick to the path of* sadhana, *or spiritual practice, and succeed are a handful.*

Your worldly intelligence cannot fathom the ways of God. He cannot be recognized by mere cleverness of intelligence. You may benefit from God, but you cannot explain Him. Your explanations are merely guesses, attempts to cloak your ignorance in pompous expressions. Bring something into your daily practice as evidence of your having known the secret of the higher life from me. Show that you have greater brotherliness. Speak with more sweetness and self-control. Bear defeat as well as victory with calm resignation. I am always aware of the future and the past as well as the present of every one of you, so I am not so moved by mercy. Since I know the past, the background, the reaction is different. It is your consequence of evil deliberately done in the previous birth, and so I allow your suffering to continue, often modified by some little compensation. I do not cause either joy or grief. You are the designer of both these chains that bind you. I am anandaswarupa *(the embodiment of bliss). Come, take* ananda *(bliss) from me, dwell on that* ananda *and be full of* shanti *(peace).*

My acts are the foundations on which I am building my work, the task for which I have come. All the miraculous acts which you observe are to be interpreted so. The foundation for a dam requires a variety of materials. Without these it will not last and hold back the waters. An incarnation of the Lord has to be used in various ways by man for his uplift.

The Lord has no intention to publicize Himself. I do not need publicity, nor does any other Avatar *of the Lord. What are you daring to publicize? Me? What do you know about me? You speak one thing about me today and another tomorrow. Your faith has not become unshakable. You praise me when things go well, and blame me when things go wrong. When you start publicity you descend to the level of those who compete in collecting plenty by decrying others and extolling themselves.*

Where money is calculated, garnered or exhibited to demonstrate one's achievements, I will not be present. I come only where sincerity and faith and surrender are valued. Only inferior minds will revel in publicity and self-aggrandizement. These have no relevance in the case of Avatars. Avatars *need no advertisement.*

The establishment of dharma *(righteousness): that is my aim. The teaching of* dharma, *the spread of* dharma: *that is my object. These miracles as you call them are just a means toward that end. Some of you remark that* Ramakrishna Paramahansa *(an Indian saint) said that* siddhis *or yogic powers are obstructions in the path of the* sadhaka *(spiritual aspirant). Yes,* siddhis *may lead the* sadhaka, *the spiritual aspirant, astray. Without being involved in them he has to keep straight on. His ego will bring him down if he yields to the temptation of demonstrating his yogic powers. That is the correct advice which every aspirant should heed. But the mistake lies in equating me with a* sadhaka, *like the one whom* Ramakrishna *wanted to help, guide and warn. These* siddhis *or yogic powers are just in the nature of the* Avatar—*the creation of things with intent to protect and to give joy, is spontaneous and lasting. Creation, preservation and dissolution can be accomplished only by the Almighty . . . no one else.*

Cynics carp without knowledge. If they learn the Sastras *or scriptures, or if they cultivate direct experience, they can understand me. Your innate laziness prevents you from the spiritual exercises necessary to discover the nature of God. This laziness should go. It has to be driven out of man's nature in whatever shape it appears. That is my mission. My task is not merely to cure and console and remove individual misery, but it is something far more important. The removal of misery and distress is incidental to my mission. My main task is the reestablishment of the* Vedas *and* Sastras *(spiritual scriptures), and revealing the knowledge about them to all people. This task will succeed. It will not be limited. It will not be slowed down. When the Lord decides and wills, his divine will cannot be hindered.*

You must have heard people say that mine is all magic. But the manifestation of divine power must not be interpreted in terms of magic. Magicians play their tricks for earning their maintenance, worldly fame and wealth. They are based on falsehood and they thrive on deceit, but this body could never stoop to such a low level. This body has come through the Lord's resolve to come. That resolve is intended to uphold the satya, or truth. *Divine resolve is always true resolve. Remember there is nothing that divine power cannot accomplish. It can transmute earth into sky and sky into earth. To doubt this is to prove that you are too weak to grasp great things, the grandeur of the universe.*

I have come to instruct all in the essence of the Vedas, *to shower on all this precious gift, to protect the* sanathana dharma, *the ancient wisdom, and preserve it. My mission is to spread happiness, and so I am always ready to come among you not once, but twice or thrice—as often as you want me. Many of you probably think that since people from all parts of India, and even foreign countries outside India, come to* Puttaparthi, *they must be pouring their contributions into the coffers of the* Nilayam *(Prasanthi Nilayam: name of Sai Baba's ashram). But let me declare the truth. I do not take anything from anyone except love and devotion. This has been my consistent practice for the last many years. People who come here are giving me just the wealth of faith, devotion and love. That is all.*

Many of you come to me with problems of health and mental worry of one sort or another. They are mere baits by which you have been brought here. But the main purpose is that you may have grace and strengthen your faith in the divine. Problems and worries are really to be welcomed as they teach you the lessons of humility and reverence. Running after external things produces all this discontent. That type of desire has no end. Once you have become a slave to the senses, they will not leave hold until you are dead. It is an unquenchable thirst. But I call you to me and even grant worldly boons so that you may turn Godward. No Avatar *has done like this before, going among the masses, counseling them, guiding them, consoling them, uplifting them and directing them along the path of* satya, dharma, shanti and prema *(truth, righteousness, peace and love).*

My activities and movements will never be altered, whoever may pass whatever opinion on them. I shall not modify my plans for dharmasthapana *(the establishment of righteousness), my discourses or my movements. I have stuck to this determination for many years and I am engaged in the task for which I have come: that is, to inculcate faith in the path of* prasanthi *(the highest spiritual peace). I shall not stop nor retract a step.*

Not even the biggest scientist can understand me by means of his laboratory knowledge. I am always full of bliss. Whatever may happen, nothing can come in the way of my smile. That is why I am able to impart joy to you and make your burden lighter. I never exult when I am extolled, nor shrink when I am reviled. Few have realized my purpose and significance, but I am not worried. When things that are not in me are attributed to me, why should I worry? When things that are in me are mentioned, why should I exult? For me it is always, "Yes, yes, yes." If you give all and surrender to the Lord, he will guard you and guide you. The Lord has come for just this task. He is declaring that He will do so, and that it is the very task that has brought Him here. I know the agitations of your heart and its aspirations, but you do not know my heart. I react to the pain that you undergo and to the joy that you feel, for I am in your heart. I am the dweller in the temple of every heart. Do not lose contact and company, for it is only when the coal is in contact with the live embers that it can also become live ember.

Cultivate a nearness with me in the heart and it will be rewarded. Then you too will acquire a fraction of that supreme love. This is a great chance. Be confident that you will all be liberated. Know that you are saved. Many hesitate to believe that things will improve, that life will be happy for all and full of joy, and that the golden age will recur. Let me assure you that this dharmaswarupa, *that this divine body, has not come in vain. It will succeed in averting the crisis that has come upon humanity.* [1]

[1]Sai Baba addresses his devotees on his 43rd birthday, November 23, 1968

11
THE
AVATAR

In the Hindu religion an *avatar* is an extraordinary being, a miraculous embodiment of the divine in human form, incarnating for the welfare of mankind. By definition the *avatar* manifests sixteen special qualities. The most profound and those which clearly distinguish him from mortal man are his complete mastery and transcendence of the physical world—including the ability to materialize objects at will; qualities of omniscience, omnipresence and omnipotence; the capacity to manifest a flow of pure and inexhaustible love; and a special grace which transcends all conditions of *karma* (compensation required for acts done in the past), manifesting in his ability to miraculously transform a person's life by an act of divine will. The last full *avatar* in the Hindu religion is traditionally believed to have been *Krishna,* who lived about five-thousand years ago.

Sai Baba makes this distinction between an *avatar* and a spiritual aspirant or spiritually evolved individual: The latter two may evolve through spiritual practice to higher levels of self-realization, perhaps even developing *siddhis* or yogic powers. The *avatar*, by contrast, is *born* with full awareness. Rather than being born on earth and ascending heavenward, or to more highly evolved planes of existence, the *avatar,* already fully divine, chooses to descend earthward.

The actions of the *avatar* are fully free. They are not bound or determined by *karma*. His life is an act of love, a great play, a pure expression of the divine. *His task is the granting of peace and joy, of a sense of fulfillment to seekers who have striven long–the fostering of* dharma *(righteousness), the suppression of evil, the overwhelming of the wicked. The descent of God to earth, the incarnation of the formless with form, is the concretization of the yearning of the seekers. It is the solidified sweetness of the devotion of godly aspirants.*[1]

The *avatar* is believed to have clear consciousness of past, present and future, with complete awareness of his mission and the course of his life. Controlling the location and family of his birth, he chooses to be incarnated in order to bring love to the physical world and to uplift its spiritual consciousness. Baba declares that he himself is a full *avatar* and that his appearance on earth has been prophesied in sacred literature, including the Bible.

Sai Baba was born in *Puttaparthi,* a remote village in southern India, on November 23, 1926, and given the family name of Satyanarayana Raju. Stories of the family and villagers tell of "miracles" which began to occur shortly before his birth. Musical instruments in the family home, for example, are said to have played by themselves. Another unusual incident is said to have occurred shortly after the baby was born. Someone noticed movement under his blankets on the floor and he was quickly snatched up. Discovered beneath the blankets was a deadly cobra, which for some reason had not harmed the baby. (The cobra, coincidentally or not, is the symbol of *Shiva,* of Hinduism's holy trinity.)

From early childhood it was apparent that young Satya was quite different from his playmates. Although his family ate meat, he himself was a natural vegetarian, who abhorred the thought of killing animals. He was extremely helpful to all in the village, doing work unselfishly, frequently bringing beggars home to be fed by his parents—though they often scolded him for what they felt to be unwarranted generosity on his part. He was called *"guru"* by his playmates, leading them in devotional songs before school and fascinating and amusing them by taking candy and playthings from an apparently empty bag.

Then a mysterious incident occurred when Satyanarayana was thirteen. One day while playing outside, he leaped into the air with a shriek, holding his bare foot. His family feared he had been stung by a scorpion and would not survive. But he slept that night without apparent pain or sickness. Then twenty-four hours later, he fell unconscious and remained so for a day. When he awoke, his behavior was strange, alternating between periods of unconsciousness and what appeared to be trance-like states. He began chanting and quoting long Sanskrit passages of poetry and philosophy far beyond the scope of his formal education.

At times he became stiff and appeared to those around him to leave his body, then described distant places which his parents said he had never visited and people whom to their knowledge he had never known. He laughed and cried, explained complicated religious doctrines. Could he be possessed by evil spirits?

Satya endured a period of torture as his parents took him to exorcists

[1]*Bhagavatha Vahini* (Sai Baba's version of the Hindu Scriptures, the *Bhagavatha*), pp. 1-2

throughout the countryside. One famous and feared exorcist, to whom the boy's demon had become a personal challenge, shaved Satya's head and cut three crosses into his skull, then poured caustic material into the wound and into his eyes until they were swollen almost shut. Finally, his parents could stand no more of this ordeal and called a stop to it, though their son had apparently not been cured.

Baba subsequently stated that he was demonstrating at this time that he is beyond pleasure and pain, beyond duality. He has disclosed that there was in fact no actual scorpion sting: *No such bite could create a Satya Sai Baba, and if it could, then scorpions should be objects of the highest veneration and worship.*

Two months after the supposed sting, in May 1940, Satya's father saw a crowd gathering around his son. He appeared to be manifesting candy and fruit out of thin air, and many people were falling to the ground, calling him an incarnation of God. Confused and frustrated by his son's strange behavior and now by this display of sleight-of-hand or, worse, black magic, Satya's father picked up a stick and approached threateningly. "Who are you . . . who are you?" he demanded angrily.

In a calm but firm voice, the boy announced: *I am Sai Baba.* Then he proceeded to relate how he had chosen this particular family for his incarnation in answer to the prayers of a devout ancestral sage. He was, he said, the reincarnation of a little-known but much respected Moslem holy man, named *Sai Baba of Shirdi,* who dressed like a Moslem but wore ash on his forehead like a Hindu. The original Sai Baba had died eight years before Satya was born—the length of time he had reportedly told his devotees would elapse before his reincarnation.

Naturally, it was difficult for many in the village to accept this boy, unusual and charming though he was, as the actual reincarnation of a man regarded by his followers as a saint. Young Satyanarayana was beginning to be quite a mystery indeed. Then a couple of months later, on Thursday—Guru Day in India—a group of questioning villagers approached him, pleading, "Show us a sign!"

With a quick and unexpected gesture, Satya threw a bunch of jasmine flowers onto the floor. There, it is reported, they clearly spelled out—in Telugu script, the language of the village—"Sai Baba."

Soon afterwards, Satya Sai Baba told his family that he belonged with them no longer, that his devotees were calling and that he had to leave. He left school in October of his thirteenth year and began to gather followers around him. They grew in number until it became necessary to establish an *ashram,* where many could live with their *guru,* and where those seeking his guidance could meet with him. The construction of *Prasanthi Nilayam* (Abode of Eternal Peace) continues even to the present in an attempt to accommodate Sai Baba's swelling number of devotees. Here and at *Brindavan,* his summer residence, Baba has received millions of people from India and around the world.

Sai Baba says that his name is significant. "Sai" denotes the female aspect of the universe and "Baba," the male aspect—the full name denoting the wedding of the two. He has also proclaimed that he is the manifestation of both *Shiva* and *Shakti* aspects of the universe, the male/female aspects of the divine. To some he seems to manifest both of these qualities, his movements at once delicate and flowing, powerful and commanding.

Baba speaks frequently about the life of *Shirdi Sai Baba,* manifesting pictures of him for his followers and further illustrating his ties to the saint by materializing *vibhutti,* or sacred ash. *Shirdi Sai Baba* had also distributed ash to his devotees but did it from a fireplace which was constantly lit. Now Sai Baba of Puttaparthi evidently has this fire burning in another dimension into which with a simple wave of his hand he reaches to draw from a seemingly unlimited supply of sacred ash.

Rare photograph of Shirdi Sai Baba (second from left) with devotees.

Most of the miracles attributed to Jesus Christ have reportedly been accomplished by Sai Baba. His followers believe him to be beyond time and space, unbound by the laws of physics. Well-documented reports by reliable eye-witnesses—many of which appear throughout this book—would seem to show that Baba is able to read minds and see into past and future; to transport himself anywhere in the world instantaneously and be in many places at once; to transform himself into different forms; and to influence the elements—such as stopping rainstorms, creating winds, instantly nullifying impending catastrophes.

There are accounts of his taking the physical illness or injury of another upon himself in order to preserve the individual's health or save his life, becoming physically ill in his place and then curing himself instantaneously. Other reports tell of his healing by materializing surgical instruments which he himself uses with expert skill, or by actually manifesting *himself* in the body of a surgeon to perform critical operations. There is virtually no illness which he is not reported to have cured—and there is evidence that he has even brought a devotee back from death.

Yogi Suddhananda Bharathi, a famous Indian mystic poet of Southern India, said while addressing a conference at which Sai Baba had presided: "I have practiced yoga for fifty years. I once observed the laws of silence for over twenty years, and I have come in contact with *Sri Shirdi Baba, Sri Ramana Maharishi, Sri Aurobindo, Sri Meher Baba*[1] and others. As a result of this *sadhana* (spiritual practice), I have now met Sri Satya Sai Baba."

I came, Baba says, *because the good men of the world—the wise, the* sadhu *and the* sadhaka *(spiritual aspirant); the* guru *and godly—panted for me. May the pure and righteous rejoice.*

On the evening of June 28th, 1963, Baba asked Mr. N. Kasturi, his interpreter and biographer, an historian and close devotee, to announce at the ashram that no more interviews would be granted for a week. Early the next morning, Baba suddenly fell unconscious.

Initially, the devotees close to him thought that he had simply gone into a trance, as he had often done in the past when supposedly traveling in his subtle or astral body to bring urgent assistance to a devotee somewhere. These trances had been known to last a few hours, but this time Baba remained unconscious for a much longer time, until his devotees became apprehensive and summoned medical aid.

In addition to a doctor at the ashram hospital, Dr. Prasannasimba Rao, Assistant Director of Medical Ser-

[1]Revered Indian holy men; see Glossary.

vices of Mysore State, was called from Bangalore. He writes, after describing the symptoms fully: "The differential diagnosis of such conditions . . . pinned me down to that of tuberculous meningitis, with perhaps a tuberculoma (tumor-like mass of inflammatory tissue due to tuberculosis infection) silent for a long time. . . ."

When the doctor tried to give the treatment indicated by this diagnosis, Baba seemed to regain consciousness and refused the injections and other medical assistance. The trouble, he said, would pass in five days' time. A devotee at a distance was about to experience a stroke and heart attack severe enough to kill him, Baba said. He had decided to take on this illness—with all its symptoms of paralysis, heart seizures, partial loss of eyesight, high temperatures and severe physical pains—to save the devotee from suffering and otherwise certain death. During the next five days he had four severe heart attacks, his left side was paralyzed and his speech and the sight in his left eye were badly affected.

Then on Thursday July 4th, Baba became sufficiently clear and strong to announce that a blood clot in his brain had been dissolved and there would be no more heart attacks. However, the left side of his body was still paralyzed, and his speech was thick and feeble. His followers believed it would take several months for him to recoup his good health.

Guru Poornima, a religious festival day, was approaching, and many visitors had been congregating at the ashram. They were of course very upset and dejected by the stories they were hearing of Baba's condition. Not knowing the cause, or believing it, they began to doubt. "If Baba is God in human form," they asked one another, "why is he afflicted with physical ailments? Why does he not cure himself?"

On the evening of *Guru Poornima,* July 6th, practically carried by several disciples, Baba descended the circular stairs from his bedroom to the crowded prayer hall below. The whole left side of his body was still paralyzed, and his speech was a feeble, scarcely intelligible mumble.

A doctor present describes the scene: "His gait was the characteristic hemiplegic one, the paralytic left leg being dragged in a semicircle, the toes scraping the floor. Seeing Baba in that condition, even the bravest wept aloud."

For a few minutes he sat in his chair on the dais before some five-thousand silent, sorrowful, deeply moved people assembled inside and outside the hall. Then he gestured for water. It was brought in a tumbler and held up to Baba's twisted lips.

He drank some; then, dipping the fingertips of his right hand into the water, he sprinkled a few drops onto his paralyzed left hand and leg. Next he stroked his left hand with the right, then followed this by stroking his stiff left leg with both hands.

T. A. Ramantha Reddy, a government engineer, was in one of the front rows and very close to Baba. He states: "In a second Swamiji's leg, eye and entire left side appeared to become normal. It was a sight for the gods to see his sudden recovery, and the devotees present witnessed the greatest of his divine powers. . . ."

N. Kasturi describes it this way: "He rose and began his *Guru Poornima* discourse. People did not believe their eyes and ears. But when they realized that Baba was standing before them speaking, they jumped about in joy. They danced, they shouted, they wept. Some were so overcome with ecstatic gratitude that they laughed hysterically and ran wild among the crowd which came rushing in from outside.

"Baba was on his feet speaking for over an hour. Then he sang a number of *bhajan* songs and finally climbed the stairs back to his room unaided. That night he ate his normal meal, and the following days saw him back in his usual vigorous, hearty health, carrying on a full program of activities. The apparent stroke, which seemed to have come at his bidding, departed within the period he had foretold, leaving no tell-tale signs behind."

In the discourse which Baba gave that night, he referred to this episode: *This is not Swami's illness, this is an illness which Swami has taken on in order to save someone else. Swami has no illness nor will he get ill at any time. You must all be happy; that alone will make Swami happy. If you grieve, Swami will not be happy. Your joy is Swami's food.* [1]

Later in the speech, Baba said: *For those who have no refuge, God is the refuge. That is exactly the reason why I had to take on the disease that one helpless devotee was otherwise to get. He would have had to suffer this dire illness as well as four heart attacks which accompanied it, and he would not have survived. So according to my* dharma *(duty) of* bhaktasamrakshana *(saving devotees from harm), I had to rescue him.*

There is another reason, too, why the eight-day period had to be observed—something I have not disclosed so far, something which I have been keeping within myself for the last thirty-seven years. The time has come to announce it. The following, in brief, is the story which Baba related to an enthralled audience.

Thousands of years ago the great sage Bharadwaja, wishing to master

[1]*Sai Baba: Man of Miracles* by Howard Murphet, pp. 128-129.

all the Vedas *(scriptures)*, *was advised by* Indra *(the ruler of the gods) to perform a* yaga *(Vedic ritual). Eager to have* Shakti *(the consort of Shiva) preside over it and receive her blessings, Bharadwaja left for* Kailas *(a sacred peak in the Himalayas), the abode of* Shiva *and* Shakti, *(male and female aspects of God), to convey the invitation. Finding them coupled in the cosmic dance, Bharadwaja waited for eight days—apparently ignored by them, although he had failed to comprehend the welcoming smile cast at him by* Shakti.

Unhappy and disappointed, Bharadwaja decided to return home. But as he began to descend, he fell in a stroke, his left side paralyzed as a result of cold and fatigue. Shiva *then approached and cured him completely by sprinkling on him water from the* Kamandalu *(vessel). Consoled by* Shiva, *Bharadwaja was granted boons by both* Shiva *and* Shakti, *who also were pleased to attend the* yaga. Shiva *promised the* rishi *(sage) that they would both take human form and be born thrice in the Bharadwaja lineage or* gothra *(religious kin group):* Shiva *alone at* Shirdi, *as Sai Baba;* Shiva *and* Shakti *together at* Puttaparthi, *as Sathya Sai Baba; and then* Shakti *alone as* Prema Sai.[1]

Further, in expiation of an illness that Bharadwaja had suffered at Kailas, Shiva *made another promise: "This* Shakti *will suffer the stroke for eight days when we both take birth as Sathya Sai, and on the eighth day I shall relieve her from all signs of the disease by sprinkling water just as I did at* Kailas *to cure your illness."*

Baba continued: *It was the working out of this assurance that you witnessed today. The assurance given in the* Threthayuga *(the age long ago when this all took place) had to be honored. The poor forlorn devotee who had to get the stroke which I took over was a convenient excuse which was utilized. The disease had to be gone through; the devotee had to be saved; the assurance carried out, the mystery cleared. The divinity had to be more clearly announced by the manifestation of this grand miracle. All these were accomplished by this one incident.*

Let me tell you one more thing: Nothing can impede or halt the work of this Avatar. *When I was upstairs all these days, some people foolishly went about saying, "It is all over with Sai Baba;" and they turned back many who were coming to* Puttaparthi. *Some said I was in* samadhi *(communion with God)—as if I am a* sadhaka *(aspirant). Some feared I was a victim of black magic—as if anything can affect me.*

The splendor of this Avatar *will go on increasing day by day. Formerly when the* govardhanagiri *(a particular mountain) was raised aloft by the little boy* (Krishna), *the* Gopis *and* Gopalas *(milkmaids and cowherdsmen,*

[1]Sai Baba says that he will reincarnate one more time in the future, as *Prema Sai Baba.*

friends and companions of Krishna) *realized that* Krishna *was the Lord. Now, not one* govardhanagiri *but a whole range will be lifted—you will see! Have patience; have faith.*

Since his declaration that he is the embodiment of *Shiva/Shakti,* the number of Baba's devotees has been increasing rapidly. *Prasanthi Nilayam will very soon become another Mathura (holy city, birthplace of* Krishna) *and Tirupati (another holy city in India), attracting hundreds of thousands of devotees; and many saints' and sages will crowd at the* Nilayam *and achieve their life's ambition of eternal bliss,* Baba has declared.

Documented accounts of Sai Baba's powers must number in the thousands. Many have been collected in Howard Murphet's exciting and informative book *Man of Miracles.* Following is one of the most dramatic stories that I have heard, related here because of its uniqueness and its bearing on what happened to me later. It concerns the reported resurrection of Walter Cowan, allegedly brought back from the dead on Christmas Day in 1971. Dr. John Hislop, a former professor and corporate executive, now retired and living in Mexico, was a witness to this extraordinary drama. Here is a summary of his account:

> "Early Christmas morning, news spread among devotees gathered about Baba that an elderly American had suffered a fatal heart attack. Upon hearing the rumor, my wife and I at once went to the Cowans' hotel, where Elsie confirmed that her husband Walter had died. She had prayed to Sai Baba for help and with great self-control and recollection of human mortality had ended the prayer with, 'Let God's will be done.'
> "Walter's body was taken to the hospital by ambulance. Later that day, when Elsie and her friend Mrs. Ratan Lal went to the hospital, they found that Sai Baba had already been there as well. To their utter amazement they found Walter alive."

Recognizing the need for documentation of Walter's death in the form of medical reports and witnesses' testimony, Dr. Hislop investigated the matter fully. "At my request, Judge Damadar Rao of Madras interviewed the doctor who had attended Walter when he arrived at the hospital. The doctor's statement was that Walter was indeed dead when he examined him, shortly after the ambulance arrived at the hospital. There was no sign of life.

> "He pronounced Walter dead, then stuffed his ears and nose with cotton. The body was covered with a sheet and moved to an empty room. The doctor then left the hospital and missed seeing Sai Baba while he was there. Upon returning to the hospital after Sai Baba had left,

the doctor found Walter alive. He was unable to explain this.

"Later that day Sai Baba informed his devotees that he had indeed brought Walter back to life. He did not disclose the reasons for doing so, however; this remains a mystery he has not yet chosen to explain."

There were two or three subsequent occasions on which Baba attended to Walter's health in an extraordinary manner. Dr. Hislop describes Baba's delivering a spiritual discourse and giving out awards at a meeting which he attended. After the meeting, Baba turned to Hislop and said, *While I was talking in the meeting, Mrs. Cowan called me. I at once went to the hospital and did what was necessary. Mr. Cowan's health had taken a bad turn.*

Hislop continues: "So even while busy on the speaker's platform, Sai Baba had gone to the hospital and performed what was necessary. Yet to the eyes of my friends and myself he had continued in speech and action on the platform the whole time. How does one explain this mystery?"

When Walter had recovered sufficiently to be moved from Madras to Bangalore, he was described by Hislop as appearing extraordinarily well. "Dr. Gnaneswaran, with whom my wife and I had been acquainted for several years, was the Cowans' attending physician in Bangalore. He had obtained Walter's medical history, with its specific laboratory tests showing severe diabetes of long standing and various other diseased conditions. He compared it with his own laboratory tests and could scarcely believe the results. Not only were the diabetic symptoms now completely absent, but the tests for other diseased conditions proved to be negative as well. He claimed in amazement, 'Only the Divine Baba, only God himself, could do this.' "

The following is an account by Walter Cowan himself of his apparent death and resurrection under the grace of Sai Baba:

"While in the Connemara Hotel in Madras, two days after I arrived, I was taken very sick with pneumonia. As I gasped for breath, suddenly all the body struggle was over, and I died. I found myself very calm, in a state of wonderful bliss; and the Lord, Sai Baba, was by my side.

"Even though my body lay on the bed, dead, my mind kept working throughout the entire period of time until Baba brought me back. There was no anxiety or fear, but a tremendous sense of well-being, for I had lost all fear of death.

"Then Baba took me to a very large hall where there were hundreds of people milling around. This was the hall where the records of all of my previous lives were kept. Baba and I stood before the Court of Justice. The person in charge knew Baba very well, and he asked for the records of all my lives. He was very kind, and I had the feeling that whatever was decided would be the best for my soul.

"The records were brought into the hall: armloads of scrolls, all of which seemed to be in different languages. As they were read, Baba interpreted them. In the beginning they told of countries that have not existed for thousands of years, and I could not recall them. When they reached the time of King David, the reading of my lives became more exciting. I could hardly believe how great I apparently was in each life that followed.

"As the reading of my lives continued, it seemed that what really counted were my motives and character, as I had stood for outstanding peaceful, spiritual and political activity. I do not remember all the names, but I am included in almost all of the history books of the world from the beginning of time. As I incarnated in the different countries, I carried out my mission—which was peace and spirituality.

"After about two hours, they finished reading the scrolls, and the Lord, Sai Baba, said that I had not completed the work that I was born to do and asked the judge that I be turned over to him to complete my mission of spreading the truth. He requested that my soul be returned to my body, under his grace. The judge said, 'So be it.'

"The case was dismissed and I left with Baba to return to my body. I hesitated to leave this wonderful bliss. I looked at my body and thought that it would be like stepping into a cesspool to return to it, but I knew that it was best to complete my mission so that I could eventually merge with the Lord, Sai Baba. So I stepped back into my body . . . and that very instant it started all over again —trying to get my breath, being as sick as you could be and still be alive. I opened my eyes and looked at my wife and said, 'You sure look beautiful in pink. . . .' "

After Hislop had heard Walter give this account, he asked Sai Baba whether Walter's experience was real or some sort of hallucination or illusion. Baba replied, *The experience was a real experience, not an illusion. It was an experience occurring within Mr. Cowan's mind, and I myself was there—directing and clarifying the thoughts.* When asked if every person has similar experiences with death, Baba said, *It is not necessarily so; some may have similar experiences, some not.*

BHAGAWAN SRI SATHYA SAI BABA

PRASANTHINILAYAM P.O.
ANANTHAPUR DT.
TELEPHONE No. 30.

BRINDAVAN
WHITEFIELD
TELEPHONE No. 33.

Date :

Message

You as body, mind or soul are a dream.
but what you really are is Existence, Knowledge,
Bliss. You are the GOD of This universe. you are
creating The whole universe and drawing it in.
To gain The infinite universal individuality The
miserable little prison individuality must go.
Bhakti is no crying or any negative condition.
it is seeing of all in all we see.
it is the heart That reaches the goal. follow the heart.
A pure heart seeks beyond the intellect. it gets
inspired.
whatever we do reacts upon us. if we do good,
we shall have happiness and if evil, unhappiness
within you is the real happiness, within you is the
mighty ocean of nectar divine. Seek it within you,
feel it, feel it, it is here, the self. it is not the body,
The mind, the intellect, The brain. it is not the desire of
The desiring. it is not the object of desire. Above all
These, you are. All These are simply manifestations.
You appear as the smiling flower. as the twinkling
stars. what is There in the world which can make
you desire anything?

With Blessings and
Love
Sri Sathya Sai Baba

12
GOLD
SPOT

After returning from my first trip to India I began to feel an inner "awakening," as if a once familiar but closed-off and hidden center was opening up and I was becoming reacquainted with a part of myself I had long forgotten. I identified the experience as one of devotion and began to wonder whether such a center lies dormant in all of us, awaiting release through some personal spiritual experience. This awakening, or opening, or unfolding, was a source of great joy, and with it came a deepening feeling of love toward Baba—and for people in general. Was I witnessing something about the dynamics of love that modern psychiatry was not aware of?

Nothing was more important than this new reality. I began to pursue with fascination the unfolding of such inner potential. Baba's teachings became a way of life. I became a vegetarian and began practicing *hatha yoga* and meditating faithfully.

In the serenity of meditation I felt an exhilaration at reexperiencing my closeness with Baba; and I soon came to realize that the only separation between us was a limitation in my ability to concentrate and focus on him, and not geographical distance. *Do not lose contact and company, for it is only when the coal is in contact with the live embers that it can also become live ember*, Baba had said. I tried to stay in constant touch.

This change in attitude carried over into my work and social life. As an extension of the meditation, I tried to carry out my daily activities while meditating on Baba's physical form and my experience with him, as if the services I did were an offering to him. I attempted to see him in all experiences, to respond as if they were in fact part of him.

This was a real challenge to my control and concentration and a marvelous way of patterning my daily experience. Keeping his form in my heart and mind brought me as close to him as I had been in India. I wanted to spend all my time focusing on this magnificent awakening —because of the joyful experience itself and also because such attention is encouraged by Baba as a way of bringing one closer to God. The purpose of our life is to realize God, he says, accomplished by bringing Him in concrete ways into all of our activities.

The divine should be expressed in mind, heart and action; in thought, word and deed. This attitude toward life, of course, entails discipline, patience and perseverance. But when directed to the task by such as Sai Baba, with such love and caring, the undertaking becomes a pleasure.

In fact, it is the rule and restriction that gives charm to the game of life. If in the game of football, any player can do anything with the ball and there is neither foul nor out, neither offside nor goal, neither throw nor penalty, then it will be a meaningless game incapable of giving ananda *(bliss).*[1]

I began to see that I must diligently engage in spiritual practice because, in large measure, I am creator of my own destiny. Baba put it this way in a message to American devotees in 1972: *You as body, mind and soul are a dream, but what you really are is existence, knowledge, bliss. You are the God of this universe. You are creating the whole universe and drawing it in.*

Baba goes on to describe the mechanism or type of spiritual work through which we can succeed in becoming the whole universe: *To gain the infinite universal individuality, the miserable little prison individuality must go.* Bhakti *(devotion) is not crying or any negative condition. It is seeing the all in all we see. It is the heart that reaches the goal; follow the heart. The pure heart seeks beyond intellect. It gets inspired.*

The conviction grew in me that all of one's strength comes from contact with, and meditation upon, God—tuning in to God's love by actually becoming the process, vibration or frequency called devotion, or meditation or reverence . . . by actually becoming God Himself. Could it be that by tuning ourselves this way—as with a radio receiver—we are able to receive deeper messages from the universe? And that we experience the reality to which we are accustomed by keeping ourselves tuned to inferior "stations," such as infatuation with sense objects and the constant struggle for prestige and power?

In Baba's teachings I saw the possibility of infinite growth and evolution. Both spiritually and professionally, my work became more alive, exciting and productive. I found myself more intuitively attuned to my patients while in a meditative posture.

Seeing these changes quickened my interest in Baba as a teacher. How could I draw closer to him? Should I treat him as I had treated other

[1]*Sathya Sai Speaks*, Vol II, p. 219

teachers: was the best way to learn by being in close physical proximity and verbal communication with him?

Within a matter of weeks after my return, I decided that I had to go back to ask this question of Baba himself. I yearned to return and continue to witness events which I now believed to parallel those of the life of Christ. I knew I was watching the unfolding of a monumental event in the history of mankind. Could I sit at the feet of this great master? Perhaps if I found work in a hospital somewhere in India and he allowed me to visit him regularly. . .

Plans were made for a trip in October 1972. This time my wife, my brother and his wife—who incidentally is my wife's sister—and a cousin were also going. We would join Indra Devi and some thirty-five other people.

I remembered that prior to the first trip my wife and I had been sitting across the table from my brother and sister-in-law at dinner one evening, discussing the forthcoming adventure. Don was quite skeptical; somewhere a screw was loose in my brain. I remember his comment specifically: "Sam, you'd never catch me dead on that subcontinent. Nothing but poverty, a primitive way of life and disease." And to think that here was this hyperscientist, a physician, joining me—completely skeptical but beginning to feel some of the excitement of the investigation, perhaps even the possibility of discovering what had so transformed his weird brother.

I had also received a long distance call from my cousin Jerry, a mathematics professor in the East, whom I hadn't seen for quite a while and who had recently recovered from a rather serious illness. Illness and death have a way of prompting us into thinking about the deeper questions of who we are and where we are going . . . is there a God and what is the meaning of our lives. Looking at the question from a purely mathematical standpoint, Jerry felt it was indeed probable that an *avatar* might exist at present. "All the stories of such great happenings in the past could not simply be figments of the imagination," he said. "They were probably infrequent but actual occurrences. And because of the similarities of the stories and the historical intervals between the appearances of such great beings, it is highly probable that such an event could happen now."

Lila, a friend of mine, was also going with us. About a year prior to the trip, before she had ever heard of Sai Baba, Lila was admitted to the University Hospital for a breast biopsy. As she waited for surgery, fearful and apprehensive, a roommate was kind enough to give her a prayer. She read this just before her operation and felt a great and immediate easing of pressure and a sense of peace. Nothing serious was found wrong with her.

Some time later, Lila and I were discussing Sai Baba and she became intrigued. She read a book about him and began to consider the possibility of meeting him herself. She was then deeply in debt, however, and there seemed to be no feasible way for her to get the money to go to India. Her husband Homer, an inventor, at that time had no steady income and had been unable to sell an invention in five years. Yet, as highly unrealistic as the trip seemed, she made plans to go and obtained her vaccinations and passport.

Then some strange things began to happen. Lila, feeling particularly depressed, had an unusual dream. Riding in a car, she looked up to see Sai Baba dancing on the roof of a house, like the fiddler in the movie *Fiddler on the Roof.* Baba's eyes twinkled and he was full of fun; he lightened up her spirits greatly.

Soon afterwards Homer hit upon an invention. After a swift and improbable chain of events, some people became interested in it, and his financial situation suddenly and quite unexpectedly improved—the first time in years that this had happened. Lila now had enough money for the trip within just a week of take-off time, and since she had made complete preparations, she found herself jubilantly boarding the plane with us.

There was a strange assortment of people going along on this trip, from those who felt they had supernatural powers to the hyper-scientific; youngsters and oldsters—people attracted to Baba from all walks of life. One older woman, whose diet had been almost exclusively fruits, became ill with abdominal pain on the plane, and I was amazed and amused by the number of healing techniques used on her. There was a chiropractor who twisted her this way and that, and a spiritual healer who said that by drinking water from a cup at a distance he could heal her by cleansing her insides. There were people who attempted meditation and calling on the spirits; and there was a psychiatrist (my-self) who tried to give her reassurance and a tranquilizer. Everyone with his own technique amidst the groaning and continual discomfort of this poor woman . . . the miracle was that she recovered halfway through the trip in spite of all of us.

After arriving in Bombay and then Bangalore, we found that Baba was in Puttaparthi; so we made our way, forty-strong in a caravan of ten cars, to the ashram. The distance from Bangalore to Puttaparthi is about 110 miles and the ride was unusually pleasant and beautiful. A short distance from Bangalore we passed a deserted air strip. A sign on the side of the road read: CAUTION WATCH FOR LOW FLYING AIRCRAFT. I chuckled. All I could see were a cow and a monkey.

The drive led us through interesting, busy little villages, hilly country and large expanses of open space, the terrain constantly changing. Partway through the ride a rain fell, cooling the air. We finally arrived in Puttaparthi at six in the evening. The sun had just set and the cool air smelled clean and fresh. We approached Prasanthi Nilayam along

Puttaparthi's main street, an unpaved roadway filled with people and animals and lined with small shacks. Pictures of Baba were displayed in the windows and fronts of shops. A tall stone wall surrounding Prasanthi Nilayam separated it from the village.

We turned left through an old gate and were within the ashram grounds. Everyone was excited. From somewhere inside we could hear the rhythmic chanting of *bhajans* and knew that people were gathered to await Baba's appearance. We had been told that he walked twice daily amongst the seated devotees, giving them *darshan,* the blessing of seeing the Lord. Frequently during these periods he selects those fortunate people whom he will see later in an interview.

We all jumped hurriedly from the cabs and made our way toward the chanting. Imbued with a sense of reverence and devotion, the vibrations gave notice that we were now on holy ground. As we approached the gathering, Baba was slowly walking around a cleared circular area in front of the temple. Here sat some fifteen-thousand devotees, eyes glued to the master. Though directed inward, his gaze seemed to contact and hold all in awe. Once again I experienced great joy from making contact with Baba . . . the moment was deeply moving.

We stood quietly at a distance until he had completed his walk and reentered the temple. Then some Americans approached and helped us get situated for the night. Prasanthi Nilayam was still in the process of construction. Although dormitories were still being built on the periphery of the ashram grounds to provide living space for permanent residents and visitors, only a few had been completed. Piles of rock and sand were everywhere, workmen creating busy background movement for an otherwise quiet and peaceful setting.

An important festival—*Dasera*, the Festival of Victory—had just ended and there were still thousands of people on the grounds, too many for the limited housing facilities. Considering the problems posed by this large group, however, operations were surprisingly orderly. Two large roofed areas, each perhaps the size of a football field, provided some shelter for hundreds who lay on the bare ground at night. Our party was among the more fortunate who were housed in the dormitories.

Even so, our situation was quite spartan. The men and the women were separated, and seven of us were directed to a room about ten by twelve feet. Those without air mattresses slept on the concrete floor. There was a water faucet available for bathing; the toilet was a hole in the ground. The women too were packed into a very small room. But blessed with a sink and American sitdown-type toilet, it was very attractive indeed.

The cultural shock for many Americans on first arriving in India is severe. I felt uneasy even placing my feet squarely on the floor in a bathroom filled with cobwebs, spiders and unpleasant smells. The sewerage system, I was told, was in poor repair because of the over-crowded conditions and a heavy rain which had flooded some of the drainage areas.

Despite the discomfort, most found Prasanthi Nilayam a special place with strong spiritual vibrations. Statues of gods, pictures of Baba, and the constant cleaning of sacred areas around the temple contributed to an atmosphere of silence charged with holiness. Many felt their meditation to be extremely high. Baba's presence permeated the ashram; during chanting one could almost feel his form in the vibrations.

Sai Baba occupies just one room on the second floor of the large temple in the center of the ashram grounds. The temple was in the process of being rebuilt and workmen were forever busy around it and on the roof. In front of the temple was the cleared area where devotees sat awaiting Baba. Although shoes could be worn around most of the ashram grounds, they were not permitted here.

Twice daily, about eleven in the morning and five-thirty in the evening, Baba appeared for *darshan*. As the exact time of his appearances was unpredictable, people generally came early and waited. For most of the Americans the major activity of the day was to sit around the temple in silence and wait, frequently for long hours in the hot sun. Many who were used to a faster pace became restless.

My brother and I had plenty of time to become very close. Although he demonstrated tremendous stamina and perseverance, he assured me that before he would consider Baba divine, certain criteria would have to be satisfied: first, Baba would have to change the course of the sun; second, he would have to stop the flow of a mighty river; third, create a cow at a distance; and fourth, turn himself into a mountain.

My cousin Jerry was eager. He got up the first morning chipper and ready for battle. He would sit by the temple all day, he said—not eating and not wasting a moment's time. Periodically during the day my brother and I stopped by to see how he was doing. He remained determined, although as the day wore on he seemed to wilt a bit. By the end of the first day with no success in meeting Baba, his spirits had dropped noticeably.

The second day, one of the men in the room developed a deep cough, high fever and periods of delirium. He was too ill to leave the room; we had to bring food and care for him. A number of people quickly decided they couldn't contend with these conditions and were going to leave as soon as possible. They would wait only long enough to see Baba privately. At the end of the second day we learned that he would see us the next morning. We were jubilant. In the morning, the forty of us crowded into a small room to wait for him.

Finally being in his presence was an exciting change from the tedium of simply waiting. He appears to be in constant bliss. His face and body are lit with an aura of energy that I've never observed in another human being. His movements are brisk and alive, his smile full of excitement. With a piercing gaze he stood a moment by the side of his chair looking at us—moving a person here and there, making sure we were all comfortable—and then he sat down. This alone filled everyone in the room with glee. With all of us sitting at his feet he began to speak lightly and jokingly.

All of a sudden he turned to Lila and in a very sweet voice recited the prayer that had been given to her a year before when she was in the hospital. He repeated it matter-of-factly, word for word, then moved his hand in the àir and produced a large religious necklace, or *japamala*, made of 108 crystal-like beads, which he threw to Lila. Now, before the trip she had told me that if Baba materialized anything for her she would want a *japamala* and had gone on to describe it in some detail. The necklace Baba gave her matched the description perfectly. Lila was stunned. Then she broke into tears.

No, no; you must be strong! exclaimed Baba.

"I try . . . I try," she said.

Baba replied, *Don't try. Do!*

Then, turning to a man, he asked, *What do you want?* The man gave no reply. In his familiar gesture, Baba made several quick little circles in the air with his right hand and suddenly produced a ring with a number of precious stones bordering the setting. Later, Paul, the recipient, said it was exactly what he had wanted, that he had described the ring in detail to someone in Los Angeles prior to the trip. It was a perfect fit.

Baba spent about half an hour with us during the interview. I felt overjoyed with his attention and love. He said he would see each of us privately in the days to come. Then my cousin Jerry asked Baba to produce something for him. He had bought a cheap ring in Greece and was wearing it on his little finger. He wanted Baba to transform this ring into something else. Baba declined.

Jerry felt let down; Baba apparently did not want to be obliging or to prove anything. Jerry decided to leave soon. He couldn't put up with the ashram conditions and was disappointed in Baba for not convincing him more thoroughly of his powers.

The primitive living conditions and inconveniences were becoming too much for many Americans. Some decided to leave after the second day. Those who were going would have personal interviews the next day and Jerry placed himself on the list.

There was a strange contrast between Baba's magnificence and the stark, physical setting where all this was taking place. It was easy to become disillusioned from the physical discomfort. The evening before Jerry's departure, Donald, Jerry and I left the ashram and walked down Puttaparthi's main street to our favorite eating place: a small establishment, little more than a hovel, but with the distinction of having the only refrigerator in town. Bottled carbonated drinks including Coca Cola were served here, and the drink we usually ordered was called Goldspot, a bottled orange drink. Since we were wary of the water, we drank mostly Goldspots, eating the cookies and ice cream there and an occasional banana.

This particular evening we were bushed from the heat and all the sitting. In a rather down-hearted mood we strolled lethargically down Puttaparthi's main street, dodging cow dung and other animal droppings. Our mood was further lowered by an encounter with a couple of beggars along the way: a deformed child and a man with cerebral palsy, who dragged himself along the ground, a begging cup dangling from around his neck.

What a physical setting to be in when just five or six days earlier we had been in the middle of American metropolitan areas smothered with material wealth and comfort. We made our way to the refreshment stand, seated our weary bodies around the table and ordered a Goldspot, banana and cookies for each of us. As the proprietor, an unobtrusive, dark-skinned man, wrapped from the waist down in a plain white cloth, walked to the back of the stand, a horde of buzzing flies rose suddenly from the orange juice squeezer. We congratulated ourselves for having chosen a bottled beverage.

The conversation quickly began to reflect our frayed mood. Nearly twelve-thousand miles from home, Donald and Jerry not only began to examine their own sanity but quite seriously decided that I should get myself into intense psychotherapy as well.

Oh, how I chuckled! I *knew* the magnificence we were observing though we were in the illusion of being in pain and privation, but at a time like this what could I say? How great a sway emotional and physical discomfort have on the balance of our state of consciousness! This imbalance happens to me frequently; I am amazed at how I can be tricked by emotions even though realizing what poor reflectors they are of reality.

When something like this happens, I vow to myself to detach more from my feelings, but soon I catch myself being overwhelmed by them again and can only mutter, "Well here we go again, Sam; I hope you get out of it soon this time." Baba speaks of the trap of the senses frequently, and I know it will take a lot of spiritual work to detach from them.

The next morning Donald and I waited in the sun outside the temple, watching the people who were leaving that morning go in for their interview. I prayed for Baba to do something nice for Jerry. He was yearning so deeply to have some glimpse of God, and I knew what peace and meaning faith would bring into his life. We waited for the better part of the morning; then all of a sudden many of the people began to depart, beaming. We began to gather stories.

Baba had been beautiful as always, so fully giving, with all his energy of love and protection emanating from him. For some he had held his hand out so that people could see objects dropping from his palm. We searched out Jerry and found him in an unusually bright and receptive mood, his face radiant.

He said that he didn't know quite what to make of his interview yet, but he was glad now that he had made the trip. Somehow the interview had made it all worthwhile. He even appeared to lose his bearings a bit: a woman in the party asked for someone to help carry her bags and he quite spontaneously volunteered. "I never do this!" he said. "I must be losing my mind."

Baba had brought him into a private room and begun speaking to him, but conversation was not what Jerry wanted. He pleaded again with Baba to do something with the ring and took it from his finger. Baba said this was not his wish. Jerry continued to plead. Finally, Baba put the ring in his hand, blew on it . . . and returned to Jerry an altogether different ring—which nevertheless fit perfectly.

This had obviously shaken him. Still, he wasn't completely convinced that the whole thing wasn't just a magic trick. On the other hand, how could he explain his great sense of joy and excitement? He needed the security and familiarity of home to reflect more deeply on his experience here.

For my wife, brother, sister-in-law and myself it was more waiting in the hot sun. We became increasingly irritable from the crowded sleeping conditions, the disagreeable bathroom facilities and our growing grubbiness. Arguments began to spring up among us and our emotional control was being vigorously tested. The young man at the far end of the room continued his coughing, fever and frantic trips to the bathroom every few minutes. My brother and I became more and more reluctant to use the hole in the ground and finally attempted to contain our regular bowel activity entirely.

Their "luxurious" Western-style bathroom aside, the women too were having their problems. As crowded in their room as we were in ours, they were even finding it difficult to dress themselves. They were attempting to dress Indian-fashion in saris but had difficulty keeping them wound around their bodies. They appeared to be constantly involved in the activity of raveling and unraveling themselves in a frustrated attempt at comfort.

Living next to them was a beautiful Indian woman by the name of Uma, the wife of a Delhi physician, who was marvelously kind and helpful. She had a most beautiful voice, and each night the women were treated to Indian music and her exquisitely sung *bhajans*. She also told them stories of Baba's magnificence, which deepened their feelings toward him.

I was impressed with the gentleness and kindness of the Indian people in general. They were extremely helpful to us at the ashram, inquisitive about our American style of life and filled with deep and humble reverence for Baba. India is the grandfather of spirituality in the world, and the religious flavor is everywhere.

One evening Donald and I visited the small hospital on the ashram grounds. I was telling him that I had heard that one of the workmen on a dormitory construction project at the ashram had recently fallen to his death. Sarcastically, Donald asked, "I wonder what Baba did then?"

"Perhaps there is no better place to die than in Baba's presence," I mused aloud. "He probably received his just reward by meeting Baba on the other side." My brother just shrugged and laughed.

We had been together almost continuously, the men staying together in one area and the women in another. The hot sun seared a bond between us. We walked around dazed, shabby and uncomfortable for close to a week.

Do not tell me that you do not care for that bliss, that you are satisfied with the delusion and are not willing to undergo the rigors of sleeplessness. Your basic nature, believe me, abhors this dull, dreary routine of eating, drinking and sleeping. It seeks something which it knows it has lost—santhi, *inward contentment. It seeks liberation from bondage to the trivial and the temporary. Everyone craves for it in his heart of hearts. And it is available only in one shop: contemplation of the Highest Self, the basis of all this appearance.*

13
PRASANTHI NILAYAM

After about a week at the ashram, we were told that those leaving soon would be permitted to meet with Baba. Thinking we would not be able to endure the physical discomfort much longer, eight of us made arrangements for an interview. At the appointed time one evening we were ushered into a small room, where we sat down on the floor in a semicircle. Baba came in and, closing the circle, directed himself to each of us. Once again, being in his presence made us all forget our discomfort. Suddenly we were joyful.

Then his manner changed. He became distant and detached, impersonal. He materialized some *vibhutti*. After a long silence, he began directing himself to each of us again but strangely, looking over our heads, smiling at times.

He would ask an individual's name and then appear to be off in a dream, nodding back and forth, smiling and laughing, as if he were talking with an imaginary person. At times he moved his hand, palm up, in a slow circle, then would make a strange motion with his fingers as if writing in the air. When someone asked him what he was doing, he said that the closest we could come to understanding was that he was reading people's minds and talking to his devotees.

He did this with almost everyone in the group. And although he didn't speak personally to any of us, we simply enjoyed being in his presence. He did make some predictions: that my brother's wife would become pregnant soon and that she would have a girl; that she already had a boy, and similar comments to others present. This is exactly what did happen. My brother and sister-in-law already had a handsome son, David, and shortly after the trip Nancy became pregnant and now has a lovely daughter named Deborah.

Baba then asked Donald if he would like to see him alone, and they went into a private area behind a curtain. They were there for a few minutes and then reappeared, my brother looking somewhat sheepish and uncomfortable and Baba beaming, filled with joy. He said we could leave and that he would see us again in the morning for personal interviews.

Outside, my brother said Baba had taken him into the room and hugged him, then asked, *Are you frightened?* Donald answered that he felt a bit awkward, and Baba said not to and hugged him again. Donald was confused, not knowing how to interpret or react to Baba's actions; his mind was being turned inside out.

"I just can't understand why everyone doesn't yell 'Uncle!' and leave." Don was amazed by the stamina of the Westerners who were able to persevere in such a primitive setting. Every once in a while when I'd see my brother sitting quietly, dazed by the sun, I'd ask him how he was doing. "I'm not saying 'Uncle' yet!" was his standard reply. I never knew, though, whether this would be said with a smile, or muttered through clenched teeth.

The morning after our interview, we awoke quite early after an uncomfortable night on the concrete floor, our cheap air mattresses having developed leaks days before. My brother raised himself on his elbows, rolled over and tapped me on the shoulder. I opened one eye and saw him pull himself laboriously toward me. There was quiet for a few seconds, then I heard in a rasping, just awakened whisper . . . "Uncle."

"What's that, Donald?" I asked.

"You heard me—Uncle!" There was another silence and then he continued, "You know, I can't figure it out. I've been watching Paul for the past week lying over there under his mosquito netting, sweating and sick with some kind of dysentery, and still he sticks it out—how can people do that?" Donald raised himself up again on one arm. "Paul!" There was a stir from across the room. "I can't understand why you haven't called 'Uncle' yet."

Paul stirred again. "Do you know where I can catch the next cab out of here?"

We prepared ourselves hastily for the upcoming interviews, then after breakfast stationed ourselves by the temple—and waited. Before long we were directed into a small back room and arranged ourselves again in a semicircle at the foot of Baba's chair. I was stationed just to the right of the chair and Sharon sat next to me. Baba came in beaming, setting his usual mood of love and openness.

He began by speaking a little with us and then briskly whirled his hand in the air to produce a huge mound of candy, rising four or five inches above his palm. He distributed a goodly portion to each of us. I felt transformed into a child, sitting at the feet of Santa Claus in some magnificent fairy tale. And I might add that I've seen the sternest, hardest, the most pompous people become children at Baba's feet.

He called my brother over to him and asked him to sit at his right, in front of me. His eyes twinkled as he asked Don what he wanted. Then he moved his hand and materialized a beautiful ring made of a heavy metal with small gold figurines of his pet elephant, Sai Gita, on each side, and a gold figure of Baba on its face. He placed the ring on Donald's finger and it fit perfectly. Donald beamed, I felt choked, and Sharon began to cry.

I was so happy that Baba should present such a fine gift to my brother, showing him such love, demonstrating to all of us his great power, that I could hardly hold back my own tears. Baba told him that he would have a long, healthy and happy life and be a very good doctor. Then people began asking Baba questions.

How would we know when he is with us when we are so far away? He turned to one woman in the group, someone he hadn't spoken to yet: *She knows when Baba is with her,* and all of a sudden she became flushed with excitement and began to cry.

Later she related the story of how she had first become aware of Baba's presence back in the United States. Against the advice of her family she had taken her mother out of a convalescent hospital to nurse at home. She did this out of love even though it was a trying and difficult task. Her mother was incontinent and in need of much attention, but the daughter looked after her with great devotion.

As time went on she would enter her mother's room, and spontaneous and inexplicable waves of emotion would sweep through her. She had no idea what was causing this to happen, although she sensed the presence of someone unknown but close to her and identified the emotion as love. Then she heard of the Sai Baba meetings held by Elsie Cowan and decided to attend one.

Going for the first time, she met Elsie, who happened to hand her a piece of material from one of Baba's robes. She touched it and was suddenly electrified, experiencing an almost convulsive state of ecstasy. Now, in the interview with Baba, she was certain that he was aware of her experience and was referring to it.

Baba began to materialize other objects and to talk knowingly to people about themselves and give advice. In response to a woman's complaint of problems with her eyes, he materialized a medallion, telling her to immerse it in water and to place a few drops of the water in her eyes every day.

Baba then saw each of us separately. Lila requested something for which she had been praying for a number of months. He responded by stepping back playfully, his eyes twinkling, his face a broad loving smile, and answered her in the very words which she had been using in her prayers to him. He simply had had no way of knowing what these words had been and she was overwhelmed.

To my wife's concerns and wishes for our children, Baba responded with a discussion which she felt reflected awareness of their individual personalities—and he materialized a medallion for one of them. He told me not to worry about money matters and talked to me about my spiritual development; aware that he knew my deepest yearnings and aspirations, I was filled with bliss. In answer to my question about spending time with him, he said, *First you have to attend to your duty back home; you will be freer after your children are grown.*

When we were sitting together again, Baba moved his hand in the air and brought out eight little calling cards with his picture and address and handed one to each of us. He was with us always, he said. After much encouragement and love, he gave out packets of *vibhutti*.

As usual, although the materializations during the interview were impressive, for me the major impact came from his uncanny awareness of each of us and his ability to show me that he is indeed literally with us even when absent physically. This concrete experience of the omnipresence of a loving being—an experience which continues right through one's life, filling it with a deep sense of security and safety—is a most miraculous gift!

BHAGAWAN
Sri Sathya Sai Baba
'PRASANTHINILAYAM'
PENUKONDA (TALUKA)
ANANTAPUR (DIST.)
ANDHRA PRADESH
INDIA

A number of questions were answered by this trip. Why Baba, for example, supposedly so great and powerful, would allow such uncomfortable living conditions to exist at his ashram. That intially perplexed me and I finally resolved it in this manner: Perhaps it was unfair to judge the conditions at the ashram at this time, for we were there during a period of construction, with many obstacles to personal comfort normal in such a situation. Even so, no one was turned away, and all were there free of charge.

Then too, the experience of suffering is widespread in the world, yet to my thinking, this is certainly no argument against the existence of God. It is now obvious to me that we ourselves have the responsibility to choose right over wrong, good over bad, and that the situations in which we find ourselves are due to our own actions, whether in this life or perhaps even in past lives. It is our responsibility to serve and heal ourselves.

I am beginning to appreciate the concept of *karma*. We reap what we sow, we are repaid in like for the good and bad that we do. *We* are entirely responsible for pulling ourselves out of the mess that we have made for ourselves, and it is foolish and futile to try to shift responsibility to someone else.

It is so easy to get caught up in the excitement of Baba—with all the changes one makes in his conceptions of the nature of reality and all the blows to one's previously held beliefs—that we may begin to feel that he will take care of everything exactly as we wish—not just on the spiritual level but on the physical plane as well. When the landmarks of old realities are taken from us, many of us flounder about quite lost, trying to hold fast to God for direction. At this stage it is easy to lose one's sense of perspective and responsibility. So it is with us when we expect Baba to assume responsibility for cleaning up the ashram: by waving a magic wand and suddenly making everything pure and beautiful.

It is more apparent to me now that Baba's appearance on earth is to give people faith in the existence of a higher reality and the truth of spiritual laws, so that we may have the strength to turn toward righteousness and steadfastly work to better our condition. If some great force cured all our illness and poverty but left us at our present level of consciousness, we would soon be at one another's throats again, and the same chaotic situation would develop in the world.

I am learning a great deal more about yogic powers or *siddhis*. Many yogis, and Baba himself, have stated that these powers frequently deter one from the spiritual path. I have now seen people get caught up in fascination with them and lose sight of the ultimate goal of merging with God. Baba reminds us that the spiritual leader as well as the seeker can fall prey to this temptation.

But Sai Baba admonishes us not to consider him a spiritual aspirant, who can still yield to such lower tendencies. His feats are simply part of his very nature, he says, since he is an *avatar*, beyond *karma* and evil, beyond space and time, beyond classification of any kind . . . beyond duality. His powers are simply an outer expression of the reality of his being merged with everything, everywhere, at all times.

In speaking of the extraordinary feats which millions call miracles, Baba has said, *They belong to the natural unlimited power of God and are in no sense the product of* siddhic *powers as with yogis, or of magic as with magicians. The creative power is in no way contrived or developed, but is natural only.* Swami *creates some objects in just the same way that he created the universe. Certain other objects are brought from where they were. There are no invisible beings helping* Swami *to bring things. His* sankalpa, *his divine will, brings the object in a moment. He is everywhere.*

Most people with paranormal powers know their limitations. The extent of their powers can be defined. They usually feel that they are channels or mediums in touch with a higher reality—perhaps used by it and, in any case, usually humbled by their relationship to it. In contrast, Baba's powers appear to be boundless. He states that not only are there other dimensions of reality and levels of consciousness—a way to greater awareness—but that he in fact *is* these other dimensions and the path to them. There is no separation between him and any dimension, or between him and you and me.

Even with his immense power there is no semblance of pompous show or image-building behavior on Baba's part—only giving, teaching, loving. In all my personal and professional experience with people and my awareness of motivation, I have never seen anyone behave this way. It is the most moving miracle I have ever witnessed.

I am also becoming aware of the nature of what in Sanskrit is called *maya:* the illusionary nature of what we consider reality—how our sense perceptions, our thoughts and our emotions orient us to the world in a way that is purely illusion. That senses and feelings have a way of blurring or tunneling our vision, seducing us from the spiritual path, was concretely pointed out to me by the way my feelings of physical discomfort and my reaction to the disease, poverty and primitiveness of Puttaparthi almost tricked me out of my appreciation of Sai Baba's greatness.

Many people coming to Baba are put through trying ordeals by which they learn the futility and frustration that comes from wanting. Some are so hurt that they become angry with Baba and turn away. For most, however, when confronted with the choice of giving up either their wants or Sai Baba, it becomes apparent that it isn't Baba who must go but the wanting.

It became clear to me that I was not supposed to be living at Prasanthi Nilayam, that I was supposed to find a way of establishing my relationship with Baba while continuing to live and work in America. I had heard Baba speak about this frequently: not to disrupt oneself and take to the woods or a cave in the mountains for seclusion, but to continue with one's duty where one happens to be . . . to be of service and to develop the relationship with Baba by putting more and more of his teachings into practice in the midst of one's daily life.

I was beginning to see that Baba is much greater than his physical form. He is more truly his teaching, his love, his truth, his caring. I had begun to see the futility of trying to get close to him physically, and to recognize that if I want true contact with him I must accomplish this by merging with him on a spiritual level. I must weave his teachings and his spirit ever more coherently into the fabric of my life, until I *become* him.

14
BURNING
TO ASH

After returning from the second trip, I decided that it wasn't important to live close to Baba physically, but psychologically and spiritually; to
have him always in my mind and heart. I began to study his teachings
more diligently and to make a serious attempt to put them into action in
my life. I began to discipline myself in yoga and meditation, initially for
short, intermittent periods and then regularly twice a day, morning and
evening. The more I engaged in this practice the more I enjoyed it;
without effort, I found myself increasing the amount of time devoted to
it. Also, I began attending *bhajan* groups and then developed a study
group myself, so several nights a week I was meeting with other Baba
devotees to study and participate in devotional services.

I was fascinated in observing what began to happen. My emotional
and mental responses began to change in a way that had not been the
case after a number of years in psychotherapy. Like strong, steady winds
blowing away an obscuring cloud cover, my spiritual practices began to
reveal an inner dimension I had never glimpsed before. I had heard of
others experiencing such things as light, expansion, timelessness and
boundless love, but I had thought such feelings imaginary or illusory.
Now I began to wonder about this vast uncharted part of myself. Just as
orgasm provides physical and emotional release after one has reached a
certain level of sexual maturity, could it be that inherent in this inner
dimension are mechanisms which when discovered and unlocked can
release us into higher levels of consciousness?

I make it a point when teaching students in psychiatry to ask whether
any of them spends time in meditation. Virtually no psychiatrist or
resident I've ever asked meditates regularly, and only one or two have
ever engaged in the practice at all. Many are completely unfamiliar with

the process—this in a group of people whose concern is the healing of mental and emotional problems and who are supposedly dealing with inner space. What then is meditation like?

Although there are many different techniques of meditation, one generally enters a state in which he ceases to be bothered by background sounds, thought fragments, fantasies and emotions. In this stillness we may experience the eternal. *Take the screen in the cinema theatre,* Baba says. *When the film is on, you do not see the screen, you see only the play; when the show is over, you see just a screen, a screen that has no message—neither voice nor name nor form nor color nor creed. That is* Brahman. *The rope gives the appearance of a snake in the dark; here, the entire screen was lost in the picture.*[1]

What are some of the experiences which might follow? *First you are in the light—next the light is in you—and finally the light and you are one,* says Baba. He teaches that one may begin to experience the light of divine energy first as something separate and outside oneself, then as penetrating and permeating one and, even though separate, as originating inside oneself. The ultimate state—*the light and you are one,* experiencing oneself as light—reflects the condition of going beyond duality, merging with the *Atma* or universal self, the God within.

As I began to experience the excitement and exhilaration of discovery in meditation and began to see in Baba a great scientist and teacher of consciousness, I again developed a yearning to be with him. I wanted to question him specifically about the various steps in meditation and to follow his directions exactly in extending myself into this dimension of consciousness which was opening up before me.

Also, having been away from Baba for six months, the thought of seeing him and experiencing his bliss at first hand again was very tempting. Well, Indra Devi was going to be making the trip soon, and after only a minimal amount of time spent considering alternatives, I decided to join her. Off I went for the third time to India.

This time I was an old hand at travel. My journey was pleasant and I welcomed the opportunity to be by myself and meditate for long periods, sitting quietly and immersing myself in the experience of Baba. After the long trip, we landed in Bombay, where the sights were now familiar and extremely enjoyable, the experience really psychedelic. The smells, images, movement—getting lost in all this marvelous activity—I was growing to love the India that I knew.

Arriving in Bangalore late that night, we found that Baba was in Brindavan, his summer residence. Early the next morning I was sitting by the side of a walkway with thirty other Americans and hundreds of Indians, waiting for him to come out of the house.

---

[1] *Sathya Sai Speaks,* Vol. II, p. 93

Next to me was a traveling companion, a young painter from Santa Barbara. As I saw the orange robe appear, my heart quickened and there returned all the familiar and longed-for love and excitement. Baba floated blissfully down the walk from the house, looking heavenly and beautiful. It was a miracle to experience myself begin to vibrate and be aware of so much warmth inside.

We were sitting to Baba's right. About ten feet away he turned to a group of people sitting on the other side of the walk and rotated his right hand with all the serene majesty I remembered. Suddenly in the hand, his sleeve rolled up, was the sacred ash, *vibhutti*. Steve, the painter, moved closer to me and said in a hushed voice, "That was worth the whole trip." He was silent for a moment, then he continued in almost a whisper: "I can feel *karma* from many years being lifted from my shoulders. I'm free! I'm soaring!"

Baba strolled amongst us, greeting us with loving smiles for fifteen or twenty minutes, then began to walk back to the house. All of a sudden he looked my way and walked over to me. *How is your brother?* he asked. I recalled with sudden vividness Donald's asking me just before my departure whether I thought Baba would remember him. I had replied, "Sure, he remembers everyone." Baba's question would be a great gift to bring back to Don, and my smile broadened and my heart went out to him. "He is very well, Baba," I said, the tone of my voice full of the big grin I could feel on my face.

Good, good! he said in English, smiling back. Then he turned and headed toward the house. Indra Devi came up to the group and said that Baba was going to invite us in and that we should wait. Later that morning we were ushered into a large sitting room. There were about thirty of us sitting quietly in the circle, the men on one side and the women on the other. Baba appeared, with his literally electrifying aura, and slowly circled the group, smiling and looking at each of us playfully. Then he asked Dr. Gokok to interpret for him and sat down with us to discourse and answer questions. He spoke for about an hour on the meaning and value of turning our lives Godward to the reality of the higher self. *The purpose of your lives,* he said, *is to purify yourselves.*

He seemed to answer everybody's questions without anyone's saying a word. His beauty was beyond description. He had some attendants bring out refreshments and after we snacked told us he couldn't see us anymore that day but would see us again soon. Everybody else left, but I was so filled with excitement that I stayed on, not willing to leave unless I was thrown out.

Unfortunately there are so many people yearning for Sai Baba that some take advantage of his hospitality, just as I was doing. I wouldn't think of imposing myself on him in such a manner now, but at that time I was still going through too many psychological changes in my relation-

View of Prasanthi Nilayam grounds, temple in background. Close-up of front of temple on following page.

ship with him to be really clear about the distinctions between courtesy and devotion. As no one ushered me out, I decided I would stay there for eternity unless someone objected.

From my vantage point I could gaze into the house and see Baba moving about, speaking to people, reading his letters and carrying on with other activities. I thought this trip was going to be really great; I was going to bed-down in the front vestibule and never leave. Then Baba went upstairs for a rest and I lay down on the hard floor to await his reappearance.

I was dozing when suddenly there was a flurry of activity. A car pulled up in front of the door, Baba appeared with a few people and jumped in, baskets of food were thrust into the car and off he went. As quickly as that, my dream of being close to him vanished. I was out in the hot sun again with only a banana for company. "How could he do something like this to me?"

Only a few of those closest to him had known he was off for Puttaparthi. I found out later that he had sent Indra Devi to Bombay to present a short address in his absence to some 200,000 disappointed people awaiting his annual appearance there. What a load to fall on her shoulders.

She was counting on Baba's help from afar, to ease their disappointment.

As for me, I decided to follow Baba. Early the next morning a friend and I were in a cab. The day had begun cool and clear. A short distance from town the hectic pace of the Bangalore streets gave way to the leisurely awakening of the countryside. The road was paved one lane each way; for long stretches there was no one in sight. My mind quieted, drifting off toward the distant foothills and large expanses of space.

We passed occasional bullock-pulled carts, the big cumbersome animals lethargically urged onward by a driver who, like his animals, appeared lost in a dreamlike state. Approaching villages were signaled by the appearance of men tending their goats, and women, wrapped in worn earth-colored saris, carrying objects on their heads. In the towns, I chuckled at the ingenuity of small Indian boys contorting themselves to ride bicycles much larger than they. The seat was usually too high and the crossbar between it and the handlebars did not allow them to center themselves, so they had to ride hunched to one side like spiders. The feat was apparently not as difficult as it looked for there were many of these little fellows on the road.

Most of the villages were completely agricultural and their pace of life was an almost cinematic slow-motion, in the merciless Indian heat. Simply taking a step was a task. A little over halfway we passed a good-sized community set back behind a large stone wall. We were informed that this had been the grounds of royalty some 800 years ago and the town was still flourishing.

It was oppressively hot at Puttaparthi. Almost no one was out in the sun. After finding a place to stay in one of the dormitories at Prasanthi Nilayam and eating a few mangoes, we placed ourselves by the temple to await Baba's appearance for *darshan*. The ashram had grown considerably since I was last there. With so few people about this time, the grounds looked cleaner and quieter. There was the same holy atmosphere—a serene silence—and the sun appeared to bake everything white and pure.

There was the same air of excitement too as the devotees gathered for *darshan*; the *bhajans* still had their special ring of devotion. We were happy to hear that the following morning Baba was going to preside at a nearby ground-breaking ceremony for a school that would be named for his mother. We would be able to see more of him then.

How unpredictable Baba's activities are! The next day a few others and myself walked to the area of the ground-breaking to find almost no one present. By the time Baba presented himself, there were no more than twenty or thirty people and a few mangy dogs to greet him. I couldn't understand why he had chosen to appear here while 200,000 people were awaiting his presence in Bombay. I just accepted the situation and enjoyed it thoroughly.

Strolling up gracefully but forcefully, Baba presented himself in a flaming orange robe, darker in color than I had seen before. Holding a coconut in each hand, he skillfully broke them by striking one against the other and sprinkled the milk over the ground, then materialized some *vibhutti* which he scattered over the milk. He was full of goodwill; after the coconut ceremony he reached for a satchel filled with little packets of cookies and began to move through the crowd giving them out. It is surprising how uncanny Baba is during his lovely gesture of distributing sweets. He misses no one.

Being caught up in the midst of this small crowd was a joyfully humorous experience: the small children jumping up and down, their smiling faces, the dancing of their eager outstretched fingers . . . and throughout, the image of 200,000 people sitting in a stadium in Bombay.

All the pushing and pulling, the laughing and excitement of this youthful band momentarily transported me back to childhood. The highlight of the event took place when Baba approached close to give me some cookies and in the commotion stepped on my toe! I felt joy from the tip of that toe to the top of my head.

The next day Baba arrived back in Brindavan and invited us in for a large *bhajan* meeting. He would lead devotional songs for us and we would sing to him in return. Indra Devi volunteered that many of the Americans knew *bhajans*. I knew only one myself and hoped fervently that Baba would ask me to sing before someone else beat me to it.

Baba seemed pleased by the occasion. He pointed to a young woman sitting across from me and asked her to sing. My heart dropped. She was singing the only one I knew. We all joined in and sang to Baba, clapping to the rhythm, filled with an excitement generated by deep devotion. I decided to keep quiet, sort of melt into the wall and go unnoticed. Then to my great discomfort, Indra Devi, her face beaming, said, "Oh! Dr. Sandweiss has *bhajans* in his home weekly, and *he* sings them." My goose was cooked.

Baba turned to me: *Go on!* he said. I hemmed and hawed, cleared my throat and finally said, "Baba, the only *bhajan* I know is *Ganesha Sharanam* and that has already been sung." There was no reply so I decided to sing my one and only *bhajan*. Perhaps if I sang with a great deal of enthusiasm the duplication would be acceptable. But after the first two words Baba gestured and exclaimed, *No, no—already been sung!* and I fell back defeated and destroyed. It took me two or three days to get over the hurt. I resolved to learn more *bhajans*.

Baba considers singing these devotional songs very important; they are supposed to have great effect on our meditation and spiritual outlook and are performed by one person singing a verse and the rest of the group repeating it. All the words in a *bhajan* are the Sanskrit names of God as he has appeared in various forms and aspects. They supposedly hold within their sound, vibrations capable of opening spiritual centers in those who hear them. Many of the words are used as *mantras*.

On Bhajans

Some people may laugh at all this bhajan and call it a mere show and exhibition and recommend, instead, quiet meditation in the silent recess of the shrine room. But coming out in company and doing bhajan like this helps in removing egoism. One is not then afraid of being mocked at or ashamed to call out the name of the Lord. One gets inspired also by the devotion of others. The company of men with kindred sentiments helps to foster the tiny seedling of devotion and to keep it from being scorched by the heat of derision.

For example, a person will sweep the floor of his room with a broom when nobody is looking on. But to do the same act when people are looking requires some mastery over the ego. In fact, Nama Sankirtana (singing bhajans in a group) will wean you away from distracting thoughts, whereas those thoughts will invade you when you do it alone. So sing aloud the glory of God and charge the atmosphere with divine adoration.

The name of God is the most effective tonic to keep off all illnesses. So do not take shelter behind excuses, but attend all bhajan sessions. If you are ill, bhajan will help the cure; or let me tell you, it is far better to die during bhajan with the Lord's name on the lips than at other times.

Do not also indulge in Nama Sankirtana as a pastime or a fashion or a passing phase, or as an unpleasant part of an imposed timetable to be fulfilled each day. Think of it as a part of spiritual training to be seriously taken for reducing the attachments to fleeting objects, and purifying and strengthening you, liberating you from the cycle of birth and death and consequently misery. It may appear a frail cure for such a dreadful malady. Nevertheless, it is a panacea.

The common excuse for escaping from this urgent duty to oneself is that there is "no time" for bhajan in the hectic schedule of activity that has become the lot of man at the present time. If the burden of a hundred odd jobs can be borne because they are unavoidable, can the extra job of Nama Sankirtana be such an undesirable addition? He who carries a hundred can surely carry one more.

Have the bhajans on as many days as possible or at least once a week. They can best be held either on Thursday or Sunday evening; however, this need not be strictly adhered to, since it is not the day of the week that counts, but the heart. Have them in a central place where all can come and join, and not in the houses of some people where all may not be welcome. Have them as simple as you can and without competitive pomp or show. Reduce the expenses to a minimum, for God cares for the inner yearning and not the outer trappings. No amount should be collected by passing the plate around, or a subscription or donation list.

God is omnipresent. He is the in-dweller of every heart and all names are His. So you can call Him by any name that gives you joy. You must not cavil at other names and forms, nor become fanatics, blind to their glory. When you sing bhajan songs, dwell on the meaning of the songs and the message of each name and form of God and roll on your tongue its sweetness.

Rama: *this name must evoke in you the* dharma *of righteousness He embodied and demonstrated.* Radha: *this name must evoke in you the supermental, superworldly love she had as the greatest* Gopi *(women who tended the cows—great devotees of Lord* Krishna). Krishna: *this name must evoke in you the sweet and sustaining love with which He drew all towards Him.* Shiva: *the name must evoke in you the supreme sacrifice of the drinking of the deadly poison for the good of all the world, the cool grace heightened by the cascade of* Ganga *(the holy river) and the moonlight from the crescent.*

Remember, every song sung in praise of the Lord is a sword that cuts the knots of laziness. It is a fine piece of social service to remind all of their duty to the Almighty who watches over them. Keep the name of the Lord always on your lips and you will find that all thoughts of envy and hatred will disappear from your hearts. If only you evince some genuine interest in your own real uplift, I am ready to stand by you and crown your efforts with success. Hence, do not waste time purposelessly. Let every moment be a bhajan. *Avoid all lesser talk. Know the purpose of* bhajan *and devote yourself wholeheartedly to it. Derive maximum benefit from the years allotted to you.*

After the singing, everyone was beginning to leave when Baba pulled aside one of the volunteers who had worked with him for many years. A gathering of young Indian boys quickly surrounded them. We all pressed closer and then the characteristic circular motion of his arm drew our eyes as if they were being pulled into the invisible vortex he was apparently creating in the air. Something silver suddenly flashed in his hand. It was a beautiful watch. The man who received the gift was humbled and overwhelmed as he took it into his hands.

That evening we were invited in for *bhajans* again. There was an American singing group there called Lite Storm, which has made a record of American *bhajans*. They played their guitars, drums and other instruments and took turns singing with the Indian men. Baba began the session in the most beautiful, clear and exciting voice imaginable, setting the tone for a very spiritual evening. The experience was a concrete demonstration of how love and the joyful singing of God's name unite people of such diverse backgrounds. As we experienced together the yearning for God, the yearning to love and merge with God's grandeur, we all became the closest of kin.

Baba gives a great deal of attention to the students at his school. They are always allowed around him, and the joyful admiration on their youthful faces is a vivid expression of the contact they experience with him. There were twenty or thirty young students sitting at his feet this evening. Their sense of ease and familiarity with the most complex *bhajans,* their special tonality and use of voice, precise pronunciation and deep devotional attitude, reflected clearly their heritage in this magnificent land of spirituality.

In contrast were the guitar, bongo drums and suggestion of a rock beat of the Westerners, who sang only the simplest type of *bhajans.* Still, it was obvious that the Indians understood our yearnings and we understood theirs. We were the same at heart.

Love, respect and a deep feeling of kinship regardless of ethnic background, nationality or religion awaken under such conditions. I was filled with the warmest glow and found myself thanking Baba for allowing me to see how we are all made brothers when in contact with the Father. There is no doubt that this reaction could happen among all people, all over the world, if they could somehow be awakened to the reality of the fatherhood of God.

One of the aspects of Baba that I find most important is his *Shiva,* or destroyer, aspect. In the Hindu religion, the three major aspects of God as creator, preserver and destroyer are represented by *Brahma, Vishnu* and *Shiva,* respectively. When I first began learning about Hinduism, I wondered why one should worship the destroyer aspect of God, but as my relationship with Baba deepened, I began to recognize its significance.

I have mentioned before that no matter how much I prepare myself as I draw closer to Baba, I begin to feel destroyed. This alway comes about as a result of being too attached to the mind—with its almost infinite capacity to doubt—and the emotions, which easily lead me into turmoil. If he ignores me, I hurt and sulk. When he admonishes me not to give in to momentary pleasures, I become angry with such "simplistic" advice. If he appears to make a mistake, I feel that this can't be the way of divinity. When he permits suffering, I doubt. When there is a clash between *my* feelings and thoughts and *his* words or actions, I feel it's like dying to give up reliance on my sense impressions and mental conceptualizations and surrender totally to his will. And though I vow not to desire or demand anything of Baba, desiring is always rekindled by my contact with him, frustrating me until I feel hurt and defeated.

I understand this reaction to be that of my ego struggling against being deposed, the struggle of the small self (mind and emotions) as its dominance begins to be overcome. But understanding does not necessarily lead to controlling. On this trip as on the others, I *wanted* the limiting small self to be destroyed, so that I could begin to merge with the greater universal self. But it is so difficult to give up identifying with emotion and mind—that which I thought I was for so long—and place full reliance on the *avatar* . . . to believe that he represents the true reality and that my senses, emotions and mind see only an illusion.

It is impossible to experience such a crucial and elemental struggle without ambivalence. There seemed no end to my ego; yet in his infinite love, Baba continued to chisel away at it. *You have been born with one purpose*, says Baba: *to die. That is to say, to kill the "I." If* Brahma*dies, you become* Brahman, *or rather to know that you are* Brahman. *All this literature, all this effort, all this teaching, is just to hold a mirror before you so that you may see yourself.*[1]

After I had been with Baba for a week, he began calling on those who would be leaving shortly to arrange for private interviews. Three other men and myself were ushered into a small room, where we sat down on the carpeted floor with Baba and Dr. Gokak, the interpreter. Baba was smiling and rocking back and forth blissfully. He turned to the fellow next to me, Jeff, and said casually, *I came to you twice in dreams.*

Now as a psychiatrist, I have certainly never heard of a colleague talking this way to a patient. Psychiatrists deal with dreams all the time—but to say, "I've come to you twice in dreams," would be somewhat disconcerting for the average patient. Such comments now, however, only serve to enlarge my conception of Baba's supernormal powers.

In this case I witnessed an occurrence which, while related to the work I do, was so far beyond it that my faith was reaffirmed many times over.

---

[1]*Sathya Sai Speaks,* Vol II, p. 210

Baba began to describe and interpret one of Jeff's dreams, and it became quite evident to me that he had in some way fashioned the psychic experience of this man, had actually created dreams for him and visited him in another dimension of reality. Everything that Baba said, Jeff confirmed. Here was the greatest psychiatrist I had ever seen!

An experience in the dream that Jeff couldn't understand had to do with Baba's cutting up a fish and distributing it to people present and giving some to Jeff, even though he is a vegetarian. Baba smiled and said, *Selfish, selfish—destroying selfishness*, using the fish, in other words, as a symbol for the small "I," the small self—a quality of which is selfishness. He frequently makes such a play on words, even in English.

Baba went on to speak of a message behind the crucifix: the small self, the small "I," symbolized by the vertical part of the cross, negated by the horizontal section—the *Shiva* aspect of God. Then I was in for a real ordeal. Baba teaches with words, but he invariably tempers the words in the heat of experience.

Jeff said that he had received a *mantra* from Indra Devi and wanted to know the correct way of saying it. Baba agreed to help. I knew that in advising people to repeat the name of God, Baba frequently instructs them to use a *japamala*, a religious necklace with 108 beads, similar to a rosary. The object is to repeat the name with each bead.

I said to myself, "Ah ha! I bet Baba is going to create a *japamala* for Jeff." As I watched him, he brought out from behind his back in his left hand what indeed appeared to be a *japamala*. He continued speaking to Jeff, and it seemed to me that nobody else was looking at his left hand, that I was the only one who noticed it. My mind began to work.

"Could it be that Baba is really just a cheap magician, who hides objects behind his back all the time—so forgetful that he takes this necklace from behind his back now and plays with it in front of my nose? . . . What a stupid thought!" But even as my mind attempted to argue away its own doubt, I could feel my heart sinking. No, I would not let him trick me into thinking he is just a bad magician. He continued to talk to us, smiling blissfully, and I continued to watch his left hand carefully.

Back it went behind his back, then out in front again, and I just knew he was going to give the *japamala* to Jeff as if he had materialized it. Then all of a sudden he made the familiar circular gesture with the right hand and there appeared in it a beautiful *japamala*—but quite different from the one in his left hand. The one I had seen in his left hand was gone.

I was stupefied by this turn of events. My doubting was certainly not new. It raises its ugly head whenever I'm beginning to take pride in my faith, beginning to believe that it is solid and unshakable. A fog of confusion comes over me; I know that Baba is destroying me, and I feel almost helpless before this reaction.

He continued to speak to the other three men, generally ignoring me. I didn't mind. I was still trying to recover from the *japamala* incident. He

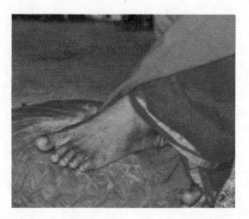

*Be attached under all conditions to the source, substance
and sum of all power: the Lord . . . and then you can draw
from that source all the power that you need. This attachment is called* bhakthi.

*For the bird in mid-ocean flying over the dark, deep blue
waters, the only resting place is the mast of a ship that sails
across. In the same way, the Lord is the only refuge for man,
who is swept by storms over a restless sea. However far the
bird may fly, it knows where it can rest; that knowledge
gives it confidence. It has the picture of that mast steady in
its mind; its form is fixed in the eye. The name of the Lord is
the mast for you; remember it ever. Associate it with the
form and have that form fixed in the mind's eye. It is a lamp
shedding light in the recesses of your heart. Have the name
on the tongue and it will drive away the inner darkness as
well as the outer. Peace within, brotherliness without—that
is the sign of a person engaged in* namajapam *(recitation of
the name of God).*

was always in direct contact with us, he said, but in case we should wish to write, he would give us a calling card; then we would have his address. He moved his hand in the air and matter-of-factly pulled out three calling cards, handing one to each of the other fellows, without giving me so much as a look.

What surprised me about this was that in a short interview six months earlier he had given me a card exactly like the ones he had just produced. Was he showing me that he remembered this, that he knew me better than, with all my doubting, I believed? He sees hundreds of people daily; he's just bombarded with people. The mere fact that he might have remembered such a trivial occurrence six months earlier seemed to me quite a feat in itself, to say nothing of the materialization of the cards and the casual manner in which he carried this all out. It certainly helped take my mind off the mysterious *japamala*.

After this kind of demonstration I've learned to say to myself, "Sam, don't fall for any of those tricks, and don't be destroyed. Just expect nothing, want nothing and demand nothing." I left the interview full of smiles rather than suspicions or hurt feelings, and Baba said we would be called back in another day or so for additional private interviews.

In a few days we were back and I felt well-prepared, able to withstand any of Baba's tricks. "He's not going to do that to me again today," I muttered with firmness to myself. "I will not be destroyed!" As we sat down, he looked at me and said, *Your mind is confused.*

I felt myself slipping but quickly reassured myself: "No, I will not be destroyed. His criticisms, his tricks—nothing will destroy me today." Baba continued to look at me smilingly.

Monkey mind, he said in a gently mocking tone of voice.

He went on to talk with the others but after awhile again addressed me: *What is it you want, sir? You have been here before.*

"Baba," I said plaintively, "I would like to merge with you."

Well, first you are in the light, then the light is in you, and then you and the light are one. . . . I was slipping again; it was too late to stop the reaction. I felt terrible pain, a terrible letdown; my fog of confusion now had a raw edge of doubt.

"This is my third trip," I thought: "Twenty-five thousand miles each time: three times I've clawed my way to the side of the *Avatar,* and listen to what he tells me—cliches. I've heard him say this a hundred times. This was my opportunity . . . and now it's gone."

Baba's words trailed off into the air. He turned to a fellow named Steve and put his arm around him, laughing and talking lovingly with him, showing him that he knew things about him that no person could know—and I began to get jealous. He noticed a rather cheap looking chain and medallion hanging around Steve's neck. *I'll give you a good one,* he said.

"Oh boy, here we go again." I began to pray that he wouldn't materialize anything for me. He hadn't made anything special for me yet, and I decided I wanted to keep it that way.

I wanted to make something good out of what I felt was neglect. "If you're going to neglect me all the time, fine!—that's great," I sulked to myself. "But in that case, *always* neglect me so I have something special on the next guy." I began to nourish the thought that Baba's not having materialized a medal for me in the past was really a status symbol. Then he gently moved his hand in the air and created four beautiful little medallions and casually tossed one to each of us. Now I had nothing on anybody. Baba had refused me even his neglect.

This *Shiva* aspect of Baba becomes painfully apparent to me as I draw closer and closer to him on a physical level. Baba is so beautiful. He is so playful. Even though on the surface he can appear to be putting you harshly to task, his is really the kindest, most loving "destruction" I've ever witnessed.

He took each of the other men into another room for a short private interview. Each returned beaming, overwhelmed, awe-stricken— completely transformed. Then he walked over to me and asked when I was leaving. *I shall see you later*, he said. There I was: the only one without a private interview, with a medallion I hadn't wanted to be given, feeling that I would never get close to Baba on a physical level—but left with the hope that, perhaps, I would get to see him later.

Within a few days summer school was to start—the school Baba had developed to teach spirituality to college students—and the ashram was buzzing with preparations. I knew it would be difficult to see Baba under such conditions, but still I had some hope. Seeing this develop in me made me shudder. I knew I might well be in for a great disappointment. Finally the last day came; students and lecturers were arriving from all parts of India. I'd been trying my best to think of ways of getting an interview.

I waited and waited in the hot sun, tried to send Baba a note, and waited some more. The day started to cool off, clouds gathered . . . and I waited. I asked where Baba was. He was checking on last-minute details about the starting ceremony for the school. I waited. The clouds became larger and more menacing. Then it began to rain. I got soaked.

I waited through the rain until it got cool and night fell. It became quite apparent that I had absolutely no chance for a private interview.

Completely drenched, I rode back to Bangalore in the back of a rickety, modified three-wheeled motorcycle, chilled to the bone by the night breeze. It had taken me three trips to discover how futile and frustrating it was to try to develop a close interpersonal relationship with Baba. I would not come back to pester him, and frustrate myself, unless struck by a clear, unmistakable and overwhelming sign to return. That was the quiet vow I made to myself on that cold, rickety night journey back to Bangalore.

15
A TRIP
OF LOVE

After my third trip to India I was sure that nothing short of lightning searing the night sky with a message to return would send me back for quite some time. I had been home four months when I received word that Walter Cowan had passed away after having lived a year and a half following his apparent resurrection by Baba. Elsie, Walter's wife, informed me that Baba had written her stating his interest in coming to America, and she was planning to go to Puttaparthi to make arrangements for such a trip. I felt that Elsie was playing a long shot, as this speculation had been going on for years. But after reading the letter Elsie had received from Baba, I decided it was the clearest sign yet that he was seriously considering a trip to this country.

Then Elsie asked me to join her. I was thrown into a tremendous dilemma. I struggled back and forth—yes, no; yes, no—and started asking for signs. I would look at chipmunks scurrying around in the yard and say, "Okay, if he jumps into that hole that means I'll go; if he doesn't, I'll stay."

Sharon, who had put up with my antics for a year and a half, said she could accept my leaving, even this fourth time, if only there was some kind of sign indicating to both of us that I should go. She mentioned this to Elsie by phone on Sunday morning. Later that day I was crawling around under the house fixing some plumbing. I was preparing for a shower afterwards when I noticed that the medallion Baba had materialized for me during my last trip was missing from the chain around my neck.

My heart dropped and my mind began to whirl as I tried to figure out where I might have lost it. It seemed peculiar to me that in all my activity over the past six months, now should be the first time for this to happen, but it would be just too farfetched to consider it a sign. Scrambling around under the house had simply pulled the medallion off its chain and it was down there somewhere in the dirt.

Then while putting on my Bermuda shorts, I was startled to find the little medal dangling from a thread in the hem of my pants leg. The small ring fastening the medal to the chain was open just enough to have allowed it to slide off and become entangled in the hem. The medal dangled playfully from my shorts, somehow reminding me of the sleight-of-hand a magician uses in pulling a coin from someone's ear.

The impact made me laugh aloud. I had the eerie feeling that this had not been just an accidental occurrence after all; I had heard many similar stories about unusual circumstances concerning Baba's gifts. Still, I could hardly call this a true sign, although Sharon's resistance softened somewhat when I told her about it. Finally, however, the temptation of being able to participate in some way with the planning of a trip by Baba to America—no matter how unlikely its chances of occurring—became simply too great to resist. I knew I would be disappointed again, I knew the destruction of Samuel Sandweiss would resume once more in earnest . . . but I decided to go back.

My loving, supportive family, having become accustomed to my frequent trips to India, saw me off with all the warmth one could possibly ask for. Away into the sky I flew, headed for Baba's feet. Coincidentally or not, the movie showing on the flight was *Man of La Mancha*. I chuckled watching Don Quixote fighting windmills and journeying after his dream. Just what *would* happen? Would I continue to feel that excruciating distance and lack of personal contact with Baba again on this trip, or would my going with Elsie permit me the intimacy with him that I desired so fervently?

As soon as we arrived at Prasanthi Nilayam it was apparent to me that I would be seeing Baba in a new light. From the start, he was very attentive to Elsie. I know Baba has the same love for all of his devotees—even though at times he appears to be actually avoiding or ignoring them; but in his relationship with Elsie I was able to see his love expressed in unmistakable fashion.

As we approached the temple, Baba sent out a small plant as a gift of welcome to her. It was remarkable: about the size of a golfball, with a short stem and round green petals, somewhat resembling a lotus. It had a marvelous fragrance, a concoction of the smells of all kinds of fruits, flowers and perfumes, the likes of which I had never before experienced. The aroma of this plant set the mood for the remainder of the trip.

Although unable to see Baba privately that evening, we had our first interview with him the next day. About five o'clock in the afternoon we were ushered into a small room with three or four Indians. Here I began to see Baba's love unfold tenderly and here I began to feel my relationship with him deepen.

Playfully, he held Elsie's hand, patting her affectionately. Turning to me, he said with mock gravity, *Elsie is weakened physically by age.* Then with a radiant smile, he added, *But she is brilliant and hard like a diamond spiritually.* Elsie beamed from ear to ear.

Walter was with him now, he said. He had been with Baba at the moment of his death in the United States, in fact; Baba had given him *darshan.* He was aware that Walter and Elsie had kept repeating his name and that Walter had been blissful at the moment of his death. Everything that Baba said, Elsie had told me prior to the trip.

Baba suddenly and unexpectedly turned toward me and pulled me closer to him. I was overcome by this great attention. *What do you want?* he asked in the most gentle manner imaginable. By this time I could say nothing in his presence and barely got out the word, "God." He smiled knowingly and patted me tenderly on the back; then, moving his arm gently in the air, produced a beautiful ring. The question of whether or not I should have come was answered: I witnessed even more of myself surrender and melt before him.

Baba manifested a *japamala* for an Indian woman, some *vibhutti,* of course, and then remarked that he would see us in our room shortly. Turning to me, he said, *I will speak to you later about the trip.* I was startled, caught off balance. Could he actually be ready to talk specifics about his trip to the United States? Elsie and her sister Floy were all merriment when they heard.

The next day we stationed ourselves close to the temple about eight in the morning and waited. Busy with interviews, Baba must have seen some twenty people while we sat there. Finally, he invited about ten Indians into the room and motioned for Elsie, Floy and Helene Vreeland, a devotee from Santa Barbara, and myself to follow. He spoke for almost an hour in Telugu, without a translator, to the Indian people, discoursing on God, higher human values and the way to peace.

Watching him speak in this foreign tongue was almost more beautiful and exciting than hearing him in English. I was transfixed by the intense energy radiating from his body and gestures. He was overflowing with serene, happy love—his gestures and laughter and bliss tangibly filling the room, sculpting broad smiles on our faces. He saw most of the Indian people individually for short interviews and produced a container of *vibhutti* for one of the Indian women and, for another, a large gold picture frame, about two by three inches in dimension, containing two photographs: one of Shirdi Sai Baba and one of himself.

Then quite unexpectedly he invited me into a small private hallway. In English, he said, *I know she (Elsie) is very anxious, and I am ready.*

"What do you mean, Baba? Do you mean coming to America?"

Yes, yes, he said. *I will come soon. I am ready.*

"When, Baba?"

I have prepared a letter with instructions for you to take to Bhagavantam in Bangalore.Work on arrangements with him. There may be a small difficulty with visas but I am ready to come immediately, before my birthday (November 23). You will stay here in Puttaparthi and I will see you once more; then leave about five o'clock in the morning and go directly to Dr. Bhagavantam. Four of us will be going: myself, Gokok, Bhagavantam and another person.

Baba motioned for Elsie to come into the hallway and repeated what he had said to me. We were aglow to think that Sai Baba would soon touch the lives of millions of yearning Americans in person, in America.

But then followed a series of events which seemed to point out the lesson that Baba continuously teaches: Life is a great game—play it. We were caught up in a most humorous display of antics, trying to set up what proved to be an extremely evasive trip. Trying to keep everything a secret, yet dashing to and fro to travel agents, running about getting papers notarized, dashing about in the rain and splashing in puddles —appearing indeed like characters out of Don Quixote, laughing with and at each other and ourselves—we were very much caught up in a great comic play. This lesson is a hard one for me to learn, for I have been a rather serious fellow most of my life; but in such a comical setting it struck home solidly.

Taking leave of Baba, we went to Bangalore to deliver the letter to Dr. Bhagavantam. He was going to see Baba the following day and it was decided that I would join him. After spending a good deal of energy with the travel agent at the hotel, working through the details of obtaining passports, visas and tickets, I called Sharon to tell her the good news. The fact that it was two a.m. in San Diego was readily brushed aside by my impatience.

We had a bad connection of course, so there I was yelling my head off with everyone in the hotel hearing me; and I'm telling Sharon to keep the news of Baba's plans quiet. Between the static of our global telephone call and her sleep, interrupted but not completely dispelled, she's still trying to determine exactly what it is that she's to keep quiet about. By the time we finally got it all straightened out, she was as excited as I was but agreed not to tell a soul until plans were concrete.

About ten the next morning I called Bhagavantam. To my surprise he informed me that he had reread Baba's letter, and as it made no mention that I should join him on the trip to Puttaparthi, he felt he should go alone. Well then, I would go to Puttaparthi myself, I replied, just in case I was needed, and would meet him there.

"Fine," he said, "but you'll have to do this on your own since Baba does not instruct me to bring you." Although disappointed, I understood that Bhagavantam was doing exactly what he should be doing: responding to the letter of Baba's directions and making sure an over-enthusiastic devotee wouldn't become a nuisance.

I rushed around to arrange for a cab. It was quickly decided that Elsie should go along too. In our flurry to get ready we could still laugh at the comic side of the whole thing. We were the cavalry, trying to cut Bhagavantam off at the pass to save our position. There was no holding Elsie back. She functioned like a field marshal, ordering advances on all fronts. You could almost hear bugle calls ringing over the foothills as we sped away to Puttaparthi.

The trip was pleasant, and Elsie had a few hours of sleep in the back seat. As we approached the little town, a mild rain began to fall and a rainbow appeared in the sky. The air took on the fresh clean smell that accompanies a light drizzle. The rickety cab continued onto the ashram grounds, where the rain had sent many for cover. As was our custom, we stationed ourselves close to the temple. Elsie sent in a short note: "Baba, I must see you immediately—urgent. Love, Rani."

As I approached the men's seating area by the door of the temple, Bhagavantam was just coming out. He had not yet seen Baba and was also going to wait. I sat for about half an hour, my eyes closed, feeling quite high and spaced-out by the drama. All of a sudden a very sweet fragrance, like that of the plant Baba had given Elsie a few days ago, caught my attention. Opening my eyes quickly, I saw Baba just leaving the temple to approach the gathering outside. The concurrence of the smell with his appearance made me even more ecstatic. The top of my head seemed to float off.

Baba walked among the crowd of people, majestic and divine. He spoke to some, distributed *vibhutti* to others and invited a few for interviews. With these he disappeared again into the temple.

After half an hour and still another group, he sent for Bhagavantam, Elsie and myself, then joined us shortly. At first he spoke only in Telugu to Bhagavantam, who in turn interpreted for us. It turned out that although Baba was ready to go, Bhagavantam had a speaking engagement in Ghana the first of November. As he was needed to translate, this would mean postponing Baba's trip.

In a cheerful, almost whimsical manner, as if playing a part, Baba said, *It's not me, I want to come—it's Bhagavantam.* My feelings crashed in on me. The expanded fantasy of a world tour with Baba—all the glory, fun and importance my monkey mind had conjured up—was destroyed in an instant.

You will go home now, and between the first and sixth of November will get word about the trip from Dr. Bhagavantam when he returns from Ghana. Keep everything a secret, Baba directed. He said he would stay seven or eight days—that he was going in order to fulfill his commitment to the Cowans and would stay with Elsie, to bring her happiness. He would be back in India for his birthday, a time of great public celebration at the ashram.

Elsie then discussed some business regarding her printing rights to Baba's books in the United States. She was having difficulty obtaining books from India and pointed out that if they were printed in this country, Americans would have readier access to the material. Baba gave his permission and directed her to work out details with the head of his Education Committee, because he was indeed interested in the dissemination of his books in the United States. He asked about letters from American devotees, and Elsie promised to bring them when she returned. With that, the interview ended and we decided to return to Bangalore that evening.

I was devastated, completely destroyed. I had again allowed myself to get caught up in expectations and fantasies, letting my mind run wild. Although disappointed on an emotional level, I knew by a higher vision that this was as it must be and, in the larger picture, absolutely right. But the negative feelings were so strong that no matter how much I understood and wanted to accept, I was swallowed by them.

We were tired on the way back to Bangalore. The ride was long and painful for me; my sense of disappointment made sleep fitful. Only slight comfort came with knowing that in a few days the hurt would heal and I would regain balance. At one point I fell into a light sleep and was startled by a vivid image of Baba appearing before me. It increased in intensity until I couldn't distinguish between dream and reality. In this strange state of consciousness I gazed uninterrupted at his brilliant form and was comforted.

After a quiet Saturday in Bangalore, Dr. M. B. Sunder Rao, an eye specialist, came to see Elsie the next day. We were pleasantly surprised to find him a very close devotee of Baba: president, in fact, of the Bangalore Central Committee, which is involved in administering activities related to Sai Baba. After checking Elsie's eyes, he explained how Baba's devotees are organized in India. In many cities there is a central committee composed of about twenty-five members. This committee meets once a month in different areas of the city or in outlying districts. In Bangalore there are some twenty local organizations which, as offshoots of the central committee, are responsible for conducting weekly *bhajan* meetings.

They are also responsible for setting up educational programs for children ages six to ten and ten to fourteen, and for organizing groups of older teenagers and young adults for service to needy segments of the community. They might help by tutoring slower students or working to solve local health problems. There is one formal evening *bhajan* meeting a week. *Bhajans* are sung for an hour and a half, followed by meditation. An hour-long study group meets on another night. Works from any religion may be read, with a certain portion of time set aside for Baba's writings.

Then once a week at four-thirty in the morning there are *Nama Sankirtana bhajans*, with devotees walking through their neighborhoods singing. Another day, mothers gather ten or fifteen children together to read religious stories and transmit Baba's teachings. The texts of all religions are acceptable as long as they have a moral or spiritual message. Once every three or four months, representatives of the central committees from all over the state meet to share and coordinate new information. Such a system is set up in other states in India as well, and perhaps once a year representatives from all the states meet in an all-India conference.

After Dr. Sunder Rao's visit Elsie received a call from Mr. Ratan Lal in Bombay, the head of Baba's Education Committee, and arrangements were made to have all of Baba's books printed in the United States. There are now many publications, biographical material as well as teachings and discourses. They are listed in the Appendix.

Early the next day Elsie excitedly called my room. "I feel very close to Walter this morning," she said. "I feel that Baba and Walter have paid me a special visit. I've been wide awake since six o'clock just full of energy."

Under Elsie's leadership we had an early breakfast and were on the road by eight-thirty, our third journey to Puttaparthi in the past eight days. The driver, a very considerate young man by the name of Lingapow, informed us that he had never driven so frequently to Puttaparthi. "Once a month or once every six months—but this often . . ." and he gave a little chuckle.

Elsie, Floy and I were joined by a travel agent who had assisted us with arrangements for Baba's trip and wanted to get *darshan* from him. We made a brief stop for some sweet-smelling flowers for him. There had been a heavy rain the day before, and because of washed-out areas we had to take a long route to Puttaparthi. We were quiet in the car so as not to reveal Baba's plans to Mrs. Swami, the travel agent.

We arrived at the ashram about noon, had lunch and took a brief nap. Even though it had rained, the heat in Puttaparthi was like the extra blanket one suffers under to sweat out a cold. Elsie had me write a note to Baba with her eyebrow pencil on a sheet of scrap paper: "Baba, I have much to discuss, Love, Rani—Room A-7." Then we set off to wait by the temple.

Baba presented himself much earlier than usual, at a quarter to four. No sooner had he finished his stroll among the two- or three-thousand people gathered and started back toward the temple, than a heavy rain began to fall. He motioned for those present to take shelter in a covered area in front of the temple. People began scurrying for cover, and in the confusion Elsie was jostled and began to fall. "I was afraid of being trampled," she said later. "Then in the commotion I looked up and saw a small brown hand, and there was Baba: smiling, peaceful and all-protective. He supported me and brought me to shelter. I was so thrilled with this sense of protection!"

At our interview that afternoon there was present an English-speaking woman in her late forties who appeared to be from the Middle East. Obviously in quite a bit of distress, she told Baba that she had two children and pleaded with him for help. She felt unloved and unhappy and worried about the care of the children because of a serious physical illness she had. *I know, I know,* Baba said sympathetically. *Feeling unloved is not unusual, it's general now in this world—one must be strong.*

He spoke about the importance of character, perseverance and faith. *Emotions come and go: pain is the place between two pleasures, pleasure is the place between two pains—transient, always changing. These come and go like waves in the ocean, like a breeze, and one shouldn't pay much attention to them. Remember, you are the unchanging, infinite, immortal.*

Everybody is saying, "I want peace," he continued. *Peace is like a letter in an envelope. The "I" of "I want peace," is the front part of the envelope and the "want" is the back. The "peace" itself is the letter inside. Throw away the envelope of "I" and "want" and keep the precious letter of peace.*

He mentioned a number of familiar sayings which took on new and deeper meaning. Gesturing expansively from his heart, he seemed almost to swoon with the bliss he naturally and spontaneously radiated to us. *Most routes to God are circuitous,* he said: *like* japa *(recitation of the name of God with the aid of a* japamala, *similar to the use of the rosary), meditation and* bhajans. *But the direct path is love.*

Start the day with love, fill the day with love, end the day with love. This is the way to God, this is the quickest path. As he said this, he gestured to the suffering woman and to all of us as if he were in heaven now, soaring in space.

"But, Baba, I am ill—I hurt," was her response.

He nodded softly and gently. *I know; your left side, it cramps—there are glands there.*

She was surprised. "Yes, Baba, glands. Yes, it is cramping hard."

I know, I know, he repeated in his soothing voice. *You don't sleep well at night, worrying this way and that. Your insides are in a turmoil; sometimes you pass blood.*

"That is right, Baba, that is right." She began to calm and soften with this experience of Baba's apparent omnipresence and omniscience.

Yes, these eyes are x-rays, he said, smiling. He continued to describe her condition, citing specific medical symptoms, which she acknowledged. She kept pleading, asking anxiously whether she would recover. *Surely, you will be all right.* he answered emphatically. *Don't worry about the body. The body is like a water bubble that disappears. You are the "I" that is behind the body, you are eternal—you will be all right.*

"But my children, Baba, my health," she persisted. He produced some *vibhutti* for her and told her to take a little in water at bedtime for three or four nights and she would sleep soundly; her side would start to get better and she would be well again.

Baba was asked about a woman who had wanted to stay in the ashram but was directed to leave by the manager of the buildings. Baba took this opportunity to speak about the need for proper discipline and to voice his disapproval of hippy-style living. *There are many undisciplined young people who come here,* he said, *who are initially by themselves but in three or four days begin to say, "She is my woman, I am married to her."*

That is not good, Baba said. *It is not good here and it is not good outside. Character, character: that is important. Pleasure without purity is not good. Duty without love is deplorable; duty with love is good. Love without duty is divine— love . . . love . . . love.* He smiled radiantly, pressing the message deep into our souls. It was during this interview that I began to see Baba less as the omnipresent controller of great forces than as a manifestation of pure love. Clearly his love for his devotees motivates his actions.

One might speculate that Baba's purpose in coming to America is to usher in a spiritual awakening in the West, or to help ease the suffering of Americans who are burdened by chaotic political, social and economic conditions; or perhaps to do something about the tinder box in the Middle East; or as part of some great design. But when we ask Baba, he smiles sweetly and says only, *I am doing this for Elsie and Walter, and to bring happiness.*

Just weeks before, Baba had participated in a conference of some 200,000 people. He is constantly visited by people from all over the world. Yet he is willing to take such a long trip simply to bring love to one of his devotees; and in so doing, demonstrate his readiness and willingness to extend himself for all devotees.

He produced some more *vibhutti* for us, and Helene Vreeland looked filled to the brim with love for him. "You've given me everything, Baba," she said. Hesitantly she asked if she could lay her head on his feet. He consented and stood up. Helene knelt, her face filled with a soft radiant glow, a mist of loving tears in her eyes, and slowly and gently pressed her cheek to Baba's feet. She rested there a moment, her eyes closed, floating in a state of peace from this contact with the divine. Baba stood quietly, smiling, recognizing the genuineness of Helene's feelings and pleased to grant this heartfelt request.

Elsie gave Baba letters from American devotees and showed him enlarged photographs of the figure of Christ on the cross which he had manifested for Dr. John Hislop. Talking business, she asked Baba if she could sell the picture and how much she should charge. He smiled: *No, no, I am not interested in the money; don't talk about money with me. Do your duty—it is your business. Money comes and goes, morality comes and grows.*

Again, such sayings take on a deeper meaning in Baba's presence. It is apparent that he really means it when he says that he is not interested in money and does not want to talk about it, that it is the source of a great deal of conflict from which he intends to stay entirely free. At the same time, he understands and accepts its significance in the lives of his devotees.

Walter and I paid you a visit this morning, he said suddenly to Elsie.

"Yes, yes! At six o'clock. I felt so filled."

No—five minutes to six, he corrected her, smiling lovingly, looking again as if he were outside his body and floating somewhere in the cosmos. *That is called realization, when you feel Baba inside,* he said. Turning to the rest of us he said, *Elsie's heart is pure. Swami loves to see a devotee's heart so filled with love and devotion.*

The love that Elsie has toward Baba is clearly the central force in her life. Here is an older woman weakened physically, having difficulty seeing and moving about, yet driven with devotion and love—always moving toward Baba. Elsie did not speak of illness or discomfort throughout the trip. Instead she urged us on further and faster toward God and toward carrying out our earthly duties and obligations.

Baba helped her up. Taking her aside for a private interview, he asked if there was anything she wanted. I heard her say that she was overwhelmed with love, then directed my attention elsewhere so as not to intrude on their privacy. I recalled a friend telling me before I had met Baba: "He is capable of filling your cup until it overflows, until you simply cannot hold more—and still he continues to give."

The sick woman who had been in such distress at the start of the interview rose to thank Baba. He smiled lovingly at her and began to stir the air with that marvelously acquisitive hand of his. Soon, there it was: a magnificent ring. This was the final touch. Crying, "Thank you, thank you," she fell into a swoon at his feet. The change from her agonizing fear at the beginning of the interview to this intense radiance of devotion and love was so overwhelming that my own heart seemed a reservoir of vicarious and personal joy, and I struggled to keep its gates from bursting.

There is so much love in the world! Never had I felt this exquisite experience so deeply. Baba showed me in an instant what years of psychiatry had not: the means for igniting this love. Such deep love is born from the devotional yearning for, the sometimes suffering journey toward, the divine.

> *Start the day with love,*
> *fill the day with love,*
> *end the day with love:*
> *this is the way to God.*

Baba distributed packets of *vibhutti* from a satchel. He poured handful after handful into Elsie's carrying case until it overflowed. She was of course speechless with pleasure. He clasped me by the shoulder: *You return with Dr. Bhagavantam the day after tomorrow and we will discuss plans further. Return to Bangalore with Elsie now.* We took leave of Baba, packed our bags, and drove off—as in all the myths and movies—into the setting sun. The sunset was magnificent, with large towering clouds, streaked and patched in reds and silver, filling the western sky.

Evening washed cooly through the open windows of the taxi as Elsie and I settled back into our thoughts and reminiscences of the past few days. Old gnarled trees lined the road. We passed dogs, monkeys, cows and sheep in the darkening fields which unfolded soothingly before us. I was dazed and amazed, yet my mind and senses were at their utmost clarity. The Indian evening was a vivid but delicately subtle collage of colors, textures, secrets, sounds. My mind settled into thoughts of love.

How intense and beautiful expressions of love can be, and what an important force they are in one's life! How they fill one's life with meaning, giving direction and serving as the basis for our expansion, growth and identity. Witnessing the play between Baba and Elsie had been profoundly touching and meaningful.

Observing my reactions toward Baba has been an invaluable learning experience in the nature of mind and emotions. Even after such high experiences with him, I find that my faith can be easily shaken, and I've found that others feel similarly—perhaps, as I've said, due to Baba's *Shiva* aspect. Experiencing him has a way of bringing out all impurities—a lack of faith, doubt, inconsistencies—to be burned. Apparently this is part of the journey toward total surrender.

Instead of transforming his home, his village, his state and his country, and thereby this world, into a Prasanthi Nilayam—*the abode of the peace that passeth understanding—man has made them all arenas for the wild passions of anger, greed, hatred and violence. Instead of making the senses—which are at best very poor guides and informants—his servants, he has made them his masters. He has become the slave of ephemeral beauty, evanescent melody, momentary softness, fragile fragrance and transient taste. He spends all his energies and the fruits of all his toil for the satisfaction of the trivial and degrading demands of these untamed underlings. Oh, the pity of it!*

The sun was just rising over the temple at Prasanthi Nilayam. I had returned from morning *darshan* and was sitting on the porch collecting my thoughts, not sure how the day would go.

Baba had told me to return to the ashram with Dr. Bhagavantam on Thursday. But when I had telephoned Bhagavantam, he informed me that he had heard nothing about this from Baba and was not expecting to go to Puttaparthi until Saturday, so the trip was not on as far as he was concerned. This seemed to be another of those famous Baba tricks. I would go on Thursday anyway, though this was a letdown, as I was scheduled to leave for the States on Friday. I would have to change my plane reservations and wait.

Next morning I had been up at four-thirty and on the road by five. A few complications arose, such as a flat tire and a motor that gave out thirty miles from Puttaparthi, necessitating a change of cabs—but other than that the ride was pleasant. On arriving at the ashram some five hours later, I learned that the day was a special holiday—*Divali* Day, a festival of lights—and Baba would present a special message. Bhagavantam was to translate and would arrive any minute. My spirits lightened as it was still possible that the three of us would meet and I could still make my plane Friday.

About three o'clock I set out for the temple, note in hand, to inform Baba that I was there and available for a talk. Wishful thinking. At about four o'clock everybody gathered at the temple for Baba's discourse. First, two articulate devotees, a prominent judge and a scholarly educator, spoke briefly about Baba's importance in their lives. Then Baba spoke for about an hour and a half on the meaning of the *Divali* Festival: the way to bring light into our lives in order to drive out darkness and to identify ourselves with the divine. Although my legs were killing me from sitting cross-legged for three hours on the hard tile, I enjoyed the discourses immensely. Afterwards, Baba sang *bhajans* and everybody was in high spirits. By that time, however, it was close to seven and I recognized that it was too late to see him. Oh well, perhaps tomorrow.

So here I was the next day, Friday, with the sun bright and warm, rimming the roof of the temple with a thin edge of gold. I wrote another note to Baba and walked with some other people to the temple to wait. Hearing that Bhagavantam had already seen Baba and was leaving, and seeing that Baba hadn't even given me a second glance since Elsie's departure, I knew I had little chance of talking to him, but I would wait anyway.

I sat for a couple of hours and finally wrote a note saying that my plane was scheduled to leave that day, and I wondered whether Baba wanted to speak to me further or had I his blessing to take leave? An hour later someone brought a reply. Baba had nothing more to say regarding his plans and I could leave—as simple as that.

Perhaps Baba had asked me to come back as a way of inviting me to hear his discourses. It *had* been a treat. In any case, I recognized that he was not going to show me any more outward attention. Maybe I would see him again soon in the United States. After packing, I returned to the area of the temple and from a distance watched Baba walking among the devotees while they sang *bhajans* to him. I said good-bye silently.

The trip home was easy and comfortable. Connections were made like the meshing of fine gears and I arrived in San Diego at ten the next evening. The trip had been a marvelous success. I was happy and filled with a great feeling of joy.

16
QUESTIONS
& ANSWERS

True belief in God and knowledge of the existence of a higher reality represent a leap in consciousness for most of us modern rationalists. Sai Baba can help many of us make this great leap, and after it is accomplished the quest for self-realization can begin in earnest. Focusing on whatever form one recognizes as an aspect of God—whether it be love, humanistic attitudes, a spiritual *mantra* or symbol or an incarnation of God—or on God as formlessness, naturally loosens the grasp of the senses, emotions and mind. One tends toward becoming that which one focuses on.

Baba directs people to keep conscious contact with whatever experience they have of God and to meditate on that experience as much as they can. One may engage in the meditation formally, sitting quietly by oneself and trying to make contact with the light within . . . or one may practice constant repetition of one of the names of God so that God is on the tongue at all times. And Baba also teaches that one should relate to every life situation as if it is God, with the same sense of responsibility, devotion and love. Thus our daily activity will become a devotional service and our life an act of worship.

Seeing God behind a multitude of forms and names is an exciting new way of relating to the world. As a psychiatrist I find this attitude powerful enough to lead one away from the world of duality, where everything "outside" oneself is seen as separate and distinct, apart from oneself, and toward recognizing the one universal principle permeating reality. The attitude also wonderfully encourages growth, because all one's mental and emotional energies are focused on an experience which is continually exhilarating. Distracting and petty thoughts seem to melt away and one is filled with a sense of peace and expansion.

The choice is ours to make: to pick God as the focus of our awareness rather than worry, pain, conflict or confusion. We do create our own universe; the trick lies in our discrimination in ordering it, our discipline and will to set ourselves to the task, our faith that we will reach the goal.

I used to think, before being awakened to the reality of the existence of God, that a state of being like this was available simply through suggestion, the use of our imagination and the psychological principles believed to govern conditioning in human behavior. Now I believe that there is actually another force at work, that we are capable in a concrete way of receiving help from spiritual levels of reality.

Baba says that if we carry out the spiritual discipline of focusing on God always, trying to take that one step toward Him, He in His grace and loving kindness will take ten steps toward us. Evidently, this is what God has been saying to us throughout the ages. Since meeting Baba I have developed a very deep trust in the truth of this loving promise.

> *You may say that progress is possible only through my grace,* says Baba, *but though my heart is soft as butter, it melts only when there is some warmth in your prayer. Unless you make some disciplined effort, some* sadhana, *grace cannot descend on you. The yearning, the agony of unfulfilled aim, that is the warmth that melts my heart. This is the anguish (the* avedana) *that wins grace.*
>
> Sadhana *(spiritual practice) must render you calm, un-ruffled, poised, balanced. Make your mind cool and comfortable as moonlight, for the moon is the diety holding sway over the mind. Be calm in speech, be calm in response to malice, caviling and praise. Calmness of senses, passions, emotions, feelings, impulses—that is real* saanthi *(peace).* He cautions: *Do not be led away by doubt and vain arguments; do not question how and whether I can do all this.*
>
> *Once* Krishna *and* Arjuna *were going together along the open road. Seeing a bird in the sky,* Krishna *asked* Arjuna, *"Is that a dove?"*
>
> Arjuna *replied, "Yes, it is a dove."*
>
> Krishna *then asked him, "Is it an eagle?"*
>
> Arjuna *answered, "Yes it is an eagle."*
>
> *"No,* Arjuna, *it looks like a crow to me. Is it not a crow?"*
>
> Arjuna *replied, "I'm sorry, it is a crow beyond a doubt."* Krishna *laughed and chided him for his agreeing to whatever suggestion was given.*
>
> *But* Arjuna *said, "Forgive me; your words are far more weighty than the evidence of my eyes. You can make it a crow or a dove or an eagle; when you say it is a crow, it will be one." Implicit faith is the road to spiritual success.*

I have had the opportunity to speak to many groups about Sai Baba. These are some of the questions asked most frequently about him.

Q: Are there people who have met Baba and doubted him?

A: There are people who have gone to India to see him who have come back disappointed and there are Indians who do not believe the stories of his miracles. There are those who criticize and attempt to demean him. But I have only rarely met an individual, no matter what his title and position, who has drawn close to Baba and remained unaffected. The usual response is for one to be deeply impressed. I am awed by the respect he commands.

When Baba was twenty years old and becoming known by people outside Puttaparthi, his older brother became quite concerned that gossip and criticism and the selfish interests of others might in some way harm his younger brother. He wrote him about his concern. Perhaps the clearest insight into the appropriate attitude to take toward this kind of gossip, as well as a clear statement by Baba of his true identity, is to be found in his reply. Dr. N. Kasturi, author of Baba's biography, describes this incident in the book *Sathya Shivam Sundaram,* Part II, p. 7:

> Baba was now twenty years of age; his elder brother, Seshamaraju, the teacher of Telugu, could not quite grasp the mystery of this phenomenon. He watched with increasing consternation and genuine fraternal love the procession of cars that came to the right bank of the river and took his simple village-grown brother away into the cities that glittered beyond the horizon, full of temptations and pitfalls. A few press comments that rose from ignorance pained him. So he wrote a letter to his brother warning him and imparting to him the lesson he had learned in life about society and human foibles, about fame and its attendants.
>
> The reply that Sai Baba wrote to him on the 25th of May, 1947, is in my possession. It is a document that reveals Baba in unmistakable terms. So I must allow you to have it:
>
> *To all who are devoted to me:* (Although the letter was written to the brother, the reply is addressed to all, including you and me, for it is essential that you and I should know the real nature of the phenomenon that has appeared for our sake.)
>
> *My dear one! I received the communication that you wrote and sent; I found in it the surging floods of your*

devotion and affection, with the undercurrents of doubts and anxiety. Let me tell you that it is impossible to plumb the hearts and discover the natures of jnanis (those who have acquired spiritual wisdom), yogis; ascetics, saints, sages and the like. People are endowed with a variety of characteristics and mental attitudes; so each one judges according to his own angle, talks and argues in the light of his own nature.

But we have to stick to our own right path, our own wisdom, our own resolution, without getting affected by popular appraisal. As the proverb says, it is only the fruit-laden tree that receives the shower of stones from passers-by. The good always provoke the bad into calumny; the bad always provoke the good into derision. This is the nature of this world. One must be surprised if such things do not happen.

The people too have to be pitied, rather than condemned. They do not know. They have no patience to judge a right. They are too full of lust, anger and conceit to see clearly and know fully. So, they write all manner of things. If they only knew, they would not talk or write like that. We, too, should not attach any value to such comments and take them to heart, as you seem to do. Truth will certainly triumph some day; untruth can never win. Untruth might appear to overpower truth, but its victory will fade away and truth will establish itself.

It is not the way of the great to swell when people offer worship and shrink when people scoff. As a matter of fact, no sacred text lays down rules to regulate the lives of the great, prescribing the habits and attitudes that they must adopt. They themselves know the path they must tread; their wisdom regulates and makes their acts holy. Self-reliance, beneficial activity—these two are their special marks. They may also be engaged in the promotion of the welfare of devotees and in allotting them the fruits of their actions. Why should you be affected by tangle and worry, as long as I am adhering to these two? After all, the praise and blame of the populace do not touch the Atma, *the reality: they can touch only the outer physical frame.*

I have a task: to foster all mankind and ensure for all of them lives full of ananda *(bliss). I have a vow: to lead all who stray away from the straight path back again into goodness and save them. I am attached to a "work" that I love: to remove the sufferings of the poor and grant them what they lack. I have a "reason to be proud," for I rescue all who worship and adore me, aright. I have my definition of the "devotion" I expect: those devoted to me have to treat joy and grief, gain and loss, with equal fortitude.*

This means that I will never give up those who attach themselves to me. When I am thus engaged in my beneficial task, how can my name ever be tarnished, as you apprehend? I would advise you not to heed such absurd talk. Mahatmas *(great souls) do not acquire greatness through some one calling them so; they do not become small when somone calls them small. Only those low ones who revel in opium and* ganja *but claim to be unexcelled yogis, only those who quote scriptural texts to justify their gourmandry and pride, only those who are dry-as-dust scholars exulting in their casuistry and argumentative skills, will be moved by praise or blame.*

You must have read life-stories of saints and divine personages; in those books you must have read of even worse falsehoods and more heinous imputations cast against them. This is the lot of mahatmas *everywhere, at all times. Why then do you take these things so much to heart? Have you not heard of dogs that howl at the stars? How long can they go on? Authenticity will soon win.*

I will not give up my mission, nor my determination. I know I will carry them out; I treat the honor and dishonor, the fame and blame that may be the consequence, with equal equanimity. Internally, I am unconcerned. I act but in the outer world; I talk and move about for the sake of the outer world and for announcing my coming to the people, else I have no concern even with these.

I do not belong to any place, I am not attached to any name. I have no "mine" or "thine." I answer, whatever the name you use. I go, wherever I am taken. This is my very first vow. I have not disclosed this to anyone so far. For me the world is something afar, apart. I act and move only for the sake of mankind. No one can comprehend my glory, whoever he is, whatever his method of inquiry, however long his attempt.

You can yourself see the full glory in the coming years. Devotees must have patience and forbearance.

I am not concerned nor am I anxious that these facts should be made known; I have no need to write these words, I wrote them because I felt you will be pained if I do not reply. Thus, your Baba.

Q: Does Baba want people to worship him as God?

A: Although Sai Baba is attracting a great following, and there is little doubt that he is the form of worship for a rapidly growing religious movement, he seeks neither publicity nor worship of himself. Even though he was born into a Hindu family and frequently speaks to Hindus about their Gods and scriptures, he does not preach any one religion to the exclusion of others. I have heard him speak about Christ to Christians and have heard that he does likewise with people of other faiths. He tries to help the individual see and attain the divinity inherent within himself: by heeding the scriptures of his own particular faith, by disciplined meditation and chanting, by gradually stilling the earthly desires of the senses, and by adhering to right action based in truth.

He teaches that we are all brothers and sisters with the same central yearning to merge with God, and he shows that this yearning is not the result of any particular church doctrine or any single manifestation of God but is the reflection of a universal truth within us all. We must learn to experience this inner truth ourselves; it is our own responsibility, no one else's. We must search for our own higher reality and the God within each of us.

Q: You talked about the extensive documentation of Baba's miracles and of his great powers. I can't understand then how the Western world can be so uninformed about him.

A: I don't know how to understand this either, but many of his devotees believe that Baba has *willed* his relative anonymity. He has said that his time schedule is different from ours, that at times he waits until he can accomplish several things at once and that he is waiting now for certain situations to develop before revealing himself to the world at large. He simply does not want publicity. I have seen people from many countries wanting to interview or photograph Baba come to the ashram and sit for days in the hot sun without being able to get close to him. They tire and leave.

I believe he has complete command over when and how people will learn about him. I feel that he is the world teacher and that the day will soon come when the whole world will know about him.

As a child Baba would dance and sing for the people of the village. He told them stories of a day when people from all over the world would flock to Puttaparthi and he would be only an orange speck on the horizon; the villagers would no longer be able even to get close to him. They just laughed at this pronouncement from the small child they loved so dearly. Now the prediction has come true. Soon, I'm afraid, this will be true for all of us.

Recently I came across something that amused me. Some reporters from *Newsweek* Magazine had traveled to India to talk to some of the lesser known *gurus* and spiritual leaders about their feelings toward the *gurus* who have come to America and made names for themselves and established a following here. There were, of course, mixed comments pro and con, but what was so funny to me was a photograph of a spiritual man, an ascetic, bearded and unkempt, lying on a bed of nails. Far in the background were a small picture of *Rama* and, next to it, a picture of Baba.

I had to laugh, because this seems to be the most publicity Baba will permit in this country. Here was this man's spiritual leader, Sai Baba, and the picture was no larger than a dot.

An hour-long color documentary on Sai Baba, with Rod Serling as narrator, was produced recently for television, and it contained good footage of Baba materializing objects and showering devotees with love and beauty. Several American devotees testified to his greatness, and I felt the objective film was very informative and powerful. Yet to my amazement I find that the company is having difficulty finding someone to distribute it.

On the other hand, the March 1975 *London Times Magazine* printed an interesting article on Baba. Word of him is spreading, but the timing of his appearance in the world is under his control.

Q: If Sai Baba has so much power, why isn't he helping solve some of the problems in India more quickly, and why doesn't he lessen the suffering of the world in general?

A: I feel that Sai Baba *is* creating vast long-term changes for the better in India as well as in the world at large. From my experience with him I know that I can't question his actions or his timetable for change because what he sees and knows is so much beyond my vision and comprehension. Baba has said, *I shall certainly achieve the purpose of this* Avatar, *don't doubt it. I will take my own time to carry out my plans so far as you are concerned. I cannot hurry because you are hurrying. I may sometimes wait until I can achieve ten things at once, just as an engine is not used for hauling one coach, but waits until sufficient haulage in proportion to its capacity is ready. But my word will never fail, it must happen as I will.*

Why does God allow suffering to exist? This issue remains one of the great mysteries in life, one which I can't begin to fathom. But after meeting Baba I have come to accept certain spiritual explanations for the meaning and purpose of suffering and have begun to realize that we the people of the world are responsible for righting the wrongs that exist. I believe that there is such a thing as free will and that suffering in the world is not brought about by God. It is the result of our own choices, freely made, and of our own deeds performed in this life and perhaps even in past lives.

In fact, the only way I can begin to make sense out of the suffering of millions of apparently innocent people is by accepting the possibility of reincarnation. I have come to accept on faith the spiritual law of *karma*. We reap what we sow; we are repaid in kind for our actions—good as well as bad—and we are responsible through our own choices for bettering our lot in the future. It seems to me that Baba can help us through the difficult period of retribution and may even be able to eliminate completely one's past *karma* or present suffering. Why he should choose to do this for one and not another is of course beyond me.

Even though Baba may choose to eliminate a physical, emotional or financial problem, he says that this is not his main task. His primary goal is to administer to our spiritual problems and cure the ill that hinders us from seeing our true nature.

I believe that the condition of the world today is due to our low level of consciousness, in which injustice and suffering are inherent. If we hurt others for gain or sensual gratification and willingly destroy the land and its creatures for money, prestige or power, we are at that level of consciousness where suffering comes about. Given our present state of consciousness and degree of awareness, if someone were to rid the world today of all its evils and sufferings, we would inevitably be back in the same mess tomorrow.

All of us together must take responsibility for righting the ills of our world. We must stop blaming God for our troubles and start searching for strength within ourselves. It is my belief that in assuming the responsibility ourselves for transcending human suffering, we will not only *improve* the human condition but *transform* it as well, into something divine. In this transformation may lie the deepest meaning and purpose of suffering.

Although I feel that each individual is responsible for his own suffering, it may be that God allows the condition to exist in the first place—perhaps even intensifies it, as in the case of Job in the Old Testament—to test and teach. Baba has said: *Do you think I would confront you with pain were there not a reason for it? Open your heart to pain as you do now for pleasure, for it is my will, wrought by me for your good. Welcome it as a challenge. Do not turn away from it; turn within and derive the strength to bear it and benefit by it. It is all my plan—to drive you by the pangs of unfulfilled need, to listen to my voice, which when heard, dissolves the ego . . . and the mind with it.*

Through my psychiatric practice I have become aware of how readily people are willing to become dependent on doctors and pills because they don't believe their cure can come from within. And I certainly can't condemn or judge another for not believing that we really have the strength to heal ourselves, because until recently I didn't believe this myself, although I had been in psychiatry nine years before I met Baba. I knew that we were supposed to have a vast reservoir of inner strength and creative potential which was largely unused . . . and that by learning to listen to some sort of voice within ourselves, we could discover the secret to tapping into this source. But although I had treated thousands of patients, and gone through my own therapy as well, I had never discovered convincing evidence of a hidden reservoir or an illuminating inner voice.

What is this inner voice; does it really exist? From my experience of Baba and meditation and my growing appreciation of the strength that is derived from devotion, as well as a new awareness of subtler energies within myself, I have come to recognize that an inner voice actually does exist. I believe that we reach a new level of consciousness when, by following it, we become aware that the strength not merely to heal but to resurrect ourselves lies within us.

Q: What are some practical, concrete examples of Baba's influence?
A: There are already over three-thousand Sai Baba centers in India, as well as many others throughout the world, with some thirty centers in the United States. Baba directs people into right conduct; his devotees become interested in doing selfless service in their communities, helping the needy in practical ways with food, clothing, housing and health care, etc. A number of hospitals, for example, have been constructed in India and dedicated to him.

Baba is vitally interested in education and has set a goal of helping to establish two new colleges in each Indian state. Already four such colleges have been completed and other facilities have been built or are in the planning stage.[1] Baba himself runs a summer school at Brindavan. Here, some of the most advanced students from all over India receive a course in spirituality and Indian culture.

[1] Sri Sathya Sai Arts, Science and Commerce College for women, in Anantapur, established in 1969; Sri Sathya Sai Arts, Science and Commerce College for men, in Whitefield, established in 1969; Sri Sathya Sai College for Women, in Jaipur, established in 1974; Sri Sathya Sai College for Women, in Bhapal, established in 1975; A hostel for male students, in Poona; A polytechnic school for learning trades, in Bombay.

Q: Is Baba profiting in any way from his popularity or his display of powers?

A: At no time during my five visits with Baba has anything of material value been asked of me. In fact it has been quite the opposite: each time, I have been housed and offered food, and Baba has asked nothing in return but my love. He warns people to beware of the spiritual leader who sells his knowledge like common merchandise and he points out that if a magician not only collected no money for his demonstrations but *gave away* everything he materialized, he would soon be out of business. The objects that Baba materializes are indeed given to his devotees to be cherished by them. This attitude toward money seems to me one of the clear signs of his authenticity.

Sai Baba's personal needs are minimal. He lives in only one sparsely furnished room in the temple at Prasanthi Nilayam . . . eats little more than rice, curds, lentiles and dahl, a variety of bean protein . . . and wears nothing but simple silk or cotton gowns. He reminds devotees that he has no need for an ashram or organization and allows these to develop only for the sake of the devotees. He permits devotees to transport him from place to place and to provide lodging and food but nothing more. Those who wish to give gifts or spend their time, energy and money in his behalf, he directs to be of service in their own communities.

Q: Do you feel that worshiping statues or pictures of human beings smacks of idolatry?

A: I used to think that I understood such things and could say that one way of worshiping God was reasonable, rational and right and another was neurotic or wrong. However, after meeting Baba I came to recognize that I am a neophyte when it comes to understanding spirituality and the dynamics and techniques of expanding consciousness.

I was reared in the Jewish religion with the idea that God is formless and therefore one should not worship golden idols or the human form. Within this attitude little if any emphasis was placed on the possibility of actually making contact with God, formless or not. This was unfortunate, for I now see that there is much in Judaism which teaches closer contact with, and awareness of, God; but this is considered a mystical side of Judaism and is given little popular expression.

The Hindu religion allows for a great range and variety in ways of relating to God, and I now feel very comfortable with these Hindu views. Baba teaches that God is the fundamental aspect of all forms, and if we can learn to appreciate this, then whatever form we direct ourselves to will eventually bring us to God.

Ramakrishna, a revered Indian saint, began his spiritual search picking as his focus and form for God that of the universal mother, the Goddess *Kali*. He worshiped her in the form of a statue, which he fed, bathed, sang to and cared for completely. His yearning for *Kali* to express herself to him through this form grew in intensity until he simply couldn't tolerate his separation from her. Finally, his worship and devotion became so all-consuming that, unable to exist a moment longer without making contact with her, he picked up a knife to kill himself. It was then, at the height of his greatest agony, that *Kali* finally appeared to *Ramakrishna*, transforming his misery to total bliss. He had realized the supreme spiritual experience.

The sheer amount of ecstasy in this kind of experience distinguishes it from a negative or disorganizing state, but what distinguishes it from the imaginary—from wish-fulfillment or hallucination—to mark it as authentic, objective spiritual experience? For one thing, when people have this kind of transcendental experience, they describe similar experiences regarding what has happened to their consciousness: what they have seen and what they then believe—and feel that they *know*—about who they are. They recognize that they are more than the body, that they are not attached to the physical plane of existence. And they describe other dimensions perceived or glimpsed during their experience in strikingly similar terms.

Another significant fact is that during such an experience people often gain access to information about events of the past, present and future which they have no "normal" way of knowing about. This information when tested by others who have not experienced the transcendental state often proves to be true—or what we presume to call "true."

Ramakrishna went on to realize divinity in other forms and by different methods of worship. He yearned to experience Lord *Rama* as *Hanuman* had in the *Ramayana*—the classic Hindu scripture of the life of *Rama*, an incarnation of God supposed to have lived a million years ago. *Hanuman,* a being in the form of a monkey, exemplified pure devotion in his worship of Lord *Rama.*

When *Ramakrishna* attempted to experience *Rama* as *Hanuman* had, he became so involved in his intense devotion that he began adopting the characteristics of a monkey. Finally, he was once again blessed with a vision of the divine, this time with *Rama* as a focal form.

Then he wished to experience Lord *Krishna,* as the *Gopis* (milkmaids) had when they lived with and worshiped this great Hindu diety. Worshiping *Krishna* from the standpoint of a woman, he began to look and act like one, until he was actually considered a woman by others. He developed a woman's yearning for the experience of *Krishna* and was finally blessed with a vision of Him. He could visualize Him moving about and playing and even entering his body, at which time he felt himself *become Krishna*.

Ramakrishna then wished to experience Christ and began to worship and yearn for him with the same intensity of his search for God in the other forms. As before, he was eventually blessed with a vision of the Christ form of God, an incarnation of pure love.

Ramakrishna was aware that God could also be experienced as formless and he apparently accomplished this as well. He was elevated to such high levels of ecstasy and expanded consciousness that he often appeared to be absent from his body, his longest "absence" an extraordinary six months. During this period his body had to be cared for by his devotees and close friends.

Baba has said there is a state so high that one has only twenty-one days left to live when it is reached. One loses interest in choosing pleasure over pain, eating over not eating. The body dries up and only spirit is left. If one remains on earth, it is only because of God's will. One exists beyond *karma* and becomes a brilliant reflection of the divine, a teacher of teachers. Such were the heights that *Ramakrishna* reportedly reached.

I now believe that one can evolve along the spiritual path worshiping any form (or no form) as long as it represents for the individual that which is divine. And it seems to me that in regard to this form one can adopt whatever relationship effectively brings one closer to attaining that divinity in his own life. God may be seen as mother, father, master, servant or friend.

I do believe that one needs a teacher; if one's own intuition isn't sufficiently developed, it is helpful to have a *guru* in the outside world. One must be very cautious of whom he picks, however. Baba has said there are very few genuine *gurus* nowadays. *The holy man must teach by example, and there are very few who earn this respect. How can a man, struggling in the same quicksand as all the others, with attachments like the others, earn the right to be called teacher and be qualified to pull the others out of the quicksand? There are very few genuine spiritual leaders these days. One must turn directly to God for guidance.*

Q: How long is Baba going to live?
A: He says he will leave his physical body at the age of ninety-five. He will come again, he says, and in his next form be called Prema Sai Baba. (*Prema* is the Sanskrit word for love.)

He admonishes us not to be fooled, that he is not limited to this body or form but is in fact immortal, eternal, infinite. He says that in this form his mission is to usher in a golden age and that during our time the world will witness an exciting spiritual revolution.

Q: What does Sai Baba say about death?

A: The moment of death is perhaps the highest point of our existence on earth, the culmination of our life's work and a moment of crucial importance for us. Baba has said that what becomes of us after death is determined by what we think at the moment of dying, and that we should prepare for it throughout our life.

If our thoughts and our heart—our being—have been with God throughout our life, and our most basic yearning has been for contact with God ... if we have so permeated our lives with this yearning that at the moment of death we still hold steadily to it, then this is precisely where we will go: to God. And, likewise, if we have been caught up in competition, pride or lust—the more animalistic elements of our nature—then we will make the transition to that level of consciousness.

For many of the educated and scientifically-oriented of our culture, it is hard to believe so unscientic a tenet as that we might actually continue to exist in some manner beyond this life on earth. Before meeting Baba I thought it futile to think about life after death and to prepare for an existence I knew nothing about. I used to rationalize that such a belief wouldn't affect one's life anyway. But I now see that one's life changes dramatically in relation to his attitudes about death.

There appears to be a growing and syncretic body of evidence from the experience of apparently credible individuals to substantiate the ancient religious teachings that death is only a transition from this plane of existence to another. We get the strongest message about the reality of dimensions beyond the physical plane from the great spiritual masters, who have experienced them through expanded consciousness. Often, they bring back evidence of the existence of these dimensions; for example, by returning with a pertinent and meaningful message from a devotee's dead relative whom the master has never met.

There is also evidence in the fascinating reports from people on the verge of dying—in fact, in some cases actually declared dead —who have experienced their consciousness move into directions and spaces they had never experienced before, and have come back to life (in this world) with the experience still vivid and sublime in their minds.

Recent psychological studies of people about to encounter what appeared to be certain death by accident, such as falling from a plane or drowning, seem to some observers to substantiate what great seers have said about cosmic consciousness and the reality of other dimensions. The reactions of the subjects to impending death were amazingly similar. They generally reported an initial desperate searching for escape, followed by a moment when they recognized that there *was* no apparent escape, at which point they fell into a state of surrender or acceptance.

For many this was accompanied by a great sense of joy, release and bliss. Some described seeing visions of their life passing before them. Others experienced a change in their consciousness, as if, they said, they were entering another realm. Many who have had heart attacks and supposedly died, have reported that they experienced "going on a trip." They lost consciousness of their body but were conscious of going to another place, where they were safe. These people have developed from their experience great faith that there is nothing to fear from death, that it is simply a transition to "another place."

In the *San Diego Union* newspaper, dated May 25, 1975, there was an article about a well-known psychiatrist who has made some interesting observations about the dying and dead. Doctor Elisabeth Kubler-Ross, who has studied the subject of death for over ten years, stated, "They 'died' and experienced peace and wholeness. The blind could see and those who suffered were free from pain. And as physicians worked to save them, they resented being brought back to 'life.' "

Author of *On Death and Dying, Questions and Answers about Dying,* and most recently *Death: The Final Stage of Growth,* Dr. Kubler-Ross said that she has drawn a number of conclusions from hundreds of interviews with people who have survived a brush with death. She has found that they resent being brought to life but after recovery are exuberant about having a second chance. Past a certain threshhold many are greeted by someone already dead, usually a loved one. None is ever again afraid to die.

She describes the case of a two-year-old boy brought to a hospital with no measurable vital functions or brain waves. He was "dead" of an allergic drug reaction. Doctors brought him back to life. "I know I was dead," the child told his mother afterward. He claimed that while he was dead he saw Jesus and Mary. It was so beautiful there, he said, that he came back only because Mary told him to "save Mommy from the fire."

In another case a woman who was suffering from a large malignancy "died" in a small Indiana hospital. Three and a half hours later, resuscitating teams brought her back to life. The woman said that, while "dead," she felt herself floating out of her body and then saw her own corpse. According to Dr. Kubler-Ross, the woman described the actions of the resuscitating team in perfect detail.

"She also described the fantastic feeling of peace and wholeness," the investigator reported. "She tried to convey to those fighting for her life to relax, take it easy. It's alright to let go. But she realized they could not hear her. The more she tried to tell them to relax, the more frantic they became. She finally gave up on them and—this is in her words—'Then I left consciousness.' "

Dr. Kubler-Ross says that her research has made her "religious in a beautifully undogmatic way."

Why are you afraid of Death?

Death is considered as something to be afraid of, something that should not be spoken about in happy circumstances. But death is neither good nor bad. You have no choice in the matter: you can't get it sooner if you welcome it, nor can you avoid it if you condemn it as bad; it is a consummation which is inevitable. From the moment of birth the march to the cremation ground has started. Some reach the place more quickly than others, some go by a roundabout route and arrive late; that is the only difference between one person and the other. Yet man walks about as if death is but a distant calamity.

Death is but a passage from this life to the next. It is a change from old clothes to new—as the Gita *says. But some cynics laugh at the comparison and ask, "What about the death of newborn infants, children, youth and middle-aged persons? Their bodies cannot, by stretching the meaning, be classified as worn out!" Well, the clothes might not be old, but the cloth out of which they were made must have been from very old stock. Though new clothes were prepared out of it, they are to be discarded soon.*

Again, there are some crooked men who refuse to believe in a previous life because they cannot recollect the events. These people cannot recollect the events of a particular magha shuddha dashami *(the 10th day of a particular month) say five or ten years ago, though they are certain they were alive on that day. How then can they remember or recollect events in past births? Forgetting events of that day does not mean that they were not alive at all; it only means that they did not pay any special heed to them and they had no special reason to keep them in memory.*

Remember death. The body is the car in which you are riding to death. You may meet death any moment while riding. Some tree or lorry, culvert or slush will bring it about. If you remember that time is running out every moment, you will not be tempted to waste time in idle talk or vain pursuits, wanton mischief or vulgar entertainment. Travel in the car carefully, slowly and with due regard for the needs of others on the road. Do not greedily try to overtake others or compete in speed. Know the limitations of the vehicle and the road. Then you will not meet with any accident. Your journey will be a happy experience for you and the rest of the people.

If someone is snatched away by death on a pilgrimage to Kashi or Badrinath, you console yourself that it was an enviable way of quitting. But if you get even a mild attack of headache at Puttaparthi, you start blaming me! According to you, those who have entered this compound once should not die; if they do, your faith wavers and dwindles. Well, not even an eyelid can close or open without the Lord's will. So try to get the Lord's grace and leave all questions to be answered by Him, according to His fancy.

Once you take on the name of the Lord, which is sweetness itself, it will awaken all the sweetness latent in you. When you have tasted the joy, you can never for a moment exist without that sustenance. It becomes as essential as air for the lungs.

Listening to some Puranic *(scriptural) tales you might say that it is quite enough if the name of the Lord is remembered at the very last moment of life. But it is a difficult task to recall that name in the end if you have not practiced it for years. In the surge of emotions and thoughts that will invade you at the last moment, the name of God will be submerged unless you learn from now on to bring that name to the top of your consciousness whenever you want it.*

There was a shopkeeper once who was inspired by the tale of Ajamila. He decided to remember the name of God with his last breath by a shortcut. He named his six sons after various gods for he knew that he was bound to call on any one of them when he was about to die. The moment came at last, and according to program he called the Lord by proxy, six times in all.

The boys came and stood around his cot and as he surveyed the group, the last thought that came to the dying man's mind, just when he was about to quit, was, "Alas, all of you have come away. Who will look after the shop now?"

You see, his shop was his very breath all through his life and he could not switch to God at short notice. The latent tendencies will have their say, whatever you may wish.

It is no mean achievement to get the name of the Lord on

one's tongue at the last moment. It needs the practice of many years, based on a deep-rooted faith and a strong character without hatred or malice. The thought of God cannot survive in a climate of pride and greed. Moreover, how do you know which is the last moment? God of death does not give notice of his arrival to take hold of you. He is not like the photographer who says, "I am clicking, are you ready?"

If you wish your portrait to be hung on the walls of heaven, it must be attractive; your stance, your pose and your smile must be all nice, is it not? So be ready for the "click" day and night, with the name ever rolling on the tongue and the glory always radiant in the mind. Then, whenever "shot," your photo will be fine.

Q: Does Baba speak about reincarnation, and who does he say he himself was in the past?

A: Yes, Baba speaks frequently of reincarnation. He says that he is the embodiment of all forms and aspects of God that have manifested themselves for us on earth. More specifically, he describes his preceding incarnation as that of Sai Baba of Shirdi, a Moslem saint who died eight years prior to Baba's birth and who at the time of his death stated that he would return to Southern India in eight years.

Baba emphasizes his relationship to Shirdi Sai Baba by materializing *vibhutti,* or sacred ash. Similar to Catholicism's holy water in its spiritual significance, *vibhutti* is also supposed to possess great healing powers. Baba has prescribed it, internally and externally, for all manner of disease and injuries and materializes it continually for his followers.

Shirdi Sai Baba is also supposed to have distributed ash to his devotees but did it from his fireplace, which was constantly lit. Satya Sai Baba evidently has his fire burning in another dimension into which he reaches to bring forth the mysteriously sweet and pungent ash.

Vibhutti not only serves as an expression of the link between the two Sai Babas, but Baba has said that ash is symbolic of the universal, changeless and infinite nature of all form. It is symbolic of the God, or *Atma,* within—that substance left when everything transient and changeable in matter has burned away. *Vibhutti* also draws a relationship between Baba and *Shiva. Shiva,* one of the three central dieties in Hindu religion, is the God of destruction, and one of his instruments is fire. By helping to burn away our desires and attachments to the body and the world of sensation—the physical plane—*Shiva* enables us to see that part of our self which is eternal.

Baba's relationship to *Shiva* doesn't end with the ash; he appears to demonstrate the destroyer aspect with many of his devotees. In the Hindu religion and in Christian tradition as well, the mechanism of breaking out of the bondage of our lower consciousness and rising to higher or spiritual consciousness is likened to dying. And frequently as one draws closer to Baba, he actually feels himself dying, experiences his ego slipping away, accompanied by very real physical and emotional pain.

One of the most unusual experiences with Sai Baba is this destruction of the small self and with it an intensification of one's love for him, as one recognizes that Baba is actually doing this in love, that it is a blessing and gift to receive this devoted attention.

This, by the way, is one of the central experiences which teaches many that there is actually no difference between pleasure and pain. We recognize that what we are experiencing as pain is in fact an immense gift and that to consider it pain is only a trick of the senses. *You do not know how to make an ornament out of gold,* says Baba, *so you give it to a smith. Why worry if he melts it and beats it and pierces it and pulls it into a wire and twists it and cuts it? Let him who knows the art shape the child into an ornament of society; do not worry.*

On April 20, 1972, while seated amongst a small group of American devotees, Sai Baba reportedly performed a miracle which, more than words could, points out the connection between Christ, *Shiva* and himself. The devotees said that with a wave of his hand he materialized this small medallion picturing Jesus on its surface. The tiny medallion was passed from person to person through the group of devotees for all to examine. Taking it back into his hand, Baba blew on it twice, transforming the image on its surface, according to those present, to that of Lord *Shiva*–pictured on the medallion here and on the back cover.

On Vibhutti

The Sivarathri *Festival (devoted to the worship of* Shiva) *as celebrated here is an example for you. You might ask, "Swami has often declared that all days are holy days, that there is no special rite that has to be observed on any single day; but Swami himself is pouring* vibhutti *on the idol and calling it* Abhisheka *(ritual washing); is this right?" Swami is doing so to teach you a lesson.*

The vibhutti abhisheka *has a potent inner meaning which Swami wants you to grasp. The* vibhutti *is the most precious object in the truly spiritual sense. You know that* Shiva *burnt the God of Desire, or* Kama, *called* Manmatha *(for he agitates the mind and confounds the confusion already existing there) into a heap of ashes.* Shiva *adorned himself with that ash and thus he shone in his glory as the conqueror of desire. When* Kama *was destroyed,* Prema *(love) reigned supreme. When there is no desire to warp the mind, love can be true and full.*

What greater offering can you give God to glorify Him than the ash signifying your triumph over tantalizing desire? Ash is the ultimate condition of things; it cannot undergo any further change. The abhisheka *with* vibhutti *is done to inspire you to give up desire and offer* Shiva *the ashes of its destruction as the most valuable of all the articles you have earned. . . . Ash cannot fade as flowers do in a day or two; it does not dry and disappear or get soiled and unpotable as water does; it will not lose color as leaves do in a few hours; it does not rot as fruits do in a few days. Ash is ash forever and ever. So burn your wiles, your vices, your bad habits, and worship* Shiva, *rendering yourself pure in thought, word and deed. Showering on him the ash purchased in packets from the shops will not please him at all.*

Q: Do you feel that the Hindu concepts of *karma* and reincarnation have any relationship to Judaism or Christianity?

A: Yes; I see more similarities than differences when I investigate these spiritual doctrines. The idea of *karma,* that we reap what we sow, that we create our future with the slightest of our actions in each moment of the present, is akin in spirit to the golden rule: "Do unto others as you would have them do unto you." This rule reflects the spiritual truth that each of us is an interrelated part of one whole, thus hurting others is the same as hurting ourselves.

Then too, most religions have a concept of afterlife directly related to our actions in this life, such as Christianity's heaven and hell. In my reading of Hebrew and Christian literature I have seen nothing to indicate that reincarnation is impossible. Paramahansa Yogananda in his remarkably rich and fascinating book *Autobiography of a Yogi,* made reference to biblical writings which indicated to him that early Christian thought accepted the idea of reincarnation and in fact suggested that John the Baptist and Jesus in their last incarnation were, respectively, the prophet Elijah and his disciple Elisha.

Q: Has Baba mentioned anything about life on other planets?

A: I haven't heard him speak specifically of this, but he does say that he is the Lord among all Lords and has complete mastery of every aspect of the universe. I have heard stories of his giving people gifts supposedly from other planets.

Q: What is Baba's relationship to Christ?

A: This is a very interesting question. I have mentioned before that he has said he is all names and all forms, that he and Christ, or any form or embodiment of God, are the same. But he has drawn the connection between Christ and himself in a number of very interesting ways. For instance, I have read of people who, questioning Baba's authenticity, have prayed before pictures of Christ or their favorite saint or master for a sign of Baba's spiritual stature, and the form in the picture has changed into that of Sai Baba. I have also heard of the picture of Christ in someone's worship room producing *vibhutti.*

Then there is the very unusual story told by Dr. John Hislop—a close devotee whose account of Walter Cowan's apparent resurrection appeared earlier in this book—of Baba's breaking two twigs off a tree and placing them together in the form of a cross. He asked John what they looked like and John replied that they looked like a cross. Baba then placed the twigs in his hand, blew on them three times and opened his hand to reveal a wooden cross with a silver statue of Jesus on it. He said that the statue was not simply an artist's representation of Jesus but an exact likeness of how He actually looked on the cross. The small crucifix on which the silver statue was mounted, he said, was taken from Christ's actual cross. This is Dr. Hislop's account:

Baba, a large group of students from the Satya Arts and Science College at Brindavan and a few other people, including myself, were walking down the bank of a road to a stretch of level sand of the dry Kekkanahalla River bed. I was walking alongside *Swami,* and as we passed a bush, he reached over and pulled off a couple of twigs and held them up like a cross. *Hislop,* he said, *what is this?*

"Well, *Swami,* it is a cross," I answered. He put the twigs in his hand, closed it and produced three rather slow breaths on it. Then he opened his hand and gave me a cross with a figure of Christ on it. *This is an image of Christ on the cross,* he said—*not as artists have imagined Him and as historians have told about Him, but as he actually really and truly was, with stomach pulled way in and ribs all showing because He had had no food for eight days.*

So I said, "Well, the cross, *Swami,* tell me about that."

He said, *This cross is a piece of the wood from the original cross on which Christ was crucified.* Then he said something very interesting. *To find a piece of that wood after two-thousand years presented a little difficulty.* I suppose that is why he breathed rather slowly three times. Usually he gives one puff, and a ring or whatever just appears.

I noticed something odd and asked, "*Swami,* what is that hole at the top of the cross?"

He replied, *That is the hole where they hung the cross on the standard.* This is something we had never even heard of before. Pictures of Christ being crucified show the cross being planted in the ground; but, according to *Swami,* it was hung on something, and you can actually see the hole through the wood.

The cross is so small that the details on the figure of Christ escape the eye. A friend, Walter Wolfe, came down to our place in Baja and took some photographs of the cross that greatly magnify the details and show the beauty of the tiny figure of christ (head size is 3/16 inches and overall length is 7/8 inches).

When he sent me a few of the prints, my wife and I were absolutely astounded. I wrote Walter that if the pictures were seen around the world, they would create an art sensation. I am sure it is the greatest sculpture of Christ that has ever been made. In the 8x10 enlargements you can see the blood flowing from His forehead where He was bruised. You can see the black and dust-caked saliva at the corner of His mouth. The expression of agony, pain and suffering in His eyes and face will tear your heart. In my estimation it is the most extraordinary object that Baba has ever produced. Why he gave it to me, I have no idea.

When Walter Wolfe brought some enlargements of the

photograph down to our house, we were standing around the table, looking at the pictures and thinking of Christ and of Baba, when suddenly—from a perfectly clear sky—there was a terrible crash of thunder. Then a very strong wind blew through the house, rattling the shutters, banging the doors and blowing the curtains. Next day an article in the *San Diego Tribune* reported that a mysterious thunder and wind had come up unexpectedly from a perfectly clear sky at five o'clock the previous afternoon. My wife reminded me that Christ died on the cross at five o'clock and that the Bible tells of thunder and earthquakes which arose suddenly.

I can only conclude that there is a tremendous amount of power in that little cross.[1]

Baba may pass someone he has never met, at our level of consciousness, and move his hand in the air and produce a picture of the individual's favorite saint or a picture of Christ. He frequently addresses Christians on the subject of Christ's teachings, occasionally purporting to clarify a particular teaching or distortion which he says has developed as the story has been passed down.

To me, the most mind-blowing event of all regarding Baba's relationship to Christ happened Christmas Day, 1972. He told a group of people: *Christ said, "He who has sent Me will come again."* To my amazement he said that he himself is the one to whom Christ was referring.

> *And the story says there was a star in the sky, which fell with a new light, and this led a few Tibetans and others to the place where the Savior was born. This story is read and taken on trust by man, though stars do not fall or even slide down so suddenly. What the story signifies is this: There was a huge aura of splendor illumining the sky over the village when Christ was born. This meant that He who was to overcome the darkness of evil and ignorance had taken birth, that He would spread the light of love in the heart of man and the councils of humanity. Appearances of splendor or of other signs of the era that has dawned are natural when incarnations happen on earth.*

[1]Excerpts from *Sanathana Sarathi* (the Eternal Charioteer), a monthly publication from Prasanthi Nilayam, April 1975, together with Dr. Hislop's comments.

Following page: two photographs of Christ figure materialized by Sai Baba for Dr. Hislop.

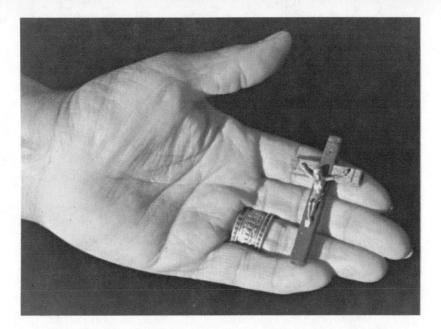

The aura of light was a sign that the darkness would be destroyed. A master arrives in answer to man's prayer: Thamaso maa jyothirgamaya (Lead us from darkness unto light).

There is one point that I cannot but bring to your special notice today. At the time when Jesus was merging in the supreme principle of divinity, He communicated some news to his followers which has been interpreted in a variety of ways by commentators and those who relish the piling of writings on writings and meaning upon meaning, until it all swells up into a huge mess. The statement itself has been manipulated and tangled into a conundrum. The statement is simple:

"He who sent me among you will come again," and he pointed to a lamb. The lamb is merely a symbol, a sign. It stands for the voice: "Ba-Ba;" the announcement was of the advent of Baba. "His name will be Truth," Christ declared. "Satya" means truth. "He wears a robe of red, a blood-red robe." (Here Baba pointed to the robe he was wearing.) "He will be short, with a crown (of hair)." The lamb is the sign and symbol of love. Christ did not declare that He would come again; he said, "He who sent me will come again." That "Ba-Ba" is this Baba.[1]

Q: How can you be sure that Baba is not a false messiah and a manifestation of the devil? This also was prophesied in the Bible.

A: I had always assumed that I knew reality, but witnessing Baba in India the first time proved to me that I had known nothing. Reality changed for me. It seemed to me that if such extraordinary power existed for the good, there must also be power that was bad, but I felt little ability to judge one from the other. I was, as a matter of fact, quite frightened, creeping back to my hotel room, fearfully peering into closets and behind the shower curtain. I suddenly felt exposed and unprotected; I was unaware of what mechanisms and strengths I possessed to ward off evil powers.

The question of how to tell the authentic from the false is crucial. With all kinds of evil and disruptive causes masquerading in the guise of "spirituality," many people have actually concluded that everything labeled "religious" or "spiritual" should be dismissed out of hand. It is true of course that a misguided spiritual-like surrender

---

[1] Exerpts from discourse by Sai Baba on Christmas Day, 1972.

to a cause can be absolutely dangerous and destructive, as has been so tragically exemplified by the Crusades, the Hitler era and the "guru"-drug scene of today—and even more recently by the brutal killings by the Manson family, who voiced a grotesque perversion of the spiritual attitude as a rationale for their actions.

Recognizing this danger and the far-reaching implications of dedicating oneself to an individual or a cause or movement, one must make such a decision only after the most careful deliberation and with a great sense of responsibility in the matter. How, then, is one to measure a being or a movement to determine its authenticity and whether or not it is indeed worthy of one's total surrender?

Since that first early fright I have gained tremendous trust and love for Baba. First of all, I have come to believe that even though we're not aware of our own powers, we have an intuitive capacity to sense whether something is good or bad, whether or not an individual is genuine. This capacity for discernment is not a function of the senses or rational mind but is an expression of our higher self, or *Atma*. As we evolve, the faculty becomes keener and keener. How much faith we place in this capacity will be different for each of us, depending on how much we trust ourselves—how good our judgment has been in the past: how stable, consistent, reliable and sensitively attuned we have been. Then too there is the measure of the man and the movement by the character and quality of the followers. Those gathering around Sai Baba are impressive indeed.

All of the highly developed souls that have experienced Baba and with whom I have become acquainted have an overwhelming intuitive sense about his greatness and goodness. Most touched by Baba become kinder, more loving, more at peace. And in all the accounts of evil forces or the devil with which I am familiar, at no time has he disguised himself as pure love, or by working in such an untiring manner for healing and the attainment of higher spiritual consciousness among people.

Finally, the life-style, activities, values and powers of a real *avatar* have been clearly defined in Christian and Hindu scriptures. The *avatar* allows himself to be measured, freely displaying his greatness to help dispel doubt. Baba, in fact, refers to his powers as "calling cards." These powers are not just the verbalization of vague abstractions and intellectual prattle which mask ulterior motives. What one observes and experiences are clear and concrete signs of his omniscience, omnipresence and love: a love measured in the promotion of health and wellbeing for all people everywhere.

Q: There are so many diverse spiritual movements springing up. What do you think of the more fanatical ones—especially where young people appear to break so with our culture?

A: Although I've found it is hard enough to determine what's going on inside myself, let alone to judge others, I do feel that it is very important to avoid hurting anyone else in one's spiritual quest. And as a psychiatrist, I feel that fanaticism and violent change usually do not reflect mature judgment. Frequently, when an individual attempts to make too drastic a change in his behavior, harmful rebounds take place. For instance, if one tries to fast without preparing for this departure from routine, the fast may end with gorging. Too unnatural a spiritual path can tire one quickly and end up leading away from God rather than toward Him. Or it can frustrate one into changing paths in a fickle manner, so that no one direction is ever maintained for long.

How does one launch upon a spiritual path; what is actually meant by surrender, renunciation, detachment? Must one make dramatic, violent changes in his way of life, torturing the body, despising the mind, throwing aside everything he has learned and taking to the forest—giving up all actions unless receiving concrete directions from spirits and entities from other dimensions?

It seems to me that spiritual doctrine is easy to misinterpret, especially when Westerners are trying to understand rather involved and esoteric Eastern practices. I myself am a beginner, a real novice in the subject of spirituality, and I wholeheartedly direct the reader to Sai Baba's own discourses for an in-depth study. His works are beautiful, his message profound.

Yet from the standpoint of a psychiatrist, I would like to point out what I consider some misinterpretations of spiritual teachings. I do this to caution some about becoming fanatical and to assure others that they don't have to become crazy or weird or dramatically change their life styles to embark on the spiritual path. Misinterpretation of religious doctrine may be in part why these ancient truths have fallen into disrepute for so many.

After my own experience with Sai Baba, I understand why it is so common for errors to be made. First of all, many of us are not very far along spiritually and, in general, have limited vision, little self-discipline and poor judgment with respect to reality and the way we should govern our lives. Add to this an intoxication with Baba's greatness and beauty and the shattering of previously held notions of reality—together with the awakening of a deep-seated yearning to merge with God—and you can see how easy it is to lose one's bearing.

I have observed many people adopting contorted and distorted behavior, trying first one thing and then another if that doesn't work in a few days, attempting in a frenzied and undisciplined manner to feel God, yet not knowing exactly what it is they are trying to attain.

I have already mentioned the confusion that exists, both in the individual and in psychiatric practice, in mistaking detachment for repression. Another of the central mistakes I have observed in

The secret of liberation lies not in the mystic formula that is whispered in the ear and rotated on the rosary. It lies in the stepping out into action, walking forward in practice, the pious pilgrim route and the triumphant reaching of the goal.

launching upon the path Baba has revealed to us is our desire to reach our destination too quickly. In this case we may repress rather than detach, play roles instead of extending ourselves honestly, appear foolish to others rather than providing a believable and inspiring example.

Buddha said to take the middle path. Baba constantly teaches patience. Yet people frequently adopt fanatical and unrealistic life styles in order to make headway fast. If one is practicing *hatha yoga* and his body is stiff and inflexible, it is dangerously foolish to attempt some of the advanced *asanas* or postures too quickly. Torn ligaments, tendons and muscles can be the result. The body must learn slowly and with patience. The art of *hatha yoga* lies in being able to sense where one's physical boundaries are; not tormenting the body and oneself because one isn't able to execute some advanced posture, but gently hovering at a particular boundary, asking and encouraging the body to open up more.

The same is true of people wishing to emulate great saints who are able to take to the Himalayas and live in the bitter cold with little food or shelter, meditating twenty-four hours a day. If we don't know what those saints know—just as our bodies are not as flexible as those of great yogis—then to try to emulate them totally is of course utter foolishness. We will only torment and hurt ourselves.

When a person is making gains in his emotional life through psychiatric therapy, there is only a gradual integration of what one learns into the fabric of what he has been. I believe this to be a sign that knowledge has been integrated into the deepest reaches of the personality, in contrast to something only cerebrally and superficially understood. When people act as if they know something when in fact their knowledge is no deeper than the cerebral level, they appear to me unreal, and I must admit that a lot of people passing themselves off as spiritual appear to me to be in this category.

Q: What is your feeling about people involved in phenomenology?
A: Many people seemed wrapped up in talking to their dead relatives or in learning how to see auras or move objects at a distance—calling upon the "karmic board" or the "purple flame," or whatever other esoteric symbol they believe in, in order to develop powers such as the ability to cure an illness or to overcome a particular problem in their lives.

I feel that our most important spiritual work is to learn to keep intimate company with God, focusing and meditating on Him always, learning to lead our lives as a devotional service and expressing this devotion and love in very practical and concrete ways in our everyday relationships with people. Baba and many others have said that yogic powers can tempt and detour the spiritual aspirant from the main goal of merging with God. People can get so caught up in excitement over what in the West we generally call extrasensory or paranormal powers that they forget that even these, like aggressiveness and sexuality, may lead deeper into the state of ego—the state of wanting and demanding, of frustration and suffering—the state of duality.

It doesn't have to follow, however, that if one breaks into higher levels of awareness and develops some extraordinary powers, he is bound to go astray. One can master and transcend these higher powers the same as the more common energies, but this calls for considerable discipline.

Q: What does Baba say about taking mind-altering drugs?
A: As a psychiatrist I have come to see that the most central human drive is to merge with God, who is our true identity—to return to the safety and strength of the Father. I see the fascination with psychedelic drugs as an expression of our yearning to lose the small self and make contact and merge with a higher reality.

There is little doubt that one of the important elements of the drug experience is the diminishment of the importance of the personality or ego as one is caught up, enveloped and submerged in a new world of swirling energies. Baba has said frequently, however, that this is not the path to true merging, but a dead-end street.

The transcendent experience brought about by drugs—however illuminating it may be of the fact that "reality" as most of us know it is in fact an arbitrary sort of tunnel vision in a world of phenomena of which we are mostly ignorant—is nevertheless false and transient itself and does not lead to true insight. Baba, as a matter of fact, has likened such experience to a plastic grape. Instant and lasting *samadhi* is apparently not to be found in a pill.

Baba is always teaching about patience, perseverance and discipline. Together with God's grace, these learned virtues are what make it possible to meet God within ourselves. Baba has promised that if we enter upon the experiment and experience of spiritual discipline, he will be with us in an intimate way, guiding us, assuring our safety, helping us to reach the goal of genuine self-realization. What more can a teacher promise?

Q: Does one have to go to India to make contact with Sai Baba?
A: No. He frequently makes contact with people all over the world in different ways. I know individuals, for example, who have been thousands of miles from him when a picture they have of him will begin to produce *vibhutti*. Or they will have an eerie feeling that he is communicating with them, or he will come in a dream to teach. I have even talked to reputable people who claim to have seen him materialize right in front of them here in this country. It is clear to me now that the dimension of prayer or meditation is as likely and as fruitful a place to make contact with Baba as is the Indian village of Puttaparthi.

Baba tells the story of a devotee who was in great danger and about to be assaulted. The devotee called upon the name and form of God to which he was devoted—picturing the diety at his place of residence, as described in Hindu scriptures, many miles away. He prayed until almost overcome by his attackers; only at the last moment did God appear and save him.

When he asked God why He had taken so long in coming, God replied that He had to come from a long distance because the devotee had pictured Him so far away. Had the devotee pictured Him within his own heart, He could have been there instantaneously.

Q: Does this mean that if we want Baba to appear to us he will come?

A: Baba says he is the indweller in each and every one of our hearts, and if we look for him there, we will find him. But as for his actions on the physical plane, it is my understanding that his movements are not determined by our wants or desires, but by our devotion, our spiritual practice and his grace. While one of my friends, a psychiatrist named Warren Gershwin, was visiting Baba recently, his wife and a young woman working as their housekeeper were sitting at home talking. Sylvia, the housekeeper, had been brought up in Tijuana, Mexico, in a rather difficult family setting and was a hardworking, stable and very healthy young woman. This evening she was a bit sad and said to Warren's wife Madelaine that even though she sang *bhajans* and wanted to believe in Baba, she simply wasn't convinced of his special powers. Madelaine was trying to comfort her but without much luck.

Sylvia looked up at the mantel where Baba's picture was hanging and silently asked him for help in building her faith. Madelaine relates that all of a sudden Sylvia's face turned ashen and she began muttering, "Oh, my God . . . oh, my God," then ran into the kitchen. Madelaine, frightened that Sylvia had seen a prowler, quickly followed her to determine what had so upset her.

"As I looked away from the mantel and into the kitchen, I saw Baba in plain view walking past the doorway," she said in an awed whisper. "Now I understand why you sing *bhajans*." She wanted to sleep there in the kitchen, and that evening they sang *bhajans* until two in the morning.

Q: If I went to India, what would be the probability of seeing and talking with Baba?

A: That is really between you and Baba. There is no way of telling what he will do, although in general it is already difficult to see him.

If you are seriously considering taking such a trip, I suggest contacting one of the Sai Baba Centers to see whether a group of devotees is planning one. There might be a better chance of seeing

Baba by going with a group. If you wish to go alone, I suggest inquiring of one of the Centers where Baba will be at the time of your anticipated visit. This information, along with a current list of the centers nearest you, may be obtained by writing the Sri Satya Sai Book Center of America. The bookstore address, together with a list of available books by and about Baba, are included in the Appendix.

I must remind you that the setting in Puttaparthi is austere. There are many obstacles to overcome and the trip is difficult in many ways. But for the real seeker, the possibility of ending your search is great.

Q: When will he come to the United States?

A: That's a good question. Nobody knows Baba's plans, itineraries or movements, and he frequently fakes his followers out of their shoes when they try to outguess him. So far, the only place he has traveled outside of India is Africa, in 1968. Americans have been asking him for years when he will come here and his answer is that he will come when we are ready.

I was present when one young man asked him this, and Baba replied that he would be going home with him—then patted him on the chest over his heart. I feel that he has indeed come to this country in the hearts of thousands of Americans who have been touched by him.

To another person he said that first one must take care of himself; and when that has been mastered, one takes care of his family, then his neighbors, then his city and finally his country; then one can go to other countries. It seems plain that he plans to focus on the healing and rejuvenation that must go on in India before he will direct himself elsewhere.

Q: How has your experience with Sai Baba affected the way you practice psychiatry?

A: I've experienced a basic change in attitude which is reflected in my work. First of all, since meeting Sai Baba I have become happier and more at peace, having lost to a great extent my fear of death while gaining a sense of omnipresent protection. This basic change in outlook and feeling of security have brought a clearer focus and sense of direction to my life, and consequently I feel able to perceive others more clearly also.

I have gone through quite a change in attitude toward the place of feelings and emotions in life. I became aware of the dangers of repressing feeling as a result of my psychiatric training, and after meeting Baba I have grown to recognize, as well, the dangers inherent in being *overly* attached to feelings and the manner in which such attachment can absolutely curtail spiritual growth.

In some strange way psychiatrists are almost trained to become agnostics and atheists. Perhaps by their over-valuation of and fascination with feelings and emotions, they overlook a spiritual order of reality beyond the senses. There naturally follows in their therapeutic objectives an emphasis on the senses and emotions. These elements of the small self have expanded in importance until they are the framework of what is practically worship in contemporary psychiatry.

I feel that there are some major limitations in psychiatric theory and practice, which should be brought to the patient's attention. It is true that untold numbers of people with emotional problems are helped to deal with them by an investigation into their feelings and thoughts. Many have to become more deeply involved with feelings in order to get to a point where they understand and can control their reactions.

But there is a limit to the amount of growth and evolution attainable through being immersed in these systems. And I think that psychiatry should make it clear where these limitations are; that, after a certain point, being immersed in feeling for the sheer joy and release of actually experiencing aggression or sexuality—without governing these feelings with a well-developed sense of morality—is dangerous.

Psychiatry must not be afraid to own up to a morality that reflects the existence of a spiritual dimension and to define proper channels of conduct which will lead to spiritual growth. Even though at one point in treatment it is appropriate to be non-judgmental and ask the patient not to censor thoughts or suppress emotions, it must be made clear that this attitude is a dangerous one if generalized as a way of life. Although most psychiatrists would say such generalization is a gross misunderstanding of the psychiatric attitude, it is my feeling that psychiatry has in some measure contributed to this distorted view by society at large. In refusing to acknowledge a spiritual dimension beyond the senses, it in effect over-values them.

Before meeting Sai Baba, I misinterpreted such monistic spiritual practices as detachment from emotions and adherence to a self-controlled, disciplined mode of morality, as generally repressive—in fact, a pathological denial of one's basic identity. I thought one's identity was primarily emotional.

So this attitude about a more limited place of emotions in a person's life, and the need for therapists more openly and clearly to discuss morality and the appropriate modes of behavior necessary for one's spiritual development, is reflected in my therapy. This can be done, I've found, without the patient's feeling punished or criticized and without stopping the flow of material necessary to reveal his repressed feelings. I came to realize that I had been taking cover under the mask of the non-judgmental observer much more frequently than was necessary or appropriate.

Psychiatry, I feel, must become spiritualized. *Education without character, science without humanity and commerce without morality are useless and dangerous,* Baba says, making the point further, while defining the limited place of the senses in one's life, by using the camera as an example.

Like ourselves, the camera is pointed to the world to receive information. The mind is the energy force that directs the camera in any number of ways toward the world. A higher aspect of the mind called *buddhi*, or intellect, directs the mind to what is important to photograph and tells it how to frame and focus. The senses are like the lens through which the information must travel to get to the film; and the film on which the image is exposed is the heart. If the intellect is wise and discriminating in its choices, one can consistently develop photographs exquisite in the truth and beauty they reveal of life.

The bliss that comes from viewing what one feels to be a moment of absolute truth captured in a photograph is analogous to the divine experience. Just as the purpose of photography is not fulfilled in stimulating the lens, neither is the purpose of life in exciting the senses. If the use of the camera is governed not by intelligence but by the sheer sensation of energy passing through the lens, then of course the images on the film will represent a chaotic picture of the world.

I now perceive in patients' verbalizations, and even in their body language, a certain vibration or element which went unnoticed before, and which I now identify as spiritual concerns and issues. While still able to identify conflicts centering around aggression or sexuality, I am more aware of the spiritual dimension—always there before but only dimly perceived—or even considered neurotic!

Where previously I saw only neurotic dependency in an adult who wanted a loving father's protection, I now also see elements of the very real sense of helplessness and isolation that comes from feeling separate from God, and perceive a spiritual yearning for merging with Him. Where I could see only neurotic fear in a patient who withdrew from expressing sexuality or aggression, I now also see an intuitive spiritual understanding which moves an individual toward detachment from emotions and which perceives the danger in being too involved with feelings.

Or in a patient overly concerned with being kind and gentle and loving, who appears to be defending against the expression of more animalistic drives, I might also see the yearning to merge with God by taking on those qualities which will lead one to Him. And with the patient I once thought dealing solely with neurotic guilt, condemning himself and anticipating punishment, I may more readily investigate his perceived past "sins" and his intuitive spiritual awareness of the need for repentance—or a fear of God he may be experiencing because of *karma*: the need to repay in kind for all one's actions.

We may even talk about the possibility of a particular condition's having arisen as the result of an action in a previous life. A patient who understands something about the concept of reincarnation may derive sufficient strength from his conception to help him through a period of mental torment or depression.

Whereas I used to see only a masochistic preoccupation with loneliness and depression in a widow or widower who would not date after the death of a spouse, I now also see the spiritual drive to treat the union as sacred . . . to observe chastity and transcend the physical plane of existence for a higher relationship with God and a loved one quite definitely experienced, although no longer at this plane of existence. I used to regard as distraught those musings by the depressed patient that he might be picking up vibrations from a loved one separated by distance or death; I am now willing to consider this a possibility.

The reality of some such human capability has been brought home dramatically to me in more than one instance. For example, I was seeing a patient who was doing well with no obvious cause for depression, who nevertheless pinpointed for me the exact time and day of the development of a rather profound depression, which lasted about ten days. Not until weeks later did she learn that her closest male friend, with whom she had not been in contact for some months, had been contemplating suicide and had at that moment placed all his pills on the table before him while making his final decision. He decided not to kill himself, and his own depression subsided at almost the same rate of recovery that I witnessed in my patient.

Spiritual issues are not the infrequent or peripheral concerns I used to consider them to be, but are in fact crucial and central ones at the heart of the patient's very existence.

A psychiatrist becomes aware of those areas in a patient's life with which he has contact in his own, and is a healer of others to the extent that he has healed himself—integrating and harmonizing his own life energies. I practice yoga and meditation daily and so bring elements of these disciplines into the treatment setting to be practiced by the patient. For example, I may suggest meditation to help a patient quiet distracting thoughts or agitating emotions; or I may introduce certain yoga techniques and postures to bring energy and fluidity into constricted areas of the body. I try to maintain a meditative state myself in the treatment setting, relying on it more than on thoughts, feelings or theories. I have developed great faith that this experience opens and sharpens my intuitive capacity while becoming transformed in some way into a method of treatment.

. . . Last, there is Sai Baba's most central message of love—a love that *must* be brought into the treatment setting. It has become apparent to me that contemporary psychiatry is grossly limited in understanding and comprehending the kind of love which he teaches.

After my initial visit to Sai Baba and experience of the awakening of a devotional center within myself, I began to realize that in this reaction I was witnessing something about the dynamics of love which had not been accessible to me in the field of psychiatry. This inner experience of devotion toward the divine is the fire in which our love becomes intensified, expanded and purified; it is the source of our deepest sense of meaning, giving rise to our most profound experience of peace and love. Baba points out how centrally important devotion is in our lives. Bhakthi *or devotion is the only path for reaching the divine destination.* Bhakthi *is the only panacea for all the ills of this world.* Bhakthi *is the only method of making you realize the truth.*[1] I knew that I had to find a way to fill not only my therapy, but my whole life, with this attitude.

Most psychiatrists, myself included, have been trained to have a rather egotistical attitude about their role in the therapeutic process. The assumption that any person can ever fully understand human nature and cure others is not only a gross illusion but also the source of a great deal of discomfort for many psychiatrists, who strain under the burden of feeling that they should know everything. Being in Sai Baba's presence and witnessing the scope of his consciousness was enough to humble this psychiatrist anyway into acknowledging how much we do not know. There followed for me an attempt to change my entire attitude about what is actually being accomplished in the therapeutic process and what its goals and purpose are.

Swami Vivekananda, an Indian holy man and disciple of Sri *Ramakrishna* said: "All the work you do is done for your own salvation, is done for your own benefit. God has not fallen into a ditch for you and me to help him by building a hospital or something of that sort! He allows you to work . . . not in order to help him but that you may help yourself. Do you think even an ant will die for want of your help? Most arrant blasphemy! The world does not need you at all . . . cut out the word 'help' from your mind. You cannot help; it is blasphemy! You *worship* when you give a morsel of food to a dog, you worship the dog as God. He is all and is in all . . . be thankful that you are allowed to exercise your power of benevolence and mercy in the world, and thus become pure and perfect. Be grateful to the man you help, think of him as God. Is it not a privilege to be allowed to worship God by helping our fellow man?"[2]

Baba has put it this way: *The play is His; the role is His gift; the lines are written by Him; He directs, He decides the dress and decoration, the gesture and the tone, the entrance and the exit. You have to act well*

[1]*Summer Showers in Brindavan,* 1972, p. 100
[2] *Thus spake Vivekananda,* Sri Ramakrishna Math Publishers, pp. 58-60.

the part and receive his approbation when the curtain falls. Earn by your efficiency and enthusiasm to play higher and higher roles—that is the meaning and purpose of life.

I have come to the belief that the therapeutic process is for the benefit of the therapist as well as the patient. I have attempted to make it an act of devotion and worship. If the therapist is meditating on the divine while in the therapeutic setting, if he sees the divine in the patient and maintains constant contact with this inner experience, he becomes more at peace, more loving and more intuitive. I believe that the transformation of our souls takes place in this kind of atmosphere. Such a setting can't help but have profound meaning for both patient and therapist.

Baba has said: *It is enough if love is cultivated—the love that knows no distinction between oneself and another—because all are but limbs of the one corpus of God Almighty. Through love alone can the embodiment of love be gained. Here no scholarship is needed; in fact, scholarship is an impediment, for it caters to egoism and it breeds doubts and desires for disputation and the laurels of victory over others preening themselves as learned.*

Besides seeing the devotional attitude as centrally important in my own life, I have more than once encouraged a patient to investigate this attitude himself. When patients discuss their sense of isolation, depression, emptiness and loneliness, I remind them, when I feel it is appropriate, of their relationship with God, suggesting that they spend time developing this spiritual relationship as well as their interpersonal relationships. I tell them plainly that their capacity to experience love is directly related to their fostering of a devotional attitude toward the divine.

I have come to realize that through love both the therapist and the patient can grow in the realization that our basic identity is *Atma*—that we in fact extend beyond time and space. People *can* experience the love that permeates and sustains the physical world.

Appreciation of the spiritual reality of love as the ultimate energy of the universe, and a realization that devotion is the means by which our love unfolds and expands, should be the goal of treatment. The purpose of therapy, in other words, should be to ease suffering in bodily, emotional and mental spheres; to thaw and loosen those areas hardened by pain. Then one can open to the vibration of the energy of love much as the lotus flower opens its petals to the sun to be in intimate communion with the source of its life and beauty.

The ultimate goal of psychiatry, I feel, is the same as that of religion: to find the God or *Atma* within, through the experience of love. Reflecting my fervent hope that psychiatry awaken to the reality of Sai Baba, I myself would rather call this still young science "*Sai*-chiatry," the *Sai*-chiatry of *Atma* consciousness, the *Sai*-chiatry of love.

17
SAI BABA'S
TEACHINGS

Who is Sai?

God is inscrutable. He cannot be realized in the outer objective world; He is in the very heart of every being. Gemstones have to be sought deep underground; they do not float in mid-air. Seek God in the depths of your self, not in tantalizing, kaleidoscopic nature. The body is granted to you for this high purpose, but you are now misusing it, like the person who cooked his daily food in the gem-studded gold vase that came into his hands as an heirloom.

Man extols God as omnipresent, omniscient and omnipotent, but he ignores His presence in himself! Of course, many venture to describe the attributes of God and proclaim Him to be such and such; but these are but their own guesses and the reflections of their own predilections and preferences.

Who can affirm that God is this or thus? Who can affirm that God is not of this form or with this attribute? Each one can acquire from the vast expanse of the ocean only as much as can be contained in the vessel he carries to its shore. From that quantity, he can grasp but little of that immensity.

Each religion defines God within the limits it demarcates and then claims to have grasped Him. Like the seven blind men who spoke of the elephant as a pillar, a fan, a rope or a wall, because they contacted but a part and could not comprehend the entire animal, so too, religions speak of a part and assert that their vision is full and total.

Each religion forgets that God is all forms and all names, all attributes and all assertions. The religion of humanity is the sum and substance of all these partial faiths; for there is only one religion and that is the religion of

love. The various limbs of the elephant that seemed separate and distinct to the eyeless seekers of its truth were all fostered and activated by one single stream of blood. The various religions and faiths that feel separate and distinct are all fostered by a single stream of love.

The optical sense cannot visualize the truth. It gives only false and barren information. For example, there are many who observe my actions and start declaring that my nature is such and such. They are unable to gauge the sanctity, the majesty and the eternal reality that is me. The power of Sai is limitless; it manifests forever. All forms of "power" are resident in this Sai palm.

But, those who profess to have understood me—the scholars, the yogis, the pundits (scholars), the jnanis (those who have spiritual knowledge)—all of them are aware only of the least important, the casual external manifestation of an infinitesimal part of that power: namely, the "miracles." They have not desired to contact the source of all power and all wisdom that is available here at Brindavan. They are satisfied when they secure a chance to exhibit their book-learning and parade their scholarship in Vedic lore, not realizing that the person from whom the Vedas emanated is in their midst, for their sake.

This has been the case in all ages. People may be very near (physically) to the Avatar, but they live out their lives unaware of their fortune, exaggerating the role of miracles, which are as trivial when compared to my glory and majesty as a mosquito is in size and strength to the elephant upon which it squats. Therefore, when you speak about these "miracles," I laugh within myself out of pity that you allow yourself so easily to lose the precious awareness of my reality.

My power is immeasurable; my truth is inexplicable, unfathomable. I am announcing this about me for the need has arisen. But what I am doing now is only the gift of a "visiting card." Let me tell you that emphatic declarations of the Truth by avatars were made so clearly and so unmistakably only by Krishna. In spite of the declarations, you will notice in the career of the same Krishna that He underwent defeat in His efforts and endeavors on a few occasions, though you must also note that those defeats too were part of the drama which He had planned and which He Himself directed.

When many kings pleaded with Him to avert the war with the Kauravas (a family group in the famous Hindu epic, the Mahabharata), He confessed that His mission to the Kaurava court for ensuring peace had "failed." But He had not willed that it should succeed. He had decided that the war would be waged. His mission was intended to publish the greed and iniquity of the Kauravas and to condemn them before the whole world.

But I must tell you that during this Sai Avatar, *there is no place for even such "drama" with scenes of failures and defeats! What I will, must take place; what I plan* must *succeed. I am Truth and Truth has no need to hesitate or fear or bend.*

"Willing" is superfluous for me, for my grace is ever available to devotees who have steady love and faith. Since I move among them, talking and singing, even intellectuals are unable to grasp my truth, my power, my glory or my real task as Avatar. *I can solve any problem however knotty. I am beyond the reach of the most intensive inquiry and the most meticulous measurement. Only those who have recognized my love and experienced that love can assert that they have glimpsed my reality. For the path of love is the royal road that leads mankind to me.*

Do not attempt to know me through the external eyes. When you go to a temple and stand before the image of God, you pray with closed eyes, don't you? Why? Because you feel that the inner eye of wisdom alone can reveal Him to you. Therefore, do not crave from me trivial material objects; but crave for Me, *and you will be rewarded. Not that you should not receive whatever objects I give as signs of grace out of the fullness of love. I shall tell you why I give these rings, talismans, rosaries, etc. It is to mark the bond between me and those to whom they are given. When calamity befalls them, the article comes to me in a flash and returns in a flash, taking from me the remedial grace of protection. That grace is available to all who call on me in any name or form, not merely to those who wear these gifts. Love is the bond that wins grace.*

Consider the meaning of the name, Sai Baba. Sa *means "Divine;"* ai *or* ayi *means "Mother" and* Baba *means "Father." The name indicates the Divine Mother and Father. Your physical parents might cultivate love with a dose of selfishness, but this Sai Mother and Father showers affection or reprimands only for leading you towards victory in the struggle for self-realization.*

For this Sai has come in order to achieve the supreme task of uniting as one family all of mankind, through the bond of brotherhood; of affirming and illumining the atmic *reality of each being in order to reveal the divine, which is the basis on which the entire cosmos rests; and of instructing all to recognize the common divine heritage that binds man to man, so that man can rid himself of the animal, and rise into the divinity which is his goal.*

I am the embodiment of love; love is my instrument. There is no creature without love; the lowest loves itself at least. And its self *is God. So, there are no atheists, though some might dislike Him or refuse Him, as malarial patients dislike sweets or diabetic patients refuse to have anything to do with sweets. Those who preen themselves as atheists will one day, when their illness is gone, relish God and revere Him.*

I had to tell you so much about my truth for I desire that you should contemplate on this and derive joy therefrom, so that you may be inspired to observe the disciplines laid down and progress towards the goal of self-realization, the realization of the Sai that shines in your hearts.[1]

There are some who are swept off their feet by the hysterical demonstrations of certain weak-minded individuals, which are described as my speaking through them or acting through them! Take it from me, I am not given to such absurdities! I do not use others as my media; I have no need to. I do not swing from side to side and prattle! Why, even those who torture their bodies and suffer the pains of asceticism for years, until ant hills overwhelm them and they become stiff as tree stumps, find it difficult to realize the Lord. How then can these idlers, who eat their fill and wander about as slaves of their senses, earn that status so cheap? Their gestures, words and actions are hollow and vain; those who burn incense before them and revere them are turning away from me and running after falsehood.

For how can the full ever dally with the paltry and wear the habiliment of the trifling? When God has come assuming form, take it from me, He will not fill inferior vessels or embellish tawdry stuff or enter impure bodies. So, do not extol these falsities and ruin those unfortunates. Deal with them severely and they will be cured. Those who have seen the brilliance of the diamond will not be misled by glass trinkets. The Lord is like the diamond, call it by any name. But a trinket cannot be turned into a diamond, however loud the praise and however adamant the claim.

[1]*Sanathana Sarathi* (The Eternal Charioteer), a monthly publication from Prasanthi Nilayam, July 1974.

Practice silence. For the voice of God can be heard in the region of the heart only when the tongue is still. . . . Silence is the speech of the spiritual seeker. Soft sweet speech is the expression of genuine love. Hate screeches, fear squeals, conceit trumpets—but love sings lullabies; it soothes, it applies balm.

The Very Breath

The nine steps in the pilgrimage of man toward God along the path of dedication and surrender are . . . (1.) developing a desire to listen to the glory and grandeur of the handiwork of God and of the various awe-inspiring manifestations of divinity. This is the starting point. It is by hearing about the Lord again and again that we can transform ourselves into divinity. (2.) Singing oneself about the Lord in praise of his magnificence and manifold exploits. (3.) Dwelling on the Lord in the mind, reveling in the contemplation of His beauty, majesty and compassion. (4.) Entering upon the worship of the Lord by concentrating on honoring the feet or footprints.

(5.) This develops into a total propitiation of the Lord and systematic ritualistic worship, in which the aspirant gets inner satisfaction and inspiration. (6.) The aspirant begins to see the favorite form of God which he likes to worship, in all beings and all objects, wherever he turns; and so he develops an attitude of vandana or reverence toward nature and all life. (7.) Established in this bent of mind, he becomes the devoted servant of all, with no sense of superiority or inferiority. This is a vital step, which presages great spiritual success.

(8.) This takes the seeker so near the Lord that he feels himself to be the confidant and comrade, the companion and friend, the sharer of God's power and pity, of God's triumphs and achievements—His sakha (friend), in fact, as Arjuna had become. (9.) As can be inferred, this is the prelude to the final step of total surrender or Atma-nivedanam: yielding fully to the will of the Lord, which the seeker knows through his own purified intuition.

You will note that the seventh step is dasyam, the servant state. That is the stage of service, which every person calling himself a social worker or volunteer or sevak has to reach. It is more fruitful than reciting the name or counting beads or spending hours in meditation, though one's service will be richer and more satisfying if done on the basis of spiritual discipline. You must look upon all as limbs of your body, and just as you try to heal any bruise or wound on any limb as quickly and as efficiently as possible, you must heal the woes and pains of others to the best of your ability and as far as your means allow.

The Lord is now worshiped by offering Him all things that you crave, by treating Him with all the honor you like to be done to yourself. The idol is bathed and washed, bedecked with jewels, fed and fanned, surrounded with fragrance, since these are things you desire. But the Lord is pleased only when you do things the Lord desires! How else can you win His grace? How else than by nursing and nourishing, succoring and saving His children? How else, then by helping them to realize Him as their Lord and

Guardian; and by cultivating faith in Him through your own straight and sincere living?

One of the first principles of straight living is the practice of silence. For the voice of God can be heard in the region of your heart only when the tongue is stilled and the storm is stilled and the waves are calm. There will be no temptation for others to shout when you talk to them in whispers. Set the level of tone yourself: as low as possible, as high as necessary to reach the outermost boundary of the circle you are addressing. Conserve sound, since it is the treasure of the element akasa, an emanation from God Himself. Reason can prevail only when arguments are advanced without the whipping up of sound. Silence is the speech of the spiritual seeker. Soft sweet speech is the expression of genuine love. Hate screeches, fear squeals, conceit trumpets. But love sings lullabies. It soothes. It applies balm. Practice the vocabulary of love; unlearn the language of hate and contempt.

The second sign is cleanliness: not outer cleanliness alone but, even more, inner. You cannot be fresh and feeling fine wearing a washed vest under an unwashed shirt or an unwashed vest over a washed shirt. Both have to be clean to provide the sense of tingling joy. So too, outer and inner cleanliness have both to be sought and won. In reality, the outer cleanliness is but the reflection of the inner achievement. There is a strange glow on the face of a guileless person. Inner cleanliness has its own soap and water–the soap of strong faith and the water of constant practice.

The third sign is that the true aspirant will have a reverent attitude to the duty he is bound with. He will carry out every task assigned to him as if it is an act of worship by which the Lord will be pleased, through which he can approach the pedestal of God. Duty is God: work is worship—that is the motto. Worship is not a uniform to be put on and taken off at stated hours of the day. Render every thought into a flower, worthy to be held in His fingers; render every deed into a fruit, full of the sweet juice of love, fit to be placed in His hand; render every tear holy and pure, fit to wash His lotus feet. The symbol on the flag at Prasanthi Nilayam is a reminder of this ideal, which you have to put into practice. It is the symbol of victory achieved by steady endeavor over the diabolic foes of lust and greed, of envy and hate, of malice and conceit. It is the symbol of the silent state of supreme bliss, won through self-control and self-realization.

Do not judge others to decide whether they deserve your service. Find out only whether they are distressed: that is enough credential. Do not examine how they behave toward others; they can be certainly transformed by love. Seva or service is for you as sacred as a vow, a sadhana, a spiritual path. It is the very breath; it can end only when breath takes leave of you.[1]

[1]*Sathya Sai Speaks,* Vol. VII, pp. 195-198.

Sai on Sadhana

Devotee: In the West, *sadhana* is generally taken to be a process of self-improvement. But does that imply identification with the changing personality?

Sai Baba: *First, there may be the urge to self-improvement. But the next stage is inquiry, the inquiry into the reality of "this" and "that." Seven-tenths of* sadhana *is inquiry.*

Devotee: *Sadhana* as it is described seems wrong, because it is a conscious effort aimed at getting a reward. It seems to me that *sadhana* is real only when it is spontaneous; that is to say, as when one naturally loves God: he cannot but help love God, and he cannot help but make inquiry.

Sai Baba: *It is as you say; but you have not experienced the spontaneous love for God. It is still just an idea. You have a conviction that love for God exists naturally in you. That conviction itself is the result of many lives spent in spiritual practice.*

Devotee: I have the conviction so strong that it is the very marrow of my bones that life is one; that others and myself are one. The *Atma* is that one and it is fully here at this moment; and I am constantly engaged in *sadhana*. So the question remains: why do I not actually experience that unity as no other than myself?

Sai Baba: *Your conviction of unity is an idea, a thought. It is not experience. For instance, when your wife has pain in the head, do you have it too? If not, where is the experience of the unity? The unity must be experienced, not just felt as an idea or entertained as a thought.*

Devotee: Swami! If *sadhana* and conviction do not bring the experience, how is one to get it?

Sai Baba: *Through* steady sadhana. *Just as with ourselves now, in this car: we need concern ourselves only with the careful driving of the car. In due course we will arrive at Anantapur, won't we? With correct and steady* sadhana *the actual experience of the One will naturally come about.*

Devotee: How does one really experience that he is the same as another? One feels for another through compassion, and compassion is idea, understanding; it is not direct experience of unity. When someone hit a dog, Sai Baba of Shirdi had the bruises. That is the actual experience of unity.

Sai Baba: *All is divine. When you are firmly established in the fact of your divinity, then you will know directly that others are divine. Compassion for others is felt as long as you consider yourself a separate entity, as a consequence of body-consciousness. The story of Shirdi*

Sai Baba that you have heard about is not fully correct. The facts are these: A lady cooked and got ready a plate of sweets for Baba and a dog ate them.

The lady drove the dog away with blows. The lady then carried another plate of sweets to Baba, who refused them, saying that he had eaten the sweets previously provided and his hunger was satisfied. The lady protested that this was the first time she had offered the sweets. Baba said, "No, you offered them and while I was eating them, you also beat me." Thus, he gave a lesson that he is omnipresent and that there is only one universal life.

Devotee: What does Swami mean by "omnipresent"?

Sai Baba: *"Omnipresent" means everywhere at the same time, all the time.*

Devotee: Swami says that at a certain stage in *sadhana* the exterior nature ceases. How is that?

Sai Baba: *There are ten stages in* sadhana, *each cognized by sounds of various types, ranging through different vibrations: bell, flute, conch, Om, thunder, etc. The tenth state is reached when the senses are transcended. Beyond the senses is the state of bliss.*

Devotee: Is that state of bliss experienced only for a time? What happens in the daily round of life?

Sai Baba: *That state remains always. In this state one thinks God, eats God, drinks God, breathes God, lives God.*

Devotee: Does everyone pass through these ten stages?

Sai Baba: *No, one may go directly to the tenth, the transcendental state, or to stage six or seven—or not progress at all. It is not uniform at all.*

Devotee: What should be one's attitude toward these stages of *sadhana*, as one encounters each stage one by one?

Sai Baba: *The states change, but the attitudes should be unchanging.*

Devotee: But what value should one give to the various states?

Sai Baba: *The* sadhaka *(spiritual aspirant) will not be satisfied with any of the states, for complete union is the goal. Desire remains strong until the transcendental bliss is realized, and then desire ceases. At that state, all is God. Thoughts, desires: all are God.*

Devotee: These thoughts that stream through the mind—are they material?

Sai Baba: *Yes, they are matter. All matter is impermanent.*

Devotee: Where do thoughts come from?

Sai Baba: *They come from food and environment. If you have* sathvic *(neither dulling nor exciting) food and desire only good things and atmosphere around you, only good thought will come.*

Devotee: Where do thoughts go?

Sai Baba: *They go no place, because thoughts do not flow through the mind. The mind goes out and grasps and gets engaged with thoughts. If the desire is for God, the mind does not go out. The best way is not to get involved in the problem: how to get rid of thoughts. See all thoughts as God. Then, only God-thoughts will come. The entire mechanism of body, mind and intelligence will work in a coordinated manner for the benefit of the higher goal.*

Devotee: Then for whom should the entire mechanism be functioning?

Sai Baba: *For the* Atma. *A small example: The earth turns on its own axis but at the same time it is revolving around the sun. The very faculties of man should do their own work, but the* Atma *is the center of their universe.*

Devotee: Swami, how can one bring these faculties under the control of the *Atma?*

Sai Baba: *When one realizes that the* Atma *is the reality, the One, then everything will function smoothly. It is a question of surrendering all to the* Atma.

Devotee: But Swami has said we should ask ourselves, "Who am I that I dare talk of surrendering my mind and intelligence to God? They do not belong to me. How can I surrender that which I do not own and cannot even control?"

Sai Baba: *It is not a question of surrendering or giving to some other one. One surrenders to oneself. Recognition that* Atma *is oneself is surrender.*

Devotee: Then Swami means that surrender is really a putting aside of that which one perceives as incorrect or false.

Sai Baba: *Yes.*

Devotee: I understand now. "Surrender" *implies* a person's offering himself or his possessions to another person. But, really, it is more like the abandoning of ideas and concepts for which one has no further use, or which one sees as inadequate or wrong.

Sai Baba: *Yes.*[1]

---

[1]From the notebook of an American devotee.

Baba Answers

Devotee: Baba! Please tell us how you are attained. I find my *sadhana* (spiritual practice) unproductive.

Sai Baba: *I know you are inflicting many austerities on yourself. I must tell you that I am attained only by devotion and by a way of life that is illumined by that devotion. Do not deprive the body of its elementary needs; it is a sacred instrument you have earned, for taking you to the goal. Lead a simple* sathwic *(balanced, pure, good) life, eat simple* sathwic *food, be sincere in speech, do loving service, be humble and tolerant, maintain undisturbed equanimity. Direct all your thoughts toward me, resident in your heart.*

Devotee: How, Baba; how can we progress in devotion?

Sai Baba: *There are different modes of devotion: that which foolishly weeps for me when I am not physically present; that which surrenders to me with wild abandon; and that which is steady and strong, ever attached to my will. I accept all these forms of devotion. The choice between one or the other is not yours, for it is I who rules your feelings, modifies them. If you try to go where I do not will, I will stop you; you can do nothing apart from my will. Be assured of that; this is the highest devotion.*

Devotee: So, what remains for me to do?

Sai Baba: *What makes you think that "doing" is so important? Be equal-minded. Then you will not be bothered about "doing" or "not-doing," success or failure; the balance will remain unaffected by either. Let the wave of memory, the storm of desire, the fire of emotion pass through without affecting your equanimity. Be a witness of these. Commitment engenders holding, narrowing, limiting. Be willing to be nothing. Let all dualities subside in your neutrality.*

Devotee: Yes, Baba, But when it is pain that one has to endure . . .

Sai Baba: *Do you think that I would confront you with pain were there not a reason for it? Open your heart to pain, as you do now for pleasure, for it is my will, wrought by me for your good. Welcome it, as a challenge. Do not turn away from it. Do not listen to your mind, for mind is but another word for "need." The mind engenders need; it manifested as this world, because it needed this. It is all my plan: to drive you by the pangs of unfulfilled need to listen to my voice, which, when heard, dissolves the ego and the mind with it.*

Devotee: Baba! I crave for your *darshan* (blessing conferred by being in the presence of a holy man), ever. Tell me where you go to and when.

Sai Baba: *I want you to pass beyond these criteria and wait in readiness, and yet with uncertainty. Location is limitation; let events manifold themselves. Be willing to be led by me, as I choose.*

Devotee: But, being so full of defects, how can we rise up to those high expectations?

Sai Baba: *Your deficiencies make you need me, and curb the arrogance of your mind. They are there on purpose, as instruments to prod you on. Through them, I am making you want me. The feeling of separation is just a trick of your mind. You form conclusions; they become beliefs, they shape your activities and attitudes.*

Devotee: It is hard to undergo your tests.

Sai Baba: *It is like baking a cake. I stir, I knead, I pound, I twist, I bake you. I drown you in tears; I scorch you in sobs. I make you sweet and crisp, an offering worthy of God. I have come to reform you. My plan is to transmute you into a successful* sadhaka *(spiritual aspirant). I won't leave you until I do that. Even if you stray away before you become that, I will hold on to you. You cannot escape from me.*

Devotee: You are so compassionate.

Sai Baba: *There is nothing I do not see, nowhere I do not know the way. My sufficiency is unconditional, independent of everything. I am the totality—all of it.*

Devotee: How then can we aspire for your grace?

Sai Baba: *I do not ask for perfect concentration or full renunciation. I ask only for love, love that sees me and serves me in all beings. I ask only that you turn to me when your mind drags you into grief or pride or envy. Bring me the depths of your minds, no matter how grotesque, how cruelly ravaged by doubts or disappointments. I know how to treat them. I will not reject you. I am your mother. No matter where you go, I am there. I can work with you everywhere.*

Devotee: I clamor for *darshan;* but you ask me to leave for my home across the seas.

Sai Baba: *Those who think that I am this outer form need me far more than you do. Their faith is more insecure, and often not at all. Their confusion arises from the habit of their mind's depending on external conditions, and drawing its sense of security from those external conditions.*

Devotee: Baba, however inadequate, I ask just this boon: make me your instrument.

Sai Baba: *All are my instruments. Perhaps you believe that I choose: this one is good, that one is worse, etc. No. Either will do. My will is the source of all that is and happens; it interpenetrates every thing*

Social Life and Atmic Sadhana

What have sociology or the social sciences to do with the sciences of the spirit or the inquiry into the human spirit? This is a question that is commonly raised. So too, many ask: What has the spiritual student and sadhaka (spiritual aspirant) to do with society and its problems? It must be said that both, these attitudes are wrong.

No society can find its fulfillment, no social ideal can fructify, without the blossoming of the spirit of man. Mankind cannot realize the divinity whose expression it is, without careful and constant attention being paid to the cultivation of the spirit. How else can this divinity express itself than in and through individuals? We can apprehend only the jagath (transitory world), this moving, inconstant fantasia; we cannot see or hear, smell or taste or touch the director of the fantasia—God. In the same manner, we can apprehend the individual, but not the entity named society. For society is no separate, distinct complex, formed out of elemental components. Society is the divine proliferation produced by the will supreme.

Man is mortal: dust he is and to dust returneth. But, in him, there shines the Atma, as a spark of the immortal flame. This is not a term of flattery invented by the Vedantists. The Atma is the source, the sustenance, of every being and every organization of beings. It is the one and only source, substance and sustenance. The Atma is God; the particular is the universal, no less. Therefore, recognize in each being, in each man, a brother, the child of God, and ignore all limiting thoughts and prejudices based on status, color, class, nativity and caste. Sai is ever engaged in warning you and guiding you so that you may think, speak and act in this attitude of love.

Society cannot justify itself by planning to divide the spoils gained from nature, either in equal shares or unequal shares. The consummation that must inspire society has to be the establishment and elaboration, in every social act and resolution, of the knowledge of the one universal Atma, and the bliss that that knowledge confers.

Sai does not direct: "The Atma has no death; therefore, kill the physical sheaths, the bodies." No, Sai does not encourage wars. Sai directs you to recognize the Atma as your closest kin, closer than the members of your family, your blood relations and your dearest descendents. When this is done, you will nevermore stray from the path of right, which alone can maintain that kinship.

Familial attachment operates even against the performance of one's legitimate duties. But attachment to the divine fills that duty with a new dedication which ensures both joy and success. It activates man as nothing else can; it confers on him, during the process of doing his duty, the highest *wisdom. Hence the advice: Do not enter the objective world* (prakriti) *in the hope of realizing the* Atma; *enter the objective world after becoming aware of the* Atma: *for then you see nature in a new light and your very life becomes a long festival of love.*

There are many who use their scholarship and intelligence, even Vedic *scholarship, in dreary debate and competitive display. They are enamored of their petty triumphs. They declare that society is an arena for winning such triumphs. But Sai calls on you to seek and strengthen another type of society, where there is no room for such trivial desires.*

Disputative Vedic *scholars crave the fruits of their endeavors and efforts, through ritual. Nature does not crave so; the clouds bring rain as an homage to God who is their Lord. But they attribute it to the efficacy of their rites and use it to inflate their egos. They play about among the far-spreading branches of the tree of Desire. They are entangled in the coils of the three "ropes"—the* thamasic, *the* rajasic *and the* sathwic.[1]

You have to go beyond the three ropes, the three bonds. You have to be, ever, in the unchanging eternal Truth. You must be established in the One, as the One, with no trace or taste of two. Earning and garnering should not interest you; you must not be caught in the pursuit of yaga *(outer-directed activity) and* kshema *(possessiveness), for you are full already and have no wants.*

The ideal of a high standard of life, instead of a high level of living, has played havoc with human society. A high level of living insists on morality, humility, detachment, compassion; so the competitive greed for luxury and conspicuous consumption receives no encouragement and will be destroyed. Now man is the slave of his desires; he finds himself helpless to conquer the thirst for pleasure and luxury; he is too weak to keep his nature under control; he does not know how to arouse the Divine Consciousness that is latent in him.

Mere moral practices or instruction cannot help you to achieve this. It can be done only by spiritual sadhana *(spiritual work), for it is a basic transformation. It involves the elimination of the mind, which is the arch-obstacle in the path. Grace of God, if invoked and won, can endow you with the power, and the grace is available within you, awaiting the call.*

---

[1]According to the *Samkhya* philosophy, *prakriti* (nature) in contrast with *Purusha* (soul), consists of three *gunas* (qualities or strands), known as *tamas, rajas* and *sattva. Tamas* stands for inertia or dullness, *rajas* for activity or restlessness, and *sattva* for balanced wisdom.

Man must give up reliance on the vagaries of the mind. He must act ever in the consciousness of his innate divinity. When that is done, his three-fold nature (composed of the gunas (qualities)—thamasic, rajasic and sathwic) will automatically express itself through only holy channels. That is the genuine manifestation.

Another point: The argument may be raised, "If one has to give up the desire for comfort, luxury and pleasure, why should one be embroiled in society?" This presupposes the belief that society is justified only by the provision of such worldly joys. But what kind of society can one build on such slender foundations? If built, it can be a society only in name. It will not be bound by mutual love and cooperation. The strong will suppress the weak. Social relations will be marred by discontent. Even when attempts are made to divide the resources of nature equally among all, the cordiality will be only on the surface, it will not be spontaneous. We can limit the resources available, but we cannot limit greed, desire and craving.

Desire involves seeking beyond the limits of possibility. What has to be done is to pluck out desire by the roots. Man must give up the desire for objective pleasure, based on the illusion that the world is many, manifold, multi-colored, etc., and not on the truth that the world, nature, all creation, is One. When one is conscious only of the One, who desires what? What can be acquired and enjoyed by the second person? The Atmic vision destroys the desire for objective joys, for there is no object distinct from the subject.

This is the true function of society—to enable every member to realize this Atmic vision. The men and women bound by mutual interests in a society are not merely families, castes, classes, groups or kinsmen and kinswomen; they are One Atma. They are knit by the closest of family ties; not only the one society to which they feel they are bound, but all mankind, is One. Vasudhaika kutumbakam, as the Sastras (scriptures) declare: the whole world is one family. This unity must be experienced by everyone.

Natural resources and wealth are now being misused for the boosting of one's ego. But when the Atmic unity is realized, they will promote the new way of life through love. What is now "mercy," or legally enforced mutual "help," will then be transformed into "divine love" that can effectively purify the recipient and the giver. This consummation is beyond the region of common politics, ethics or economics. They cannot transform the receiver and thrill the giver, however much they attempt to equalize. They do not have the appeal and they have no power to sustain. The equality they establish will be haunted by a shadow, the shadow of the ego. This shadow can disappear only when identity as One is known and felt.

It may be said that not all desires are wrong; the rajasic ones which harm and exploit others can be condemned, but why renounce the sathwic *desires? But desire is desire, though the object may be beneficial and pure. The fruit of effort, the mind that seeks it, the vitality that activates the mind, life itself—every one of these has to be turned towards the Lord, with devotion born out of the vision of the One.*

Those who argue that the spiritual path is for the individual only, and that the society should not be involved in it, are committing a great mistake. It is like insisting that there should be light inside the house, and saying that it does not matter if there is darkness outside. Devotion towards God goes ill with hatred towards fellow-men.

Fellow-men and the world must be seen ever in the mirror of Sath-chith-ananda *(existence, knowledge, bliss; the Supreme state). Kinship based on this recognition will alone last. That is the Sai kinship. When you deepen that kinship, the true presence, the constant presence of Sathya Sai, will be yours. Do not be led away by your fancies into the jungle of words and feelings. Be firm, true to your innermost nature.*

Good and evil are based on the reactions of individuals; they are not inherent in things or events. Vedanta *or atheism is accepted or rejected when one likes or dislikes it. They do not depend on logical acceptance or rejection. Only experience can establish their validity. Who can delineate Godhood as thus and thus? Those who do so are indulging in a futile exercise. They have no authority for declaring it. If they claim the right, they are but conceited people relying on their limited intellects.*

Divinity is fully immanent in everyone; it is patent for the eyes that can see clearly and deeply. Whoever denies this is only cheating himself of his reality. He cannot dismiss it by denial, either from himself or others.

The conclusion, therefore, is inevitable: that it is the duty of man to see in society the expression of divinity, and to use all his skill and effort to promote the welfare and prosperity of society. Man must cultivate this expansive feeling, this inclusive thinking and this intuitive vision. Without these three, man is but an inert being; if he derides these three, he loses his title to be human.

The spirit of renunciation, adherence to virtue, the eagerness to cooperate, the sense of kinship—these are the characteristic signs of man. Life which considers these as encumbrances cannot be valued as life.

The brotherhood of man can be translated into life only on the basis of the Atmic *vision. All men thirst for peace, happiness and bliss. They are the precious heritage which is man's right, for they are God's treasure. They can be earned only by recognizing the bond that knits man to man. All men are of one lineage; they are of divine lineage.*

All men are cells in the one divine organism, in the divine body. That

should be your faith, your fortune, your fort, your fullness. Awareness of this alone gives you the right to call yourself a man. Learn to live as men. This is the sadhana, *this is the message, of Sai.*

Maxims

1. Prema *(love)* should be considered as the very breath of life.
2. More than all other forms of prema, *man's first effort should be to fix his love on the Lord.*
3. Such love directed toward God is bhakthi *(devotion); that is the fundamental test: the acquisition of* bhakthi.
4. Those who seek the bliss of the Atma *(the soul, the spark of God within) should not run after the joys of the sense objects.*
5. Satya *(truth)* must be treated as life-giving as breathing itself.
6. *Just as a body that has no breath is useless and begins to rot and stink within a few minutes, similarly, life without truth is useless and becomes the stinking abode of strife and grief.*
7. *Believe that there is nothing greater than truth, nothing more precious, nothing sweeter and nothing more lasting.*
8. *Truth is the all-protecting God. There is no mightier guardian than truth.*
9. The Lord, who is Sathyaswarupa *(the embodiment of truth), grants His* darshan *(blessing of visualizing the Lord) to those of truthful speech and loving heart.*
10. *Have undiminished kindness toward all beings and also the spirit of self-sacrifice.*
11. *You must also possess control of the senses, an unruffled character and non-attachment.*
12. *Be always on the alert against the four sins which the tongue is prone to commit: speaking falsehood, speaking ill of others, back-biting and talking too much. It is best to attempt to control these tendencies.*
13. *Try to prevent the five sins that the body commits: killing, adultery, theft, drinking intoxicants and the eating of flesh. It is a great help for the highest life if these also are kept as far away as possible.*
14. *One must be always vigilant, without a moment's carelessness, against the eight sins that the mind perpetrates:* kaman *or craving,* krodham *or anger,* lobham *or greed,* moham *or attachment, impatience, hatred, egoism, pride. Man's primary duty is to keep all these things at a safe distance from himself.*
15. *Man's mind speeds fast, pursuing wrong actions. Without letting it hurry like that, remember the name of the Lord at such a time or attempt to do some good deed or other. Those who do thus will certainly become fit for the Lord's grace.*
16. *First give up the evil tendency to feel impatient at the prosperity of others and the desire to harm them. Be happy that others are happy.*

Sympathize with those who are in adversity and wish for their prosperity. That is the goal of cultivating the love of God.

17. *Patience is all the strength that man needs.*

18. *Those anxious to live in joy must always be doing good.*

19. *It is easy to conquer anger through love, attachment through reasoning, falsehood through truth, bad thoughts through good and greed through charity.*

20. *No reply should be given to words of the wicked. Be at a great distance from them; that is for your good. Break off all relations with such people.*

21. *Seek the company of good men, even at the sacrifice of your honor and life. But be praying to God to bless you with the discrimination needed to distinguish between the good men and the bad. Use the intellect given to you for such discrimination as well.*

22. *Those who conquer states and earn fame in the world are hailed as heroes, no doubt; but those who have conquered the senses are heroes who must be acclaimed as the conquerors of the universal.*

23. *Whatever acts a good or bad man may do, the fruits thereof follow him and will never stop pursuing him.*

24. *Greed yields only sorrow; contentment is best. There is no happiness greater than contentment.*

25. *The mischief-mongering tendency should be plucked out by the roots and thrown off. If allowed to exist, it will undermine life itself.*

26. *Bear with fortitude both loss and grief; try to search for plans to achieve joy and gain.*

27. *Assume silence when you are invaded by anger, or remember the name of the Lord instead. Do not remind yourself of things which will inflame the anger more. That will do incalculable harm.*

28. *From this moment, avoid all bad habits. Do not delay or postpone; they do not contribute the least joy.*

29. *Try as far as possible within your means to satisfy the needs of the poor, who are really* daridranarayana *(God's poor). Share with them whatever food you have and make them happy at least that once.*

30. *Whatever you feel should not be done to you by others, you should avoid doing to others.*

31. *For faults and sins committed in ignorance, repent sincerely; try not to repeat the faults and sins again. Pray to God to bless you with the strength and the courage needed to stick to the right path.*

32. *Yield not to cowardice; do not give up* ananda *(bliss).*

33. *Do not allow anything to come near you which will destroy your eagerness and enthusiasm for God. Want of eagerness will cause the*

decay of the strength of man.

34. Do not get swelled up when people praise you and do not feel dejected when people blame you.

35. If your friends hate one another and start a quarrel, do not attempt to inflame them more and make them hate each other more; try, on the other hand, with love and sympathy to restore their former friendship.

36. Instead of searching for others' faults, search for your own faults; uproot them, throw them off. It is enough if you search and discover one fault of yours; that is better than discovering tens of hundreds of faults of others.

37. Even if you cannot or will not do any punya, or good deed, do not conceive or carry out any papa, or bad deed.

38. Whatever people may say about the faults that you know are not in you, do not feel for it; as for the faults that are in you, try to correct them yourself, even before others point them out to you. Do not harbor anger or vengeance against persons who point out your faults; do not retort by pointing out the faults of those persons themselves, but show your gratitude to them. Trying to discover their faults is a greater mistake on your part. It is good for you to know your faults; it is no good your knowing others' faults.

39. Whenever you get a little leisure, do not spend it in talking about sundries, but utilize it in meditating on God or in doing service to others.

40. The Lord is understood only by the bhaktha (devotee); the baktha is understood only by the Lord. Others cannot understand them. So do not discuss matters relating to the Lord with those who have no bhakthi (devotion). On account of such discussions, your devotion will diminish.

41. If anyone speaks to you on any subject, having understood it wrongly, do not think of other wrong notions which will support that stand, but grasp only the good and the sweet in what he says. True meaning is to be appreciated as desirable, not wrong meaning or many meanings, which give no meaning at all and cause only the hampering of ananda.

42. If you desire to cultivate one-pointedness, do not when in a crowd or bazaar scatter your vision to the four corners and on everything, but see only the road in front of you, just enough to avoid accidents to yourself. One-pointedness will become firmer if one moves about without taking one's attention off the road, avoiding dangers and not casting eyes on others' forms.

43. *Give up all doubts regarding the* guru *and God. If your worldly desires do not get fulfilled, do not blame it on your devotion; there is no relationship between such desires and devotion to God. These worldly desires have to be given up some day or other;* bhakthi *feelings have to be acquired some day or other. Be firmly convinced of this.*

44. *If your* dhyanam *(meditation) or* japam *(recitation of the name of God) do not progress properly, or if the desires you have entertained do not come to fruition, do not get dispirited with God. It will dispirit you even more and you will lose the peace, however small or big, that you might have earned. During* dhyanam *and* japam *you should not be dispirited, desperate or discouraged. When such feelings come, take it that it is the fault of your* sadhana *(spiritual work) and endeavor to do it correctly.*

It is only when in your daily conduct and in all actions you authentically behave and act in this manner and along these lines that you can attain the divine principle very easily. Therefore, hold on to these maxims firmly.[1]

---

[1]*Sandeha Nivarini* (a book of questions and answers by Sai Baba), pp. 52-59.

18

LOTUS
FEET

Soon after returning from my fourth trip to India, I began working with the Sri Satya Sai Baba Book Center of America, which is engaged in reprinting and distributing Baba's teachings. Finding there to be a dearth of such material by Westerners, I began writing this book, in February 1974.

The following October my brother Donald decided to visit Baba again. I had completed enough of the book by this time to present it to Baba and ask his direction, so I decided to join Don. I had felt all along that the book would meet with his approval and that, in fact, he was giving me direction the whole time . . . but I wasn't really sure.

I began to worry. How will he receive me? Will he recognize the book as a devotional piece to him; will he accept it as a manifestation of the deepest yearnings of my heart to be close to him? Will he tell me to go ahead with it, that he is pleased—or will he tell me to burn it? We left on December sixth.

This fifth time I could no longer ignore a certain amount of guilt about leaving my wife and family so much over the past three years. *Thank God* that Sharon had had strong and unique experiences with Baba herself! They had led to her own deepening relationship with him and had given her insight into my increased involvement. The changes and pressures in our marriage had been great, and although Sharon accepted and supported my direction in life now, this had not come about without a good bit of pain and hardship.

I remembered with a smile what must have been her initial impression of me when I returned from the first trip. I had left, a contemporary, free-thinking psychiatrist, and returned in a condition comparable to being tattered, covered with ashes, muttering incomprehensible

Sanskrit words and asking everyone in the area to join in singing devotional songs to the Lord.

She had witnessed my jumping from bed before dawn to sit still as a lamp post in meditation. Add to this, teachers calling her concerning strange stories told by our children about a man who could take gifts out of thin air, and the concern of relatives who perceived the change as a defiant rejection of my own past and religion.

Then there was the continual influx into our lives of Baba devotees from all walks of life—bearded and barefoot or straight-laced—with all that this entailed in the way of *bhajan* groups, study groups and incessant talk of God. On top of this, my returning to India time and again, my lately becoming immersed in a book which frequently took me from family activities . . . and now running back to India for the fifth time.

Fortunately, Sharon's first experience with Baba had been so moving that it and subsequent experiences had sealed a bond in her relationship with him, giving her the strength to cope with all these changes. At our first meeting, Indra Devi had shown some films of Sai Baba. At one point I noticed Sharon suddenly become excited and begin to move about restlessly in her chair. I wondered what had happened but said nothing and continued to watch the film. Finally, she blurted out, "Indra Devi, when is Sai Baba's birthday?"

"November twenty-third," was the answer. Sharon was electrified. Not only was this the same date as her own, but somehow she had absolutely *known* that she and Baba shared the same birthday. We were both quite surprised because Sharon had never demonstrated any clairvoyant or precognitive abilities before.

This was the first of a number of experiences. On another occasion —just before she was about to leave with me on her first trip to India, and at a time when she was greatly afraid of flying—Sharon was driving home from the supermarket, her thoughts quite apart from Sai Baba or the trip. Suddenly she became aware of a strong scent of *vibhutti,* which lingered in the car for several minutes. The experience was accompanied by an eerie sense of Baba's presence, a presence she continued to feel and which actually helped her through the difficulties of the trip. Then one evening some weeks after our return, Sharon and the children were talking in our living room about Sai Baba. Was he *really* real, they wanted to know. "I think he's real; I saw him do some amazing things," Sharon said.

"I don't know if he's real," one of the children answered hesitantly. At that very moment a large picture of Baba suddenly crashed to the floor from a nearby table, stunning everyone. Then in awed whispers they all began to affirm: "He *must* be real!"

Subsequently, Sharon has had five or six dreams in which she is with Baba and is being taught by him. She asks questions and he responds with such love and warmth that she has felt a lasting glow from the dreams. She considers them far more than her mind's imagination. They have been invaluable in helping her reconcile Sai Baba's increasing influence in our lives with her Jewish upbringing.

Although initially Sharon had reacted to the intensity of my enthusiasm, perhaps her greatest distress had come from observing the proliferation of Baba's photographs throughout the house. Since in the Hebrew tradition it is taboo to worship a human as divine, she was uncomfortable when her Jewish friends and relatives came to our home and saw such an array.

The conflict between Baba and Judaism was gradually resolved, however, as Sharon began to discover the universality in Baba's message . . . when she learned that he encourages people to follow their own familiar religion and teaches that since God is behind all names and forms, everything is a manifestation of God. Any form can be used for the focus of worship if it symbolizes divinity for the devotee. *Worship God as the picture and not the picture as God,* Baba says.

> *The Lord can be addressed by any name that tastes sweet to your tongue, or pictured in any form that appeals to your sense of wonder and awe. You can sing of Him as Muruga, Ganaphathi, Sarada, Jesus, Maitreyi, Sakti; or you can call on Allah or the Formless or the Master of all Forms. It makes no difference at all. He is the beginning, the middle and the end; the basis, the substance and the source.*

This universal appeal is seen at Prasanthi Nilayam, for here one enters a mysterious and marvelous world where people from all faiths and all walks of life, from every imaginable social position, are undergoing profound internal changes together, being molded into a brotherhood of spiritual aspirants. The varieties of people drawn to Baba, and their stories, are remarkable. On the fifth trip, for example, I met a Buddhist monk from Sri Lanka (Ceylon) who is the head of a Buddhist monastery, two Christian medical students from England, a Sikh from the Punjab of Northern India; Europeans, Nepalese, Japanese and Africans—all with miraculous stories that send one's head reeling.

Sharon gradually started witnessing changes inside herself which began to turn her more strongly toward Baba. She found herself beginning to enjoy opening our home for religious activities. In the process of giving to people, she was receiving much more than she had anticipated. She began to experience greater calm and a new feeling of joyfulness in her life, and witnessed her long-standing fear of death subside. But perhaps her greatest joy, she told me when we worked together on this part of the book, came from seeing her husband become a more giving, loving and contented person.

As for our four lovely daughters, children have a beautiful, apparently innate grasp of the spiritual. Whether because of their dependent relationship with parents or because, as Wordsworth said, they have just come from God, "trailing clouds of glory," it seems entirely natural to them that there should be a loving God with whom to relate. The innocence and sincerity with which they sing spiritual songs and say prayers is heartwarming; there seems such direct communication between little ones and God. Sharon and I felt initially that conflicts might arise in teaching the children about both Sai Baba and Judaism, but we haven't found this to be true. Their questions can be answered from either or both spiritual orientations. This has proved a living example to us of the one truth inherent in all religions.

Such were my thoughts on boarding the plane this fifth time. I felt deep love and gratitude for the freedom Sharon was allowing me in making this trip, while she stayed home with the children. And I recognized that although there might still be some trying times along this path, the dimension it added to all of our lives more than outweighed the inconveniences and hardships it entailed. I left knowing that Sharon felt Baba's entrance into our lives had been a profound blessing, that through this contact our lives were being filled with greater meaning and love.

The sun on this beautifully clear, cool Sunday was warm and rejuvenating. About a thousand people were gathered here on the grounds at Brindavan, with Don and myself sitting on the edge of the crowd. After forty hours of traveling and very little sleep, it felt good just to sit here and soak up the sun's energy, anticipating Baba's appearance.

Then suddenly the figure in orange emerged. I kind of gauge the spiritual work I've done between trips now by my reaction on first seeing that orange robe. It's gotten so I have no control at all anymore. Suddenly I start shaking all over and experiencing inner reactions that I feel at no other time. I wonder, "My God, am I turning into some kind of hysteric?" All I can do is just sit there and hope no one is watching me.

At least I felt less conspicuous sitting as far back as we were. As Baba approached us, he raised his hand in a sign of recognition and greeting and flashed the sweetest smile one could imagine. A glance and a wave of his hand, and I just fell apart. Everyone else started running after him, and all I could do was sit there for half an hour trying to regain my composure. Later Indra Devi came out and notified us that we would have an interview the next morning.

I began to worry. It's one thing to be in San Diego, theorizing about Baba's omnipresence and omniscience; but quite another to sit next to him and, when the cards are on the table, say, "Look, I wrote a book about you and wonder what you think of it." When one has all this yearning to give everything one has, surrender everything to the divine,

it's always nice if the divine is really there to take it. If you come up to Baba wanting to spill out your heart and he says, "Who are you and what are you doing here?" that smarts a bit. But when the circuit is completed and the love is accepted and returned, the joy and fulfillment are overwhelming.

We had been invited in for a group interview. Baba spoke with clear and simple eloquence for an hour. Then I stood up: "*Swami*, can I see you about the book I have written?" Gently taking my hand, he led me into a private room. *Okay, what do you want?* he asked.

I began to shake. Oh my goodness, this reaction again . . . will I be able to handle myself? I took out my manuscript and began fumbling through an explanation, not making myself at all clear. Does he really know, I thought, or am I just looking foolish? "I have this book that I just wrote about you, Baba," I said.

When one gets close to him, there is a side that looks so human—as limited and fallible as anyone else—and I was now wondering seriously whether he even understood what I was saying. He looked questioningly at me so I made another attempt to explain. I was beginning to feel completely misunderstood. Then he looked up smilingly and with a knowing eye said, *Fine, you come back on Thursday and we will talk for an hour on all the specifics of the book. Dr. Gokak will be there, and you bring your brother too.*

"Okay," I said, stunned. I wandered in some confusion back to the group, and again all I could do was sit on the floor for some time to regain my composure. I'm still amazed to witness myself break up like this, although I have heard that many people have such reactions as they draw closer to Baba. The tears just well up and the heart goes out, and it seems the closer I get the less control I have.

Baba gave the book to Dr. Gokak to read. Under Baba's supervision, he heads the Sathya Sai Baba Educational Foundation and administers the summer school for spirituality and Indian culture. As we studied the book together the next few days, one of his comments proved to be quite an eye-opener for me.

So much is written about India's poverty, especially by Westerners accustomed to material comforts. Frequently they point to it in a critical manner, with no thought that the West is in any way responsible. Dr. Gokak assured me that the Indians abhor this sense of poverty and broken spirit and have initiated a number of far-reaching programs to deal with it. But he stated that the West must not refuse its share of responsibility for helping to create it in the first place.

Until about the sixteenth century, according to Dr. Gokak, the East and West were on about the same material level. But as the West began to gain knowledge of the physical world from its burgeoning new science, it guarded and refused to share it, he said—gradually becoming wealthy at the expense of those countries without technological know-how. These countries were used as resource suppliers, literally being bled dry. The other side of the coin of Western material wealth and power has been the poverty and subjugation of many peoples.

A story told to me by a number of educated Indians was very moving, expressing the hurt which must lie deep in the Indian psyche. A group of weavers in Dacca—now in Pakistan—had developed the weaving of beautiful muslin cloth into an extremely refined art, passed from generation to generation within families. These artists in cloth grew long fingernails, beneath which they placed delicate wheels as part of their technique in weaving. Unfortunately, this fine cloth woven with such exquisite care was competing with cloth made in the West. Therefore, I was told, the English cut off the fingers of the weavers of Dacca.

. . . Yes, it is easy for us Westerners to point to the East and say, "Look what a mess they've gotten themselves into. Why don't their *gurus* take care of it for them?" But it is becoming increasingly apparent to me that everything is interconnected on this globe, and we all share responsibility for the suffering in the world.

The day of the interview came. There were nine of us present, including two young medical students from England, two other Americans from Los Angeles, and an elderly Indian woman whom Baba introduced as one of the first politically active women in India, who had done much to help in India's fight for independence.

Sitting there rocking to a gentle inner rhythm, he began to speak his words of love. He is always the same. Most of us dwell in a "reality" shaped by the illusive transient nature of our minds, fashioned by our desires and wants. Thus, for most of us, reality is constantly changing. When we are awake, one set of circumstances appears real; when we are dreamlessly asleep, another set; when we are dreaming, still another. We perceive reality differently according to our age as well. A child sees one reality, the adolescent another, the mature and then aged and dying adult still others. It is not reality that is changing, of course, but our state of mind.

Is reality then just a manifestation of the mind? Or is there a degree or level of reality that never changes—a reality separate from our mind's distracting creations? Can we be centered someplace—or perhaps more correctly, all places—where our experience is the same no matter whether we are asleep or awake, dreaming or not, at any age at any time in our lives? Are we capable of realizing a changeless, timeless reality, where all is one and all is the same ... where there is no difference between past, present and future and where one is in constant touch with his immortality, immutability and infinite capacity—his ultimate identity with the divine? Sai Baba's sameness is convincing evidence of such a reality.

I used to wonder what would bring thousands of people, sometimes traveling for weeks on end, over great distances and often overwhelming obstacles, to come and sit at the side of the road in the scorching Indian sun, just for a glimpse of a holy man. The secret has been revealed to me by witnessing such a vision myself. There is a unique quality, an incredibly subtle vibration, which when sensed, speaks with absolute conviction of the glorious and eternal moment man is capable of attaining.

When people speak of materializations and all the other yogic or paranormal or "psychic" powers, they refer to the tip of an iceberg —whose full magnificence can often be measured best by one quick glimpse of the master. This is really the great blessing of *darshan*. The soul's conviction that one is visualizing the form and embodiment of the divine is a gift that has sent millions into a life of devotion.

... To my delight, as Baba began to address the nine of us at the interview, he focused on the book. For fifteen minutes he enveloped me in his marvelous aura of energy—answering all my prayers, assuring me that the circuit had been completed and he was receiving my offering in a way I could never have imagined. He spoke about the purpose and meaning of the book as I had visualized it and in a way which convinced me that he understood and accepted it. Finally, regarding me with love and gentleness, he said, *I am satisfied.* Then he looked into each of our eyes with an almost mischievous smile and added, *And I haven't even read this book yet.* I cracked up: the relief from tension was enormous.

During this trip as with the others, I continued to be treated to the most extraordinary stories about Baba by people from every walk of life. One such story came from Dr. S. Ramakrishna, the son of Dr. S. Bhagavantam, whom I have already mentioned. Ramakrishna grew up in the scientific tradition like his father, has a PhD in engineering and is a professor of aeronautical engineering at the Indian Institute of Sciences, in Bangalore. He related an incident which occurred some years ago when he was twenty-three.

One day he and four of his friends were riding in the country with Baba. It was about noon and everyone was thinking of lunch. Baba called a halt and asked the group what kind of fruit they liked. Suspecting that something unusual might occur, they decided in unspoken agreement that each should pick something different. One picked a mango, another an apple, another one an orange and so on. Baba smiled and listened patiently, then, according to Ramakrishna, motioned them to a small tree by the side of the road and told them to pick the fruits they had chosen. To their utter amazement, dangling from the branches were the very five fruits they had chosen, each on its own stem. Dr. Ramakrishna looked straight into my eyes and smiled.

One evening Baba called six of us in for an interview and directed us to ready ourselves to leave with him early the next morning. We would take a cab a mile out of Puttaparthi at about five o'clock and wait for him. *This will be your good chance,* he said. *I am leaving for Brindavan and you will ride behind me. It is my intention that you may ride in my car with me part of the way.*

We were so excited. Mum's the word; don't tell a soul, we all agreed, since we knew that whenever Baba travels he is followed by swarms of people. We secretly mapped out our strategy and were quite sure we could execute the plan without giving ourselves away.

The next morning Don began letting the air out of his air mattress at about one-thirty. "Not yet," I whispered. By three-thirty, unable to wait any longer, we got up and moved stealthily about, quietly brushing our teeth, tip-toeing, luggage in hand, to our taxi.

Waiting there, packed to the hilt, with their motors warming up, were ten other taxis and what seemed like five-hundred people gathered about. It was uncanny . . . how did they find out? Foiled again! We waited at the designated spot outside Puttaparthi, but when Baba came by we were left in a cloud of dust. We couldn't even see his car there were so many people ahead of us.

The next day, Thursday, Baba invited some twenty Americans in for another interview. After producing some *vibhutti*, he materialized little medals for the children present. These would protect them in time of danger, he said, by sending a message to him so that he could respond instantaneously. Then he moved his hand in the air and, as I was watching, where there was nothing . . . suddenly there was a large ball of rock candy about three inches in diameter.

He cracked some of it and gave it to the children. Then turning to me, he said that the rest was for my wife and children and Don and his family, and that he would give us something more for the children later. The candy was quite tasty.

Thursday is a day when *bhajans* are sung continuously and Baba appears twice for *darshan*. He had told Don and me in our personal interview that we were going to get a ride in his car after all. By four-thirty we began waiting for him at the gate to the inner grounds of the ashram. He appeared at about five o'clock and as he passed, motioned us to his car, then went out to the thousand or so devotees gathered for *darshan*. Before long we were driving down the driveway through the outer ashram grounds to the street.

As we made our way slowly through the grounds, I witnessed something I could not have imagined in my wildest dreams. This huge wave of humanity, hearts open, faces filled with yearning, enveloped the car, focusing energy on it with an intensity that was almost unbearable. The memory of one of my first encounters with Baba suddenly struck me: when I was watching him from outside the stadium in Bombay.

Then I had been one of thousands, with Baba in the center; now here I was at the center myself, sitting next to him. I can't begin to fully convey the experience. I felt terribly conspicuous and wanted to shrink to the floor.

The incident introduced a new dimension in my relationship with Baba. He says one should attend to spiritual practice and devotional work in the faith that one is drawing closer to the Lord. I was beginning to experience this movement in a very concrete way. So many of us think our lives are long and without movement, that we are going nowhere. Perhaps we are bored—time is dragging and nothing is happening. In reality we are hurtling through the space and time of our lives at breakneck speed.

It is at a time like this, as I concretely witness myself drawing within three years from the periphery to the center, that I know this to be true. We *do* shape our destiny. We *do* make movement. We can draw closer to the divine. *You must grow day by day, not only physically but in the spiritual life also. How long are you staying on in the primary school, writing down the alphabet? Get up, demand an examination, pass and move forward to the higher class!*

With regard to our responsibility in directing ourselves along this path, Baba writes: *God is not involved in either rewards or punishments. He only reflects, resounds and reacts! He is the eternal unaffected witness! You decide your own fate. Do good, be good, and you get good in return; be bad, do bad deeds, you reap bad results. Do not thank or blame God. Thank yourself, blame yourself!*

Baba was allowing me to feel the movement close to the center. Here he was: no self-consciousness, no awkwardness, smiling and waving, appearing fully merged with his devotees. I turned to gaze at him and was suddenly enveloped in his bliss myself, caught up in his love in a way which melted all self-consciousness. Then he looked over at my brother and with an impish smile, his eyes just twinkling, said, *All the Americans are very jealous. I don't know why.*

That just cracked me up. Baba can be so mischievous sometimes in intensifying the fire of the ego, bringing out its impurities and jealousies so they can be seen and transcended. He seems to play his role as its destroyer as part of a great game. Many people have told me they feel that Baba, in no small measure, seems to set up one ego, one faction, one quarrel against another.

What a thrill to experience Baba's personality so closely during this drive! He seemed so human, so fallible—being with us at our level to allow us to become friendly and familiar with him. The experience of being permitted to witness the *avatar* as friend is described beautifully in the *Bhagavad Gita,* in the relationship between *Arjuna* and *Krishna. Arjuna* much preferred being a friend to *Krishna* to being fully aware of all his power and glory. At one point (in Chapter 11) *Arjuna* asked to see *Krishna's* full reality and glory, and the vision was at once so glorious and terrifying that *Arjuna* was completely overwhelmed and pleaded for *Krishna* to return to his familiar limited form.

In an interview with the American spiritual newspaper *The Movement* in October 1974, during his visit to the United States, Dr. Gokak commented on this special relationship as follows:

Interviewer: It must be strange at times relating to Baba, being so close to him and knowing him. How do you relate to him—as a friend or as a vehicle for God to come through this shell called Sai Baba? How do you relate to that situation?

Dr. Gokak: He's the friend I love, the God I fear and *Krishna,* at whose enigmatic hands I love to be slain, making myself immortal. This is how I relate to him. I am prepared for everything. For my doing, for my undoing, for all that. And I am also prepared for the human relationship. In the morning when I am in the next room and the *Avatar* walks in and says, "Do you have a shaving brush?" I give him mine because he has forgotten his own. I relate to him in this way also. He is so intensely human. He can be so divine.

Interviewer: Does this seem like a paradox to you?

Dr. Gokak: No, even when I am aware of all that he stands for, when I am near him and he cuts jokes with me, I forget all that he is and I begin to talk as a friend. It is only when I get away from him and come to America, for example, and see what is happening to him in all these homes, with all these photographs everywhere, that I say, "Is this the Baba with whom I'm staying?" I begin to experience a sense of awe.

Once I said to him, "When will you show me your cosmic form?" He said, "Wait, wait, I will show you." He said, "Why do you think I have taken you so close to me? For that reason I have taken you close." But actually, I don't know what else he is going to show but what I have seen already. When I am near him, I still forget that he is Baba. I think of him as very great and all that, and near to me. I can take liberties and joke now and then—when he smiles, not otherwise. But then I forget the rest of it. When I go to other places and see *vibhutti* showering in photographs and images appearing from nowhere, people going into ecstasy repeating his name, then I say, "Yes, this is the cosmic form." [1]

And so I too was being allowed closer contact with the personality. As we started our drive, Baba leaned forward, resting his elbow on the back of the front seat. His actions were animated and he appeared to be in a joking mood. *I like to make jokes,* he said. Turning to the young driver of the car, he began to chide him playfully to drive more slowly. He was the epitome of the nagging backseat driver: *Slower . . . slower . . . slower,* he kept demanding, until the poor fellow was driving about five miles an hour.

To the left, over more to the left—smiling all the while. (Cars drive on the left side of the road in India.) A small rickety car passed to our right. *I like small cars,* he commented. Then he began to talk about our families and our marriages. *I'll give something to the children;* and he materialized six postage-stamp-sized pictures.

For part of the ride he appeared to be thinking—relaxing and unwinding from a busy day. But he wasn't still for long. His speech and movements became quick, at times almost staccatto. He kept up a steady

[1]*Sanathana Sarathi*, p. 340, January 1975.

stream of conversation in a casual, friendly tone which put us at ease.

Partway through the drive Baba directed the driver to stop and invited us out for a walk. In a few minutes we were walking along the side of the road like old friends. The sun was setting and the Western sky was a radiant orange fan. Far down the road behind us we could see headlights approaching.

You men surround me and we will walk in this fashion so that no one can see me, because if that is a bus and they see me, they will stop and put an end to our walk. I was momentarily taken aback by Baba's instructions, having been put at such ease in his presence that I'd almost forgotten his immense stature and popularity; then I reminded myself that, after all, here I was with an *avatar.* He was simply saying what was true.

> *In truth, you cannot understand the nature of my reality either today, or even after a thousand years of steady austerity or ardent inquiry, even if all mankind joins in the effort. But, in a short time, you will become cognizant of the bliss showered by divine principle, which has taken upon itself this sacred body and this sacred name. Your good fortune which will provide you this chance is greater than what was available for monks, sages, saints and even personalities embodying facets of divine glory!*
>
> *Since I move about with you, eat like you, and talk with you, you are deluded into the belief that this is but an instance of common humanity. Be warned against this mistake. I am also deluding you by my singing with you, talking with you, and engaging myself in activities with you. But, any moment, my divinity may be revealed to you; you have to be ready, prepared for that moment. Since divinity is enveloped by humaness you must endeavor to overcome the* maya *(delusion) that hides it from your eyes. This is a human form, in which every divine entity, every divine principle—that is to say, all the names and forms ascribed by man to God—are manifest.*
>
> *How fortunate you are that you can witness all the countries of the world paying homage to* Bharatha *(India); you can hear adoration of Satya Sai's name reverberating throughout the world, even while this*

body is existing—not at some future date, but when it is with you, before you.[1]

. . .Rama and Krishna *and Sai Baba appear different because of the dress each has donned, but it is the selfsame entity, believe me. Do not be misled into error and loss. The time will soon come when this huge building or even vaster ones will be too small for the gatherings of those who are called to this place. The sky itself will have to be the roof of the auditorium of the future; I will have to forego the car and even the airplane when I move from place to place, for the crowds pressing around them will be too huge. I will have to move across the sky; yes, that too will happen, believe me.*[2]

The four of us gathered around him, all sort of hunched over and wearing big grins; it was obvious that we were hiding something. The headlights bore down on us—and seemed to be taking an awfully long time to get there, while we clambered over each other like cattle—until we could see that it was only a truck. The drivers hardly bothered to look our way. I'm sure if they had they'd have stopped just to see what we were hiding. Baba had been smiling the whole time, apparently enjoying the play very much.

On the way back to the car, my brother was about to step into a pile of dung when Baba playfully grabbed his arm and pulled him to safety. *Cow dung,* he said, pointing down, then proceeded to give us a short lesson on the correct pronunciation of "cow dung" in Telugu. We were all laughing when we reached the car. Then again in his play, and as if he didn't know, Baba asked us the number of children in our families—only to give us another glimpse of his infinite knowledge as he created six beautiful little silver medals, one for each child, with a swirl of his hand.

As we started off again, Baba resumed his chiding of the driver and for the most part the conversation was light, but we touched on some deeper subjects as well. To a question about economic inflation and depression, Baba answered: *Not until man learns to value mankind will anthing else find its proper value. There will be a time of unrest and change in the world, a time when mankind will turn more toward the spiritual for guidance.*

"Baba," I asked, "Will your message soon be known throughout the world?"

[1]*Sathya Sai Speaks*, Vol VI, pp. 211-212
[2]*Sathya Sai Speaks*, Vol. II, pp. 90-91

Not soon, he said: *slowly. It will be hard for people to understand my message—it will only come about slowly.*

"When will you come to America?" I asked.

Before one can go out to others he has to put his own home in order, he replied, *and some* gurus *have given the Indian holy man a questionable reputation.*

But I will come, I will come . . . and I am always with you—always . . . always . . . always. As we approached the entrance to the ashram grounds, he turned to us and said, *It has been your good fortune to spend this time with me. When you are back home, remember this experience. It will be meditation for you.*

It was eight o'clock in the evening and my brother and I would have to depart the next morning. Baba invited us into a private room. I felt that perhaps this very special ride marked the beginning of a more personal relationship with him. In spite of all my earlier rationalizing to the contrary, I asked him if I could come live by him. *It is only in your imagination that there is distance,* was his patient reply. He allowed me to place my forehead on his lotus feet . . . and I left.

Good news about the presence of Sai Baba among us will spread quickly throughout the world, I am sure—even though, as he says, it will take awhile for us to comprehend his full significance or the meaning of his message. It has been my good fortune to draw close to him at a time when it is still possible to become friendly with him on a personal level and see the clear signs of his greatness in a close and intimate way. Yet I feel that soon Baba will become but an orange speck on the horizon, surrounded by millions of eager faces. And like the people in his village who were once blessed to know the sweetness of his being from daily personal contact with him, I too will one day be saddened by having to view him only from a distance.

But it is enough to know that Sai Baba exists at all. I feel deeply fortunate to be able to play a part, in some small measure through this book, in an evolutionary phenomenon moving inexorably toward realization: world consciousness awakening to its own glorious potential, and to the presence of a being who may indeed be ushering in a golden age.

Photograph materialized by Sai Baba for a devotee.

Be simple and sincere. It is sheer waste of money to burden the pictures and idols in the shrines and altars of your homes with a weight of garlands, and to parade costly utensils and vessels and offerings, to show off your devotion. This is deception; it demeans Divinity, imputing to it the desire for pomp and publicity. I ask only for purity of heart to shower grace. Do not posit distance between you and me; do not interpose the formalities of the guru-friend relationship, or even the attitudinal distinctions of the God-devotee relationship, between you and me. I am neither guru *nor God; I am you; you are I; that is the truth. There is no distinction. That which appears so is the delusion. You are waves; I am the ocean. Know this and be free, be divine.*

APPENDIX

Other books by and about Sai Baba are listed below. Most of these can be obtained by contacting the

Sri Sathya Sai Book Center of America
P.O. Box 278, Tustin, California 92680
Phone: (714) 835-5206

They include:

Title	Description
Sathya Sai Speaks:	
Volume I	Discourses, 1956-1960
Volume II	Discourses, 1960-1962
Volume III	Discourses, 1963-1964
Volume IV	Discourses, 1964-1965
Volume IV (Indian Edition)	Discourses, 1964-1965
Volume VI	Discourses, 1967-1968
Volume VII	Discourses, 1968-1971
Volume VIII	Discourses, 1970-1973
Volume IX	Discourses, 1974-1975
Sathyam Sivam Sundaram	Baba's Life
Sathya Sai Baba	American edition of Part I
Part 2	1926-1961
Part 3	1969-1972 (hard cover)
Sri Sai Satcharita	Life and teachings
	of Shirdi Sai Baba (hard cover)
Summer Showers in Brindavan 1972	Summer School Discourses
Summer Showers in Brindavan 1973	Summer School Discourses
Summer Showers in Brindavan 1974	Summer School Discourses
Bhagavatha Vahini	Baba's version of the *Bhagavatha*
Geetha Vahini	Teachings on the *Bhagavad Gita*
Dhyana Vahini	Teachings on meditation
Jnana Vahini	Teachings on knowledge
Upanishad Vahini	Writings on spiritual discipline
Prema Vahini	Inner peace through love
Prasanthi Vahini	Peace within
Sandeha Nivarini	Questions and answers by Baba

Chinna Katha	Stories and parables by Baba
What is Truth	Teachings on truth
Selected Jewels	Verses about Sai Baba
Sai Baba, Saint of Shirdi	Biography by Mani Sahukar
The Incredible Sai Baba	Biography of Shirdi Sai Baba
Sathya Sai Geeta	Selected discourses (pocket-size)
Teachings of Sri Sathya Sai Baba	
Sanskrit/English Dictionary Vol. 1	
Sanskrit/English Dictionary Vol. 2	
Bhajana Songs	Devotional songs 1st edition (words only) 2nd edition (words, index and glossary)
Sai Baba: Man of Miracles	By Howard Murphet
Sai BABA Avatar: A New Journey into Power and Glory	
Sai Baba and His Message	Compilation of articles by Eastern and Western behavioral scientists. Edited by Dr. S. P. Ruhela, Professor of Sociology (India) and Dr. Duane Robinson, Professor of Sociology (U.S.A.)
Bhagavan Sri Sathya Sai Baba: The Man and The Avatar	An interpretation of the many facets of Sai Baba's personality by Dr. V. K. Gokak
Sai Baba and Sai Yoga	By Indra Devi
The Divine Master	Articles by close devotees from East and West

A selection of cassette tapes, super 8 and 16mm films can be obtained by contacting the Sathya Sai Baba Center of Hollywood, 7911 Willoughby, Los Angeles, California 90046 — Phone (213) 656-9373.

GLOSSARY

abhisheka Ablution, ritual washing.

akasa Ether/or space, the first of the five elements evolved from *Brahman;* the subtlest form of matter.

ananda Bliss, joy. Bliss is considered to be the very substance of God (God *is* bliss, not "has" bliss).

anandaswarupa Of the very form or nature of bliss; ananda.

Arjuna A hero of the *Mahabharata* (a famous Hindu epic) and the friend of *Krishna.*

asana Easy, comfortable sitting pose. *Hatha* yoga posture.

asanthi Grief, anxiety (absence of peace).

ashram Hermitage, monastery.

atma The soul, the spark of God within.

Avatar An incarnation of God.

avedana Yearning for the Lord.

Baba Father.

Bhagavad Gita The Hindu "Bible."

bhajan A song in praise of God.

bhakta, bhakti A *bhakta* is a devotee, one who has *bhakti;* virtue, self control, faith, devotion.

Bharath India, the land that has *rathi,* or attachment to *Bha* or *Bhagavan,* the Lord.

Brahma The Creator God of the Hindu Trinity, the other two being *Vishnu* and *Shiva.*

Brahman The immanent principle, said to have three aspects: creation, preservation, destruction. The Absolute, the Supreme Reality.

Brindavan Place where Sai Baba frequently resides when away from Prasanthi Nilayam, his ashram. Also, the name of a town on the banks of the Jamuna river associated with Sri *Krishna's* childhood.

buddhi The intellect, intelligence or discriminating faculty.

chakra Centers or "lotuses" of potential energy arrayed upward in man from the base of the spine to the crown of the head.

darshan To see a great person and receive his blessing— literally, "to breath the same air as."

Dasera Festival celebrating the victory of good over forces resisting progress toward light.

dharma Righteousness, duty, code of conduct—one of the four ends of human pursuit.

dharmaswarupa Of the very form or nature of righteousness; *dharma.*

dhyana Meditation.

Ganesha, Ganapathi Names for the elephant-headed god, son of *Shiva.*

Ganga	The Ganges.
Ganja	Marijuana.
gopas	The cowherd boys of Brindavan, playmates of Sri *Krishna*.
gopis	The milkmaids of Brindavan, companions and devotees of Sri *Krishna*.
guna	Human characteristic or quality.
guru	Teacher, guide to spiritual liberation.
Hanuman	One of the most devoted of the *bhaktas* of *Rama*, represented as part monkey, part man; mentioned in the *Ramayana*.
hatha yoga	A school of yoga; the practice of *asanas* or yoga postures for the purpose of physical well-being and for awakening spiritual centers.
Indra	The King of the Gods.
jagath	The objective, transitory, untrue world.
japa, **japam**	Recitation or repetition of the name of the Lord.
japamala	Religious necklace.
jnana, **jnani**	A *jnani* is one who has *jnana*, knowledge of God attained through reasoning and discrimination.
Kailas	A peak of the Himalayas regarded as the sacred abode of *Shiva*.
Kali	A name of the Divine Mother; the Primal energy.
karma	Action; the law that governs all action and its inevitable consequences on the doer; the law of cause and effect, of moral compensation for acts done in the past.
Krishna	An avatar of *Vishnu*. "He who draws you by means of the joy he imparts."
kshema	Preservation of that which one has acquired.
kundalini	Spiritual energy lying dormant in all inividuals.
mahatma	A great soul.
manas	The mind.
mantra	Chant, sacred words or formula.
Mathura	Town where *Krishna* was born.
maya	Ignorance obscuring the vision of God; the primal enticing illusion called the world; attachment.
moksha	Stage of liberation from both joy and grief, freedom from birth and death—the goal of spiritual practice.
nagara-sankirtan	Singing bhajans in a group while walking slowly through the streets; done in the early hours before dawn.
Nilayam	Prasanthi Nilayam: abode of Eternal Peace. Name of Sai Baba's *ashram*.

Om   The primal sound, pronounced A-U-M—the most sacred word of the *Vedas*. It is the symbol of God and of *Brahman*.

prakriti   Primordial nature, which in association with *Purusha* (Eternal Conscious Principle) creates the universe.

prana   The vital breath that sustains life in the physical body.

Prasanthi Nilayam   The abode of undisturbed inner peace. The name of Sai Baba's *ashram*.

prema   Divine love of the most intense kind; universal, unconditional, unblemished love.

premarasa   The flavor of *prema*.

pundit   Scholar.

pura   The physical body.

Purana(s)   Books of Hindu mythology.

Purusha   Eternal Conscious Principle; soul.

Puttaparthi   The quiet and remote village in southern India where Sai Baba was born (November 23, 1926) and where he now has his *ashram*, Prasanthi Nilayam.

Radha   The beloved of *Krishna*.

rajasic   The active, passionate aspect of nature.

Rama   An *avatar* of God, a divine being. An *avatar* whose name means, "he who pleases; he who fills with *ananda* (bliss)."

Ramakrishna Paramahansa   Revered and Christ-like Indian master.

rishi   A sage, one leading a life without desires, with attachment only to the *atma*. A seer of truth.

saadrisya   Acquiring divine nature.

saalokya   Existence in God.

saathi   Calmness of senses, passions, emotions.

sadhaka   A spiritual aspirant engaged in conquering his egoism and greed, the sense of "I" and "mine."

sadhana   Spiritual discipline or practice, through activities such as meditation and recitation of holy names.

sadhu   A good man, detached, devoted, virtuous, wise.

sakhya   One of the five attitudes cherished by the dualistic worshipper toward his chosen ideal: the attitude of one friend to another.

samadhi   Perfect equanimity, devoid of ups and downs, untouched by joy or sorrow—communion with God.

samkhya   One of the six systems of orthodox Hindu philosophy.

sankirtan   Reciting or singing with joy.

samsara   The physical world.

samskara   The tendencies inherent from previous births.

sanathana dharma   The ancient wisdom, the eternal path of righteousness.

Sanathana Sarathi   The eternal charioteer—name of monthly publication from Prasanthi Nilayam.

Sastra	The scripture that illumines, the moral code.
satchitananda	The supreme state, usually translated as existence, knowledge, bliss.
sathwic	Pure, good, pious; the principle of balance or wisdom.
sathya	Truth—that which is the same in the past, present, future.
sevak	One who is dedicated to service.
shakti	The great universal power or energy—the creative power of *Brahman*; a name for the Divine Master.
shanti	Peace, undisturbed peace. A benediction often repeated three times after *Vedantic* prayers.
Shirdi Sai Baba	Indian holy man from whom, says Sai Baba of Puttaparthi, he was reincarnated.
Shiva	The Destroyer God of the Hindu trinity, the other two being *Brahma* and *Vishnu.*
siddha, siddhi	A *siddha* is one who has attained *siddhis* (occult powers).
Sri Aurobindo	1872-1950: his ashram at Pondicherri, in southern India, was turned into a community of spiritual seekers from all over the world, called Auroville. A prolific writer, his works include *The Life Divine, Essays on the Gita, The Synthesis of Yoga, Letters on Yoga,* and many others.
Sri Meher Baba	1894-1969: quarters known as Meherabad. He observed a vow of silence for many years; traveled throughout Europe and America; wrote *Discourses by Meher Baba* and *God Speaks.*
Sri Ramana Maharshi	1879-1950: He was an illumined rishi of southern India; taught non-duality through self inquiry—one should constantly ask himself, "Who am I?" His *ashram* was located on a sacred hill called Arunachala.
sudarshana	Holy vision.
swami	Lord, spiritual preceptor.
swarupa	Form, body.
tapa	Religious austerity, sacrifice, asceticism.
thamasic	Dull or inert quality.
Treta Yuga	The second of the four *yugas* or cycles or world periods. Hindu mythology divides the duration of the world into four *yugas; Satya, Treta, Dwapara,* and *Kali.* The first is known as the Golden Age as there is a great preponderance of virtue among men, but with each succeeding *yuga* virtue diminishes and vice increases. In the *Kali yuga* there is a minimum of virtue and a great excess of vice. We are supposedly in the *Kali yuga* now.
vahini	Current, flow, river.
vandana	Reverence toward all life.
veda	Knowledge.

Vedanta   One of the six systems of orthodox Hindu philosophy, formulated by Vyasa (compiler of the *Vedas*).

Vedas   The most sacred scriptures of the Hindu religion, regarded as revelations to great seers and not of human origin. There are four *Vedas:* the *Rig-Veda,* the *Yajur-Veda,* the *Soma-Veda* and the *Arthava-Veda.*

vibhutti   Sacred ash, frequently materialized by Sai Baba.

Vishnu   The Preserver God of the Hindu trinity, the other two being *Brahma* and *Shiva.*

yaga   Outward-directed activity; sacrifice.

Yasada   Foster mother of *Krishna.*

yoga   Union of the individual soul and the Universal Soul; also the method by which to realize this union. It is the general term for the several types of devotional practice that are disciplines for controlling the mind and transforming it into an instrument for realizing God.

yogi   One who is given to simple living and who practices *yoga.*